The Return of Private Property
Rural Life after Agrarian Reform in the Republic of Azerbaijan

What makes private property valuable, desirable, and workable? The starting point in this book is the observation that many rural dwellers in postsocialist Azerbaijan do not cultivate the land they received for free through the country's agrarian reforms, enacted in 1996. The author asks whether those who have recommended private ownership of land as the primary and even sufficient motivation for use of the land have been wrong. Did Azerbaijan's long socialist experience as a Soviet republic erase memories of the experience of private ownership and convince rural communities of the superiority of collective property and state agricultural organisation?

Lale Yalçın-Heckmann focuses on social and economic dimensions of private property since the agrarian reforms. She looks at the kinds of land and cultivation strategies that emerged in the decades after the break-up of the Soviet Union and asks why many rural households in Azerbaijan were unwilling to cultivate their privatised land shares, despite the threat of rural poverty. She also considers households that did engage in cultivation, including households of internally displaced persons who were formally excluded from privatisation but who nevertheless became successful farmers. How far can private property thrive on its own, she asks, without being embedded in efficiently functioning markets and without the implementation of appropriate economic policies by the state? What role did the considerable emigration from the region play in enabling people to market cash crops in the Russian Federation and in supporting rural households in western Azerbaijan? Have women been winners or losers in privatisation and new trading activities in the market economy?

Through the lens provided by economic anthropology, the author combines concepts of political economy with an actor-oriented approach and the notion of moral economy. In doing so, she chronicles the way the historical legacy of authoritarian state structures has shaped micro- and macro-economic struggles over property in independent Azerbaijan after socialism.

AF201886

 **Halle Studies in the Anthropology of Eurasia**

General Editors:

Chris Hann, Thomas Hauschild, Richard Rottenburg, Burkhard Schnepel

Volume 24

LIT

Lale Yalçın-Heckmann

The Return of Private Property

Rural Life after Agrarian Reform
in the Republic of Azerbaijan

LIT

Cover Photo: Cultivating clover on *pay* land, Təzəkənd (2005)
(Photo: Lale Yalçın-Heckmann).

This work was prepared for the *Habilitation* degree at the Martin
Luther University Halle-Wittenberg.

Gedruckt auf alterungsbeständigem Werkdruckpapier entsprechend
ANSI Z3948   DIN ISO 9706

Bibliographic information published by the Deutsche Nationalbibliothek
The Deutsche Nationalbibliothek lists this publication in the Deutsche
Nationalbibliografie; detailed bibliographic data are available in the Internet at
http://dnb.d-nb.de.

ISBN 978-3-643-10629-2

A catalogue record for this book is available from the British Library

©LIT VERLAG Dr. W. Hopf Berlin 2010
Fresnostr. 2   D-48159 Münster
Tel. +49 (0) 2 51-620 320   Fax +49 (0) 2 51-922 60 99
e-Mail: lit@lit-verlag.de   http://www.lit-verlag.de

Distribution:
In Germany: LIT Verlag Fresnostr. 2, D-48159 Münster
Tel. +49 (0) 2 51-620 32 22, Fax +49 (0) 2 51-922 60 99, e-mail: vertrieb@lit-verlag.de
In Austria: Medienlogistik Pichler-ÖBZ, e-mail: mlo@medien-logistik.at
In Switzerland: B + M Buch- und Medienvertrieb, e-mail: order@buch-medien.ch

In the UK: Global Book Marketing, e-mail: mo@centralbooks.com

In North America by:

Transaction Publishers
New Brunswick (U.S.A.) and London (U.K.)

Transaction Publishers
Rutgers University
35 Berrue Circle
Piscataway, NJ 08854

Phone: +1 (732) 445 - 2280
Fax: + 1 (732) 445 - 3138
for orders (U. S. only):
toll free (888) 999 - 6778
e-mail: orders@transactionpub.com

Babam Aydın Yalçın'ın hatırasına

Contents

List of Illustrations

Figures

Maps

Plates

(all photographs were taken by Lale Yalçın-Heckmann, 2000-2008)

Tables

Acknowledgements

This book evolved out of my Habilitation dissertation, which I wrote while I was a member of the research group working under Chris Hann on the theme of rural property in postsocialist countries at the Max Planck Institute for Social Anthropology in Halle/Saale, Germany. The theme and the area of my research were new to me, and I learned much from colleagues in the group. I would like to thank them all for many fruitful discussions. Bruce Grant was a great colleague for discussing many aspects of my research, especially during our common field stays in Baku. My friends and colleagues Deema Kaneff, Frances Pine, John Eidson, and Patrick Heady read various versions of my chapters, and Chris Hann read all of them and provided valuable criticism and commentary. Richard Rottenburg and Ingrid Schindlbeck also made suggestions for improvements. I have followed most but not all of these suggestions, and I alone am responsible for the remaining flaws.

Many people in Baku and in my research sites in Azerbaijan became friends over the years and contributed immensely to my knowledge and well-being during my stays in Azerbaijan. They have welcomed me every time I have returned there since 2000. I thank them all – anonymously – for their support, friendship, and patience. I deeply regret that my mentor and friend, the late Atiga Izmailova, could not see this work finished; she was an invaluable and lively discussant of my ideas and observations during field-work.

Chris Hann offered me the opportunity to publish my Habilitation dissertation as a book, and I am grateful to him for his encouragement in opening up Azerbaijan to ethnographic knowledge and discussions in economic anthropology. The staff at the Max Planck Institute for Social Anthropology generously supported the research for and production of this book. I thank Berit Westwood for her help in the final stages; Jutta Turner and Robert Goßmann for cartographic work; and student assistants Norman Prell, Anne-Christine Wahl, and Alexander Kramer for ensuring me the best support for this project. Jane Tienne and Jane Kepp undertook the language improvement, and I appreciate their work.

Note on Transliteration

Azerbaijani usage follows the Latin transcription adopted by the Republic of Azerbaijan in 1991. Russian usage follows the United States Library of Congress system, with established exceptions such as 'Yeltsin' rather than 'El'tsyn'.

Chapter 1
Introduction

Politicians and bureaucrats of the independent Republic of Azerbaijan declared in the mid-1990s that one of the main goals of agrarian reform in their country was to prevent the decline of agricultural production. In 1996 Azerbaijan passed extensive reform laws concerning ownership of agrarian land (Əliyev 1997: 140–146; Ibrahimov 1998: 5). Since then the output of agricultural produce has increased. Although total production by mid-2000 had not yet equalled the level of 1990[1], the radical reform measures, the almost total privatisation of formerly state-owned land, and the distribution of that land to rural dwellers had allowed politicians to boast about the increase in agricultural production. Before his death in 2003, President Heydər Əliyev (who was succeeded by his son, Ilham Əliyev) said that agricultural land was almost completely in the hands of private producers. In the eyes of Western and international economic and financial overseers and development and financing agencies, this was a highly desirable outcome, probably envied by other former Soviet countries.[2]

The picture looks different, however, when one focuses on specific places, such as the district (*rayon*) of Şəmkir in western Azerbaijan, and within it the village of Təzəkənd, where I carried out my anthropological research (map 1). Without addressing how representative such a case study

---

[1] This outcome is not an anomaly among Commonwealth of Independent States (CIS) countries, as Stephen Wegren indicates (2006: 535, citing Lerman, Csaki, and Feder 2004: 168).

[2] See reports by the World Bank on Azerbaijan such as Dudwick, Fock, and Sedik (2005) and writings by agrarian experts and rural economists such as Lerman (2006) and Rozelle and Swinnen (2004). However, not all reports on the agricultural sector are that positive. For instance, researchers referring to agriculture's share of GDP in Azerbaijan point out that the figure fell from 34 per cent to about 18 per cent between 1990 and 2000, and investments in agriculture decreased steadily during that period, reaching zero in 2000 (Temel, Jansen, and Karimov 2002: 3–4). Agricultural produce contributed 9 per cent of GDP in Azerbaijan in 2008 (www.azstat.org/region/az/01.shtml, accessed 16 March 2010).

might be, let me formulate the question I was concerned with in relation to privatisation, changes in property regimes, and land use.

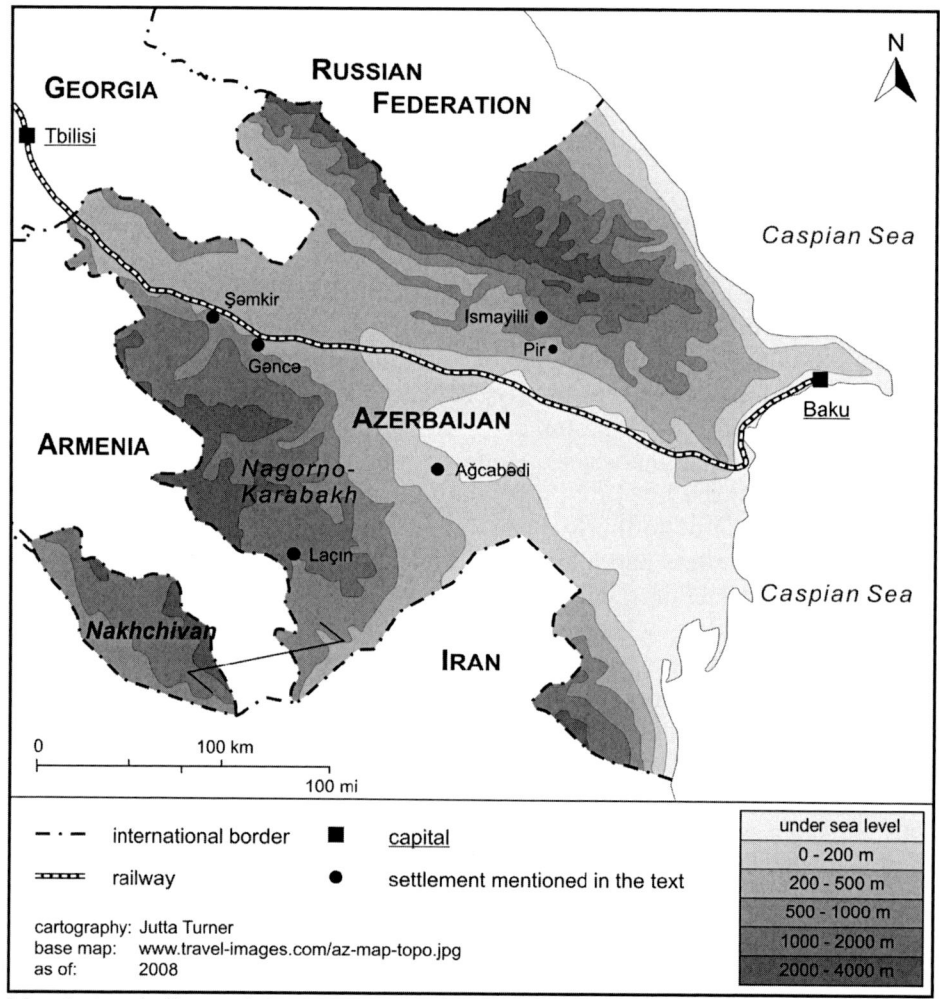

Map 1. Azerbaijan and the field sites.

During the Soviet period and into the present day, Şəmkir was referred to as one of the wealthiest districts in Azerbaijan. It has suitable geographic, climatic, and agricultural conditions, including sufficient water and adequate irrigation systems, for cultivating cash crops such as wine grapes and cotton (*Azerbaijan Soviet Encyclopaedia* 1987: 464). A flat region on the lower slopes of mountains (*dağətəyi*), it is considered to be relatively fertile.[3] Yet as of 2000, agricultural production in Şəmkir, in terms of output and area under cultivation, still had not returned to the pre–agrarian reform level of 1990.

Some positive developments had taken place in Şəmkir since the agrarian reform. Although the area used for cultivating grains and wine grapes declined between 1995 and 2000, the area devoted to potatoes, vegetables, and fruit increased significantly – that for potatoes, by 9 times, and that for vegetables, by 17 times. Productivity, calculated as *sentner* (100 kilograms) per hectare, was said to have doubled for potatoes between 1995 and 2000, to have tripled for vegetables, and to have increased for all listed kinds of produce (*Azərbaycanın Regionları* 2001: 521).[4] Altogether, though, the area under cultivation for wheat, vegetables, cotton, and fruit in Şəmkir in 2000 had reached only 80 percent of the level of 1995 (*Azərbaycanın Regionları* 2001: 520), and productivity had still not recovered to the level of 1990.

Agricultural economist and World Bank expert Zvi Lerman, in his studies of agrarian transition in the former Soviet countries (Lerman and Mirzakhanian 2001; Lerman 2004, 2006), has argued that in Azerbaijan and the other Transcaucasian countries – Georgia and Armenia – increases in the numbers of individual farms and average sizes of landholdings have led to increases in agricultural productivity. Lerman (2006) and others also point out the significance of sales and commercialisation of agricultural produce in the postsocialist countries (see Sikor and Tuong Vi 2005), underscoring that the new farmers are far beyond being simply subsistence farmers. Lerman, for instance, sees increased farm size as the reason for the increase in sales, which leads to an increase in household income.[5]

The Azerbaijani agrarian reforms of 1996 required that privatised land shares (*pay torpağı*) be distributed to all rural residents, including former agricultural producers and non-producers such as teachers, hospital workers,

---

[3] Qərib Məmmədov (1998: 192) described the agro-ecological zone of Gəncə-Qazax, where 47 per cent of the cultivable area was devoted to vineyards (*üzümçülük*), 14.4 per cent to animal husbandry (*maldarlıq*), 12.6 per cent to wheat and the like (*taxılçılıq*), 7.3 per cent to additional sheep husbandry (*qoyunçuluq*), 5.2 per cent to potatoes (*kartofçuluq*), and the rest to fruit and vegetable cultivation and silkworm breeding (*baramaçılıq*).

[4] Figures given by the State Statistical Committee of the Republic of Azerbaijan show that productivity for potatoes more than doubled between 2000 and 2009, doubled for fruits, and increased for all other agrarian produce in the Gəncə-Qazax region (www.azstat.org/region/az/004.shtml, accessed 16 March 2010).

[5] Wegren (2006: 539) is critical of this appraisal of farm size and points out that agricultural efficiency has less to do with collective labour and the sizes of farms than with the macroeconomic environment and policies.

technical personnel in other sectors, and traders. Nevertheless, rural poverty persists, and economic inequality has increased. Azerbaijan receives funds for reducing rural and urban poverty from the International Monetary Fund and the World Bank and is monitored by those organizations through re-search and special programmes.[6] The World Bank's 2006 Country Brief for Azerbaijan observed that 47 percent of the population was below the na-tional poverty line in 2002.[7]

My central question, then, is the following: Why do a substantial pro-portion of land recipients in Şəmkir district not cultivate the land they were given for free, when they are clearly experiencing economic difficulties such as unemployment, poverty, and economic exclusion (although not hunger and alcoholism, as one finds in many other former Soviet countries)? How is this social and economic phenomenon to be explained and understood? Might an anthropological study make it possible to understand this phe-nomenon more precisely than the explanations given by agrarian economists, who suggest institutional adjustment problems or corrupt political and eco-nomic elites as the reason for misgivings about the agrarian reforms?

A further factor might also be causal in this case of under-cultivation despite thorough privatisation. Like some neighbouring and formerly wealthy western Azerbaijani districts, Şəmkir continues to suffer from high emigration, mainly to Russia and other former Soviet countries. No reliable figures about the emigration exist, because it involves differing types of movements of people back and forth between these countries, to which they can still travel without visas. Figures for the whole of Azerbaijan range from the conservative estimate of about 1 million people (out of a total of slightly more than 8 million inhabitants of Azerbaijan in 2006) working outside the country to the more extreme estimate of 2 million people, or one-fourth of the population. My figures from Təzəkənd, where in 2001 I surveyed a random sample of 77 households, indicate that more than one-third of the households had at least one member working abroad. Although I have no exact figures to prove the significance of emigration from the northern and western *rayon*s of Azerbaijan, I observed a general consensus on the extent of the phenomenon as women in these districts talked about it jokingly. In Azerbaijan, the slaughtering animals is done by men, following the Islamic prescription. Small animals such as chickens can be slaughtered by young men and even boys. The women said they were having difficulty finding a

---

[6] For instance, see International Monetary Fund, Country Report 03/105, 2003.
[7] See http://web.worldbank.org/WBSITE/EXTRENAL/COUNTRIES/ (accessed 23 August 2006). According to official Azerbaijani sources, only 10.9 per cent of the population was below the national poverty line in 2009 (www.azstat.org/MDG/MDG_.shtml, accessed 16 June 2010).

man to slaughter a chicken and had to grab any boy passing by in the street to do the job.

The issue of privatisation of state-owned land but continuing under-cultivation or low productivity is not unique to Azerbaijan. It has been identified and discussed in relation to other postsocialist privatisation schemes (see Wegren 1998, 2006; Lerman and Mirzakhanian 2001; Spoor 2003; Rozelle and Swinnen 2004). Analysts usually argue that the reforms are unsuccessful because they have been delayed, carried out too slowly, or carried out incompletely. The Transcaucasian countries are seen as exceptions to the general trend of unsuccessful reforms because the indicators there are positive, if not yet fully satisfactory.[8] The problems are seen to lie in the extensive fragmentation of land through full privatisation and in failing infrastructure, corrupt local structures, and politically weak governments, which are unable to push through the reforms in all parts of the new states.

In this book I want to differentiate and explore these diagnoses and offer a nuanced understanding of how rural communities in postsocialist Azerbaijan received and adjusted to its agrarian reforms. I look at both the commercialisation of agricultural production in the postsocialist context and the micro-level structures of economic dependencies and historical connections between regions, *rayons*, and local economies. I examine the viability of certain economic strategies at the household and individual levels, along with the way values and norms of sharing, reciprocity, and kinship solidarity function as background for these strategies and whether and how these norms might be violated.

My question regarding Azerbaijan involves at least three dimensions: under-production, total land distribution, and emigration. The connections between these dimensions need to be explored in order to understand whether causal or other types of interrelationships exist among them. Further questions can be posed. Why do the rural residents of Təzəkənd and many other villages choose to emigrate instead of cultivating the land shares they have received? Who chooses to emigrate and who remains on the land to cultivate it? What happens to land shares that are not used by their new owners? How do actors decide whether or not to cultivate land and which crops to grow on it? If land received through privatisation is not being culti-

---

[8] This was especially the argument of Rozelle and Swinnen (2004: 438), who wrote that 'total factor productivity [TFP] … increased strongly in Armenia and Georgia [but not in Azerbaijan], two Transcaucasian countries that implemented strong individualized land rights and dramatically shifted to individual farming even though the nations were recovering from a series of natural disasters and war-related incidents. In contrast, TFP declined in the Central Asian republics in which reforms lagged most'.

vated, can this be seen as resistance?[9] What does this specific case tell us about property relations, the postsocialist transition to a market economy, and the meaning of land in independent Azerbaijan? Is under-production an effect of a not yet fully developed and profitable agrarian market? Does land hold different economic meanings for different rural dwellers, such that landless displaced persons, for example, see it as a desirable asset while people who have free access to land but lack other inputs or profitable markets view it as a liability?

Later I discuss the way the foregoing questions are embedded in debates over property, but the Azerbaijani case has also been part of larger discussions and theories about economic transformation and agrarian change in postsocialist societies. These issues have been explored by numerous anthropologists, especially those working in central and eastern Europe (e.g. Abrahams 1996; Verdery 1996, 2003; Hivon 1998; Leonard and Kaneff 2002; Perrotta 2002b). The way anthropological analysis contributes to understanding the economic transition in postsocialist states and societies has also been a topic of edited volumes (e.g. Bridger and Pine 1998; Buroway and Verdery 1999a; Hann 2002; Mandel and Humphrey 2002; Hann and the Property Relations Group 2003).

The Caucasian countries of the former Soviet Union, however, have been analysed less from the perspective of economic and agrarian transformation than from the perspective of post-war ethnic and nationalist conflicts and identity change (for anthropological studies, see Abrahamian 1997; Dudwick 2000; Platz 2000; and Pelkmans 2006; for historical and political analyses, see Suny 1993; Swietochowski 1993, 1994; Goltz 1998; and Derlugian 2005). The economic processes of postsocialist transformation amply documented for other countries have been treated only secondarily in these studies, because of the dominance of political and military conflicts leading up to and continuing during the independence period. Even more recent discussions of transitions in Azerbaijani society and economy have taken either a 'conflictological' perspective (O'Ballance 1997; Cornell 2001) or the perspective of energy and security politics (Karagiannis 2002). Changes in rural Azerbaijan are scarcely discussed outside the framework of rural economists, who are interested primarily in macro developments such as the

---

[9] Wegren (2006) rightly pointed out that in many postsocialist countries, rural dwellers have not refused to accept free land and have not protested against neo-liberal reforms, as has happened in South America, for instance. He acknowledged that after land distribution, some people won and others lost, but he maintained that one could not speak of a general resistance (2006: 531). Although I agree with his nuanced critique of some other writings about postsocialist agrarian reforms, I still think one can try to conceptualise the strategies of rural households and individuals as forms of indirect resistance, if these are systematic, long-term strategies of, for instance, choosing out-migration or abandoning farming.

establishment of rural markets and the improvement of marketing methods and infrastructural support systems. Such scholars tend to treat privatisation as a finished and functioning, albeit problematic, phenomenon.[10]

How the issues of under-production, land distribution, and emigration are interrelated is scarcely discussed in an analytical way or at a micro level, either –something I aim to do in this study. I then integrate local and regional developments into larger discussions while examining how far the general theoretical models of postsocialist transformation are relevant for explaining local phenomena. My findings confirm the fruitfulness of the approach taken by some other anthropologists who have studied postsocialist transformations, namely, those who have explored the uses of path-dependency models for explaining variations in adjusting to a market economy (Burawoy and Verdery 1999b; Kalb 2002). As Don Kalb (2002: 323) argued, path-dependency models help establish links to the past ('paths in time') as well as 'paths through space'. This approach enables 'a systematic study of the spatial inter-linkages and social relationships that define territories and communities'. Kalb called for 'studying upward and outward, to set intensely local experiences and local outcomes in the wider contexts of commonalities and divergences'.[11] To meet this challenge, I return to the starting point of this study: a focus on postsocialist property relations.

Unpacking the Puzzle

The framework in which this study took place was the work of the Property Relations Focus Group at the Max Planck Institute for Social Anthropology. The fellows in this group studied the transformation primarily of rural property regimes in former socialist countries, using approaches and theoretical models ranging from political economy to E. P. Thompson's (1991) 'moral economy'.[12] All the countries studied shared a history of socialist property that had undergone privatisation measures and market economy forces. Not all cases involved the same kinds of property. In rural Siberia, for example, reindeer were the main objects of property (Stammler 2005; Ventsel 2005), and in some areas, fellows looked at forests (Cellarius 2003) or houses

---

[10] See the contributions to the edited conference volume *Azərbaycan Respublikasında milli iqtisadiyyatın inkişaf etdirilməsi istiqamətləri* [Directions for developing national economy in the Azerbaijani Republic] (2004).

[11] For a similar concept of studying up and outward, see Burawoy's appeal for globalisation from below, or 'grounding globalisation', in which he advocates starting from the real experiences of people, spatial and temporal, and exploring their global contexts (Burawoy 2000: 341).

[12] For collections of presentations and summaries of these projects, see Hann and the Property Relations Group (2003) and Hann (2005a).

(Leutloff-Grandits 2006). Agricultural land was important in all the eastern European, Russian, and former Soviet Union cases (Cartwright 2003; Gambold-Miller and Heady 2003; Gray 2003; Hann and Sárkány 2003; Kaneff and Yalçın-Heckmann 2003; Torsello 2003), but the policies and processes of privatisation differed from one country to another, even within the former Soviet Union (Gambold-Miller and Heady 2003; Gray 2003; Visser 2006).

Agrarian reforms followed almost identical patterns in all the southern Caucasus countries (Lerman and Mirzakhanian 2001; Bezemer and Davis 2003; Lerman 2004, 2006) but were very different from those in Ukraine, the Russian Federation, and the newly independent republics of Central Asia (Kandiyoti 1998, 2002; Wegren 1998; Gambold-Miller 2002; Perrotta 2002a, 2002b; Allina-Pisano 2003; O'Brien 2005; Visser 2006). What were the reasons behind these different paths of reform? Why did the southern Caucasus countries follow almost identical paths of agricultural transformation and rural property reform?[13] I take up these questions in chapter 3, where I show how the independent states of the southern Caucasus had a heritage of regional cooperation and had shared administrative and political structures for longer than just the Soviet period.

The members of the Property Relations Focus Group were concerned with concepts and forms of social inequality, notions of moral economy, and processes of political economy (Hann 2003: 6). Chris Hann has argued that values linked to collective property were strong in many postsocialist countries, such as Russia and Bulgaria, but not in all of them (2003: 28–29; see also Hann 2005a, 2007). He saw a strong concern for moral economy in the cases under study by the focus group, which he attributed to people's concern for the socialist agrarian organisations that had served their communities and were then being dismantled, without replacement (Hann 2003: 34, 37).

In Azerbaijan, concern for the moral economy seems to have been weak, and if it existed at all, it was articulated in religiously coded – hardly socialist – terms. Concern for collective property, too, was missing, apart from the bitterness people felt about how the property of the former state and collective farms had been completely and unfairly carried away. 'It was all demolished (dispersed, stolen, ripped apart) [hamını dağıtıblar]'[14], was the

---

[13] For instance, Bezemer and Davis (2003) provided examples from their study in Armenia indicating the early privatisation of agricultural land there, too, and the similar development of and interdependency between agricultural production and rural nonfarm economy (see also Lerman and Mirzakhanian 2001).

[14] The Azerbaijani word dağıtmaq means 'demolish' and 'disperse' in a negative sense but also 'dissipate' in at least a neutral sense. The connotation of having been robbed was evoked more by extension than by literal meaning. The distribution of land, however, was referred to

statement I often heard in reference to the movable and immovable property of the socialist farms. Private property was seen in opposition to state property, rather than in opposition to what one might understand as belonging to or symbolically or materially representing the collective. This opposition between the private and the state – not the collective – is one of the key points I pursue in this study. Catherine Alexander (2004: 253), in her analysis of privatisation and property in Kazakhstan, raised a similar point, writing that the state was 'a crucial element in the way people talk about the reconfiguration of persons, things, and relations [of privatisation]'. Where Azerbaijani villagers talked about 'demolished and dispersed' state property, Alexander's informants used the rubric of 'theft' for describing what happened to the property of state factories in Almaty.[15]

The concept of property as a 'bundle of rights' between persons over objects, first used by Henry Maine in 1861 (Hann 2007: 291), has by now become canonical. The bundle of rights metaphor 'has been used to conceptualise … arrangements, mostly in two ways: first, to refer to the totality of property rights and duties as conceptualised in any society, and second, to refer to any specific form, such as ownership, which by itself can be thought of as a bundle' (von Benda-Beckmann, von Benda-Beckmann, and Wiber 2006: 15). The metaphor was adopted by many others after Maine, such as E. Leach, J. Goody, M. Gluckman, F. von Benda-Beckmann, C. Hann, and K. Verdery (von Benda-Beckmann, von Benda-Beckmann, and Wiber 2006: 15, note 16). Such authors have amply discussed the way rights over objects can be differently distributed and separately exercised and applied. Some writers have emphasised the need to distinguish access to property from property itself. That is, the ability to use and benefit from property is different from simply having rights to property (Ribot 1998; Ribot and Peluso 2003).

In exploring such rights and people's ability to use various kinds of property in my Azerbaijani fieldwork sites, I collected and examined stories about how property and agricultural produce were used, valued, and disposed of in late Soviet times and how those practices contrasted with contemporary ones. These narratives are telling about social relationships surrounding property and about people's relationships with the authorities who define, prescribe, and administer property. An analysis of all kinds of property and of all the complex layers of property relationships in western Azer-

---

as *paylamaq*, meaning that shares were divided and distributed, thus suggesting a fair distribution.

[15] For other discussions of how land can 'vanish' or be 'stolen', see Berry (2002) and Verdery (2003).

baijan, however, is beyond the scope of this study. My arguments concern primarily agricultural property, and specifically, agricultural land.[16]

Economists and rural sociologists have been interested in questions about property similar to those that have interested anthropologists.[17] Economists in many socialist and former Soviet countries have widely studied the fate of socialist property after market economic reforms and privatisation. Their theoretical premises derive from liberal economics, which has been critical of socialist economies for favouring collective property over the individual. The prevailing assumption is that once property is privatised and ownership secured, it will be used productively and innovatively by individual producers (see Hann 2003: 7). Such economists began to look at the significance of property 'in managing the social and economic effects of scarcity so that human needs can be efficiently satisfied. Maximisation of scarce resources is optimised where institutions clarify and regularise access to resources' (von Benda-Beckmann, von Benda-Beckmann, and Wiber 2006: 8).

Anthropologists such as the von Benda-Beckmanns, Hann, and Verdery argue that economists have been concerned with the maximisation of efficiency in resource use and the meeting of human needs. Economists have also been concerned with rural productivity as central to all agrarian reforms. Anthropologists are not indifferent to these concerns (see Visser 2006). Pauline Peters (2006: 99) urged anthropologists 'to go beyond calling attention to the "embeddedness" and "complexity" of property rights' and take up a serious dialogue with dominant economic paradigms of economic progress through property reforms:

> The neoclassical economic/neoliberal logic posits that *property in land* is the vehicle to ensure a *market in land* and thereby guarantee *individual incentives* to produce and improve income. For this faith to be rejected requires a notion not of embeddedness but of fetishisation. Rather than fetishising the market and property, we need a political, economic and cultural analysis of 'real' targets of human health, income and work. ... we need an approach 'historically

---

[16] For analyses of other kinds of property and property relationships, see, for instance, Malinowski (1935) on the relationship between magic and land among Trobriand Islanders; Strathern (1988) on the relationship between ideas of person, gender, and property in Melanesia; Weiner (1992) on ideas of gift exchange and property; and Woodburn (1998) on the distinction between sharing, ownership, and the generalised system of exchange among hunter-gatherers. For a more recent discussion of property within the system of values and of property objects as 'things', see Humphrey and Verdery (2004).

[17] In fact, these were the only scientific experts I met in Azerbaijan who showed any real interest in my topic of research. Local ethnologists were mostly astonished at my choice of theme and the questions I was posing.

grounded in the societies under consideration for which capital and capitalism, for example, are more appropriate as both material and cultural categories than are the universal notions of property, institutions, and ideology' (Peters 2006: 100, emphasis in original).

Anthropology has a considerable tradition of engaging with the theories of rural sociologists and economists. The Russian agrarian economist A. V. Chayanov, who developed a model of household production by peasants, argued that 'the amount of labour that peasants committed to farm production related to tax and rent obligations, replacement of equipment, the consumption needs of the household and their subjective evaluation of leisure against the drudgery of working in the fields' (Ortiz 2005: 59). His model has been embraced by Marshall Sahlins (1972) and many others working on peasant households and rural change (Meillasoux 1981; Ellis 1988; Netting 1993; Durrenberger and Tannenbaum 2002).[18] At the same time, Chayanov's model has been extensively criticised for not explaining why peasant households should have needs limited only to feeding themselves (see Wilk and Cliggett 2007: 24) and for treating the peasant household as an undifferentiated unit, ignoring intra-household relations of gender and generation.[19] I follow these critical appraisals of Chayanov's work and show where his model does or does not hold in the Azerbaijani case.

Taking peasant households and especially heads of households as social actors in decision-making in rural production was a common point of critique in the 1970s and 1980s. Nevertheless, giving primacy to individual actors seems to be common in agrarian policies and practical applications of economistic models, as was the case during agrarian reform in Azerbaijan. But even if, under economistic models, individuals have free agency, not all individuals have the same capabilities or possibilities for social action. Individual actors are significant because they make decisions and apply them – in western Azerbaijan, for example, to get together to cultivate a field, to travel as traders abroad, or to spend household capital on goods consumed during life-cycle ceremonies. The task at hand is to explore and explain the conditions, possibilities, and restrictions in which such decisions are embedded and carried out.

In Azerbaijan, agrarian reforms and privatisation gave property rights to individuals, apparently making the individual the main actor in the economic field. Yet the law made the rural household a collective social actor by treating it as a unit for holding private property. That is, members of a household were given land adjacent to one another so that they could – and

---

[18] For appraisals of Chayanov's work, see Durrenberger (1984), Shanin (1990: 319–340), and Schulze (2001).

[19] For good overviews of these critiques of Chayanov, see Harris (1981) and Wong (1984).

would have to – manage the privatised plots collectively. Thus the logic of the agrarian reforms was such that they gave the individual primacy in economic action only conditionally, by embedding him or her in the unit of the household. Why this should be so is something I examine later, from different perspectives.

The question I raised earlier, about why villagers in western Azerbaijan do not cultivate the privatised land shares they received, cannot be explained mono-causally as the failure of the liberal economic remedies of agrarian reform and transition to a market economy. On the one hand, neo-classical predictions are correct in that villagers who received privatised shares did not cultivate the land if doing so was economically unviable. As this theory suggests, they maximised their economic interest. On the other hand, the neo-liberal assumption that secure land ownership is the main incentive for rural people to cultivate and increase their gains does not hold, because Azerbaijani producers did not always cultivate the land even when given ownership of it for free.

These and similar contested areas in the understanding of economic behaviour need to be untangled. In order to do so, I look at four domains of possible explanations.[20] The first domain, which I discuss in chapters 2 and 3, is that of the relationship between the history and geography of economic integration in my fieldwork region and the larger economic and political structures of empires and states.[21] I show how economic links and embeddedness in larger structures have changed over time but maintained a strong disposition towards market orientation and economic flexibility. I provide the historical background for the region and describe the legal institutions of property and changing property forms.

The second domain involves village households, their composition and structure, and their strategies for agrarian and economic activities (chapters 4 and 5). This domain reflects concretised property relations (see von Benda-Beckmann, von Benda-Beckmann, and Wiber 2006: 19–22), as in the way the agrarian reforms made the individual rural resident the legal unit for receiving privatised land shares. In this domain, I deal with theories of

---

[20] To some degree, these domains correspond to the four analytical layers of social organisation suggested by von Benda-Beckmann, von Benda-Beckmann, and Wiber (2006: 14–23; see also von Benda-Beckmann and von Benda-Beckmann 1999) as important in examining property: cultural ideals and ideologies, legal institutions, actual social relationships, and social practices.

[21] I use the term *integration* in a conventional sense, borrowing from state theories; others use *encapsulation* in a similar sense, to describe how ethnically marginal groups and peripheral areas get incorporated 'into structures of larger and more powerful entities such as the nation state and international institutions' (Tadesse 2005: 2–3).

household production and consumption in order to build on the explanatory models of the history of regional economic integration.

The third domain is that of the ideology and practice of kinship, reciprocity, and exchange (chapter 6). In western Azerbaijan, the ideology of kinship, with its emphasis on solidarity and support, is as significant as the actual social practices of exchange (of property and other valuables such as gifts and dowries) and reciprocity between kindred households. Because property is a part of kinship exchange and reciprocal systems, its accumulation and disposal do not always accord with rational economic behaviour and thinking. The role of household plots under the former socialist system and in contemporary cash crop production for international markets is a central issue in these discussions. I illustrate why people may cultivate their long-held household plot but not their privatised land share.

The fourth domain I consider is that of property as part of Azerbaijanis' relationships with the state and its local representatives. Central to both socialist and liberal economic models of property is a dichotomy between private and collective property (see Hann and the Property Relations Group 2003; also Hann 1998; Verdery 2003). In Azerbaijan, however, the operative dichotomy is that between private and *state* – which is seen as different from collective – property. Part of the explanation for this opposition lies in the historical fact that collective farms (kolkhozes) had already been changed into state farms (sovkhozes) before the collapse of the Soviet Union, apparently without affecting people's relationships with either the objects of property or the agricultural organisations themselves. In their narratives, people mentioned the change from kolkhozes to sovkhozes only in passing, as if it involved just another administrative rearrangement of production and distribution.[22] Even if property in Azerbaijan under the Soviet system was in some way labelled 'collective', people perceived it as being under state management and subject to state power. The socialist state was the provider, the manager, the authority that could make property valuable and take property away, and the entity to cheat in order to pursue one's individual and household interests. Furthermore, the state as manager was organised hierarchically through offices and committees, all occupied by people with whom one could establish relationships that might be used to one's benefit.

This notion of property as existing within the realm of the state, overwhelming any importance of the collective, had an important bearing on the privatisation of property in western Azerbaijan and on people's expectations

---

[22] For a contrasting case in the former German Democratic Republic, see Eidson (2006), who describes how the change from one form of *landwirtschaftliche Produktionsgenossenschaft* (LPG) to another was resisted by participants and even by farm administrators.

of benefiting from private property. The change was understood as a change from state – not from collective – property to private property. The Azerbaijani case well illustrates Katherine Verdery's point (2003: xiv) that decollectivisation should be seen not as 're-making private property but as transforming socialist property'. Moreover, for people in rural Azerbaijan, the state had resided in distant, autocratic Moscow and had disappeared after 1990. They might acknowledge 'those above' as governing the new Azerbaijani state, but their common feeling was of being left 'headless' and without protection (*yiyəsiz*, 'ownerless').

Fieldwork Sites and Methodology

I chose both of my fieldwork sites in rural Azerbaijan by chance, through the first contacts I made during my initial visit to the country in March 2000.[23] Although I knew or made contacts with supportive anthropologists and other intellectuals in Baku, these people had few close connections with rural areas. I received news from a friend in Turkey that her distant aunt in Təzəkənd, a village in western Azerbaijan, might allow me to stay with her. With my friend's letter in hand, I went looking for her relative, Könül, who became my hostess and closest friend in Təzəkənd.[24] By extension, I became incorporated into Könül's family like a distant relative from Turkey; indeed, many townspeople believed I was a relative of hers. This allowed me to be easily accepted in the village, and I was seldom questioned by other residents or officials.

In Təzəkənd I spent time accompanying people on visits to neighbours and acquaintances, which was the most fruitful way of getting to know families in order to visit them again for talks and informal interviews. I did not record interviews when I wanted to ask about agricultural production, work, and life involving the sovkhoz or kolkhoz, because significant fraud and corruption cases had taken place in the area and the people involved were still around and sometimes held influential positions. Discussions of such topics were considered sensitive, and my interlocutors reacted with suspicion at any suggestion of my making recordings. Almost all my information and quotations, therefore, are based on notes that I wrote either during interviews or daily from memory.

My host family's neighbourhood was in the centre of the village, where few agricultural workers and cultivators lived. I extended my contacts

---

[23] I spent a total of ten months between 2000 and 2002 and another month in 2005 doing fieldwork in Azerbaijan. I visited the field sites again briefly in August 2007 and August 2008.

[24] All names of people in my field sites have been changed.

to other neighbourhoods primarily by getting to know families whom I selected as a random sample for a household survey. I developed my own contacts in other neighbourhoods and tried to follow the activities of cultivators through frequent visits to families who worked either their fields of privatised land or, mostly, their household plots. Some of these families were also involved in selling produce from household plots, so they became contacts to follow up during a brief visit I made to Moscow and the vegetable wholesale markets there.

I developed close relationships with some families who had newly acquired economic wealth, but not with many of them. It was difficult to establish any relationship of trust with people who had acquired wealth by holding governmental positions and who were said to be taking bribes, such as some police officers, the state attorney (*prokuror*) for the *rayon*, and the head of the oil depot. I collected stories about such people but was unable to establish an insider's perspective, apart from occasional conversations with several such persons. The newly elected municipal administration and its members had less at stake, and because I had contact with them by knowing their relatives well, I had fruitful talks with them about how administrative structures functioned, how wealth was being accumulated, and whether or not property and land played any role in these processes.

Besides collecting people's stories and information from discussions of certain themes, I relied heavily on information I gathered as part of my household survey, which enabled me to enter people's homes. People would otherwise avoid me, for reasons ranging from the shame they felt over being poor and unable to host me for even a few hours of visiting to their feelings of anxiety about my inquiries concerning land distribution and access to agricultural resources and technology. I managed to become friends with some people who at first avoided me, but by no means with all of them.

Finally, I made an effort to get to know some of the administrators and intellectuals in the nearby town, mostly people who had links to relatives or acquaintances in Təzəkənd. Followed these links between village and town helped me understand how villagers' relationships with administrative and power centres worked.

My second research site was a settlement of internally displaced persons (IDPs), the settlement of Pir in the *rayon* of Ismayilli. I was interested in contacting Kurds in Azerbaijan, of whom hardly any study existed, because of work I had done earlier in Turkey. My contact with the Kurdish IDPs changed my initial research interest, because their ethnic identity and status as IDPs presented an important and complementary link to the privatisation of state land and people's access to and use of agricultural land. I learned that IDPs were 'hungry' for land, and I decided to explore why this was so.

I stayed with a leading family in Pir for nearly five weeks in 2001, after having made contact with the head of the household through a wealthy relative of his who lived in Baku. In Pir I carried out a household survey concerning the IDPs' access to land and their farming and pastoral production. I made frequent visits to the main town of Ismayilli, where I was assisted by a group of former agrarian economists and technicians who had recently organised themselves into an NGO to give credit to local farmers. I was able to have detailed and informative talks with these agrarian specialists about former and contemporary problems of agrarian production, land reform, and rural livelihood. I also spent many hours with their families and was able to observe the significance of kinship and friendship links for economic survival and accumulation. Although these families had a very different economic status from that of the IDPs, both groups had to engage in agricultural production within the same rural economic structure of dry farming and livestock husbandry. In the final chapter of this book (chapter 7), before a brief conclusion, I examine the kinds of strategies the IDPs used in order to guarantee their right to use agricultural land in a legal situation in which they had no right to own land.

Chapter 2
Western Azerbaijan in Pre-Soviet History

> There ought to be no 'relationship' between history and anthropology, since there should be no division to begin with. A theory of society which is not also a theory of history, or vice versa, is hardly a theory at all.
> – John L. Comaroff, 'Dialectical Systems, History, and Anthropology'

Approaching the centre of Təzəkənd, a village that feels more like a small town, one drives down a main street shaded by big trees on either side, mostly cherries and mulberries. Although the typical houses of the region are built of stone and feature courtyards shielded from the gazes of passers-by by high outer walls, some houses along this road are in the half-timbered architectural style, with old tiles, deep cellars, and wooden porches facing the street. Similar houses and streets exist elsewhere in Azerbaijan, as in the *rayon* centre, the city of Şəmkir. The style originated in old rural settlements in southern Germany, and in Azerbaijan it is a remnant of settlements founded by German colonists in the late nineteenth century. Local people know that ethnic Germans lived in the region until they were deported during World War II, but otherwise they have been largely forgotten.

More recent – and more strikingly absent from public discussion – was the exodus of Armenians from the region. Only occasionally and with great reluctance did my neighbours and acquaintances in Təzəkənd recall or speak of the existence of Armenians in the village. They had all 'left' during the years of 'chaos' (*hərc-mərclik*, 'anarchy', in Azerbaijani). That is the way people usually refer to the years between 1988 and 1990, when the Soviet Union was disintegrating. Immediately afterwards came the declaration of independence of the Azerbaijani Republic in 1991, followed from 1992 to 1994 by the war with Armenia over the autonomous region of Nagorno-Karabakh. During a conversation about a circumcision ceremony to be held in the neighbourhood, I was told that the grandmother of the child to be circumcised was in fact an Armenian, but no one would talk about it openly, let alone to her face, so as not to cause her pain. A woman I knew from the marketplace was said to have an Armenian mother, but no one would talk about it in the presence of outsiders like me. The muted histories of both the Armenians and the Germans fascinated me and made me aware of the many levels of interpretation that ensue from evoking and forgetting the past.[25]

Azerbaijani history, like many other complex, contested regional histories, involves colonial encounters, expansions and deportations, migration and re-settlement, the establishing of roots as well as uprooting, and the 'constant mixing of populations, blurring of ethnic boundaries, intermarriage, bi- and tri-lingualism, to the point of some people becoming other people, and some disappearing into others' (Suny 1997: 2).[26] In this chapter I want to account for this complexity, which must be understood if the nature and extent of property concepts are to be explored. What is the historical background of existing property concepts in Azerbaijan? How deeply rooted are property relations? What are the parameters of people's memories of the relationships pertaining to certain property objects and the rules and regulations surrounding them? Which aspects of property do they seem not to remember?

In order to decipher the historical layers of property relations in the region, it is necessary to explore patterns of settlement in the region, the kinds of state and societal relationships that existed, the integration of the region into larger economic and political structures, and the types of social and ethnic boundaries that prevailed at certain times in history. All these factors affected property regimes and concepts. In exploring the history of property regimes, it is essential to consider the ways property objects were conceived of in the past and the ways particular groups of people positioned themselves in relationship to the objects and to one another, expressly because property is about the relationships surrounding objects and between people.

Azerbaijani historians often seem to stick closely to political guidelines, in that they seek to replicate, in local histories, an overall 'History'. Here I want to look at the exchange and interaction between History and histories and to deduce from this interaction which aspects are relevant for understanding the social and economic formations and relations in the region. Some of the questions I raise in this context have to do with the degree of the region's economic integration into world markets and with the exis-

---

[25] For a recent and excellent study of the connections between modern societies and forgetting, see Connerton (2009).
[26] On the issue of how history continues to be a politically and, now, nationalistically informed science in postsocialist Azerbaijan, see Adam (2005).

tence of landlords or state property prior to the Soviet period of collectivisation.

I begin with Russian colonial expansion into western Azerbaijan, the changes that colonisation brought to the region, and the effects of those changes on property regimes.[27] I am concerned with placing the region within the overall history of Russian expansion, not with arguing for historical determination. I want to explore the historical roots of certain configurations, especially insofar as the historical information supports or challenges assumptions about contemporary property relations and regimes.[28] If my arguments sometimes sound speculative, it is because historical sources for western Azerbaijan are limited, often contradictory, and contested, and the data they provide are distributed unevenly across time and the region.

Western Azerbaijan before the Russian Conquest

Many princedoms, empires, and other political entities, large and small, have at different times exercised influence and control over the provinces now known as Azerbaijan. Certain periods of this history are contested from the perspectives of contemporary Azerbaijani, other Caucasian, and non-local historians (see Altstadt 1992: 2–3; Shnirelman 2001: 93–197).[29] In particular, historians of the region still contentiously debate the pre-Christian and pre-Islamic statehood of Caucasian Albania, which in the first century BCE was a kingdom in northern Azerbaijan, allied to Georgia and Armenia. Christianity became the state religion there during the fourth century CE.[30] From the seventh century onwards, Azerbaijani territories fell under the influence of Islam, although there were occasional uprisings against the Muslim Arab rulers and caliphs. The nature of the Christian and Muslim denominations and the link between the Albanian and Armenian churches continue to be other controversial issues (Altstadt 1992: 7).

The city of Ganja (in this work, Gəncə), in western Azerbaijan, is said to have been established during the third century CE and was a trading,

---

[27] I rely here on the standard historical works, the seven volumes of *Yeddi cilddə Azərbaycan Tarixi,* published by the Azerbaijani historians of the Azerbaijani Academy of Sciences from 1998 through 2003. I also draw on Altstadt (1992), Swietochowski (1995), Suny (1996), Swietochowski and Collins (1999), and Mostashari (2006).

[28] For an inspiring study of historical anthropological sources and cultural history of gift giving, kidnapping, and exchange, see Grant (2009).

[29] For a review of the main points of contestation over Azerbaijani history among local historians, see Mustafayev (2007).

[30] Albania was a vassal of Sassanian Iran in the third and fourth centuries CE and joined Sassanian armies fighting Muslim Arab invaders in the seventh century, becoming a vassal of the Arab caliphate at the end of that century (Altstadt 1992: 2–5; Swietochowski and Collins 1999: 38).

crafts, administrative, and cultural centre of Caucasian Albania (see Məmmədova 2004: 15–19).[31] The district of Shamkir (Shamxor, Şamxor, or, in this work, Şəmkir, its contemporary transliteration), some 30 kilometres west of Gəncə, would have been under the same rule.[32] Persia, with its ethnically mixed ruling dynasties and its expansion to the north, including the territory of modern Azerbaijan, played an important role during the following periods of history. From about the ninth century onwards, small dynastic states existed in the region, each headed by a prince, who usually made alliances with other princes and became a vassal to a stronger king, shah, or sultan in one of the surrounding political bodies.

The settlement of Turks and the rise of Turkic influence in the region are other points of historical dispute. According to Peter Golden (1992: 97–104, 382–386), Turkic nomads of the Oguz tribes were involved in Transcaucasian affairs as early as the sixth and seventh centuries, through the Khazars and the Bulgar tribal federations to the north (see also Altstadt 1992: 6). By the eleventh century, the arrival of the Seljuks completed the Turkisation of eastern Caucasia, which was more fully consolidated with migrations of Turkic elements during the thirteenth-century Mongol invasions (Altstadt 1992: 7; Golden 1992).[33]

---

[31] Since the last deportations from Armenia (1988–1990), some Azerbaijani historians have referred to the territories of Armenia that were historically claimed and settled by Azerbaijanis as Western Azerbaijan (e.g. Ələkbərli 2000, 2002, 2006). I do not follow this usage; I refer to western Azerbaijan as including the western *rayon*s of the present Azerbaijani Republic, which are often referred to locally as 'Qazax-Gəncə zonası'. I thank Volker Adam for drawing my attention to the different uses of the term.

[32] Contemporary Azerbaijani historians mention Ganja as an ancient city and say that the surrounding area was densely populated (see *Gənjə Tarixi Oçerk* 1994: 3–4). Some sources cite Şəmkir as having been an important town of Caucasian Albania (Tapdıqoğlu 2005: 127).

[33] For discussions of how devastating the Mongol invasions were for the countryside and production systems at the time, see *Azərbaycan Tarixi*, vol. 3, 1999: 52–60.

Plate 1. Ruins of Şəmkir castle.

In the twelfth and thirteenth centuries, *atabeg*s and shahs were ruling autonomous states in Azerbaijan.[34] The rule of the Shirvanshahs, for example, lasted until the rise of Safavid rule in the sixteenth century in southern Azerbaijan, in today's Iran, and then was incorporated into the Safavid administrative system (Altstadt 1992: 5; Mustafayev 1999; Swietochowski and Collins 1999: 119). During the reign of Ismail I, the first shah of the Safavids, who ruled from 1501 to 1524, Twelver Shia became the state religion.[35] At least one writer sees this development as having sealed the division of Azerbaijani Turks from those in the Ottoman Empire and from the Shibanids in Central Asia, on the basis of religious differences. This evaluation needs to be critically interpreted in terms of the meanings and

---

[34] *Atabeg* or *atabak* was the title given to high dignitaries under the Seljuks and their successors. By the twelfth century, Azerbaijani *atabeg*s had made this title into a hereditary possession of governorship and had begun suppressing the power of sultans by depriving them of local resources (Cahen 1986a: 731–732).

[35] On Twelver Shia, see Brunner and Ende (2001).

uses of ethnic and religious identities in those centuries and in light of the political organisation of multi-ethnic and pre-national states and empires.[36]

The dominant features of the historical formations of the pre-Russian period, in short, were that these states were ruled by *atabeg*s of Mamluk dynasties (see Bünyadov 2004: 44–104); the society was composed of nomadic and settled groups and federations; and the religious and ethnic affiliations of rulers and subjects varied greatly (see Golden 1992; Bournoutian 1996; Suny 1997). The region of Gəncə was subjected to substantial re-settlement by *kizilbash* tribes who were brought to the region from Iran during Shah Abbas's reign, towards the end of the sixteenth century.[37] The city of Gəncə was re-established after this population movement.

On the eve of the Russian conquest, after the end of the Safavid dynasties, local rulers were fighting among themselves and asserting some autonomy, until Nadir Shah of the Afshars came to power and established some law and order among them. He also made alliances with neighbouring Georgian princes, giving, for instance, land in Gəncə to be ruled by Kartveli-Kakheti princes (*Gəncə Tarixi Oçerk* 1994: 15). Nadir Shah was killed in 1747, by which time the population had become a mixture of settled people, nomads, and semi-nomads, of Georgians, Armenians, Jews, Kurds, Turkomans, and Lezgis.

Concerning law, administration, and property regimes prior to Russian rule, historians point out that secular and religious laws co-existed, as was common throughout most of the Islamic world. Until the Russian conquest, the administrative and legal systems derived primarily from the Safavid rule of the sixteenth century onwards. Under the Safavids, the territory they called Azerbaijan was divided into four units (*beklerbeklik*s), administered by governors (*beklerbek*s). The units were Tabriz, with its centre in the city of Tabriz, in today's Iran; Shukhur-Saada, centred in the city of Nakhjivan; Shirvan, centred in Shemaki; and Karabagh, centred in Gəncə (Altstadt 1992: 9).

From the Safavid period until the mid-eighteenth century, Azerbaijan was ruled as individual khanates. The rulers, *beklerbek*s and then khans,

---

[36] According to Altstadt (1992: 5), 'Shi'ism was adopted by Ismail at least partly as a political tool in his ongoing conflict with the two neighbouring Sunni Muslim Turkish empires, the Ottomans to the West and the Central Asian Shibanids on the Northeast. For the Turks of Azerbaijan, the result was twofold: (1) a strengthening of the bonds with the Iranian state and what was by the sixteenth century its Turco-Persian culture (the Safavid court language … was Turkish), and (2) a sectarian division from other Turks'. For a critical view, see Adam (2001).

[37] *Kizilbash* refers in general to a variety of Shiite sects, mostly from Turkmen tribes, which flourished in Anatolia, Kurdistan, and Azerbaijan from the late thirteenth century onwards. The name arose from the red headgear worn by members of the sect. See Savory (1986).

were also tribal leaders, and their primary loyalty was to their tribes. Under this system, all land was considered the personal property (*mülk*) of the khan. Close relatives of the khan were given the title of *bek* (*beg, bəy,* 'notable'). They served the khan, had their own retainers, were exempt from taxes, and enjoyed a great deal of local authority (Altstadt 1992: 9–10). Tadeusz Swietochowski (1995: 2–3) described the eighteenth-century khanates as

> miniature replicas of the Iranian monarchy. ... their socioeconomic structure was based on state ownership of land, an outgrowth of the medieval institution of *iqta*.[38] Plots were distributed to landholders, *bəys* and *ağas,* as nonhereditary grants for services rendered to the ruler, the khan. The khanates were often subdivided into *mahal*s (regions), territorial units inhabited by members of the same tribe, a reflection of the strong residue of tribalism.

The rulers depended on the landed nobility for taxes and soldiers. Once the khanates came to an end, both the larger and lesser administrators were absorbed into the local land-owning nobility (Altstadt 1992: 10).

Another historian of the region, George Bournoutian, looking at the majority of the population – Armenians and Muslims who lived as peasants and nomads – described their socio-economic conditions before the Russian conquest:

> Villages were divided into farming and communal grazing areas in an open field and common pasture system. The elders divided the agricultural plots according to the number of animals, people, and labourers in a family. The lands of large villages were farmed communally; in small villages each plot was farmed by a single family. Agricultural lands followed the two-field rotation system; half the plot was planted, half left fallow. ...
>
> In many villages large individual farms belonged to one clan, who lived together in one household. Usually the land of these clans could not be sold unless the family became too large or quarrelled among themselves. The family organization was patriarchal. The sons all inherited an equal share, the daughters half a son's share. If a daughter married during her parents' lifetime, she forfeited any inheritance and received only a dowry. ...
>
> Unlike other parts of Persia [during the last decades of Persian rule] there was no rebellion or large emigration. ... Banditry and violence in the cities ceased to exist. Another positive indication of

---

[38] For more on the *iqta*, or *ikta*, as a non-inheritable administrative grant, see Cahen (1986b: 1088–1091). For discussions of the history of the *iqta* system, see Golden (1996: 57–58), Bünyadov (2004), and Mundy (2004).

the well-being of the population was the small number of landless peasants (*ranjbar*) in the region. In general the inhabitants of [this region] received numerous services for their taxes, a condition which did not prevail everywhere in Persia. The amount of trade activity, the number of domestic animals, [and] the sizeable bureaucracy all attest to the socio-economic stability of the region during this period (Bournoutian 1996: 83–85).

On the whole, Azerbaijan before the Russian conquest is depicted as having always been a region of agriculture, nomadic herding, garden cultivation, and trade (Altstadt 1992: 10). Crafts and trade were widespread and developed. Interestingly, from very early on there was also trade in oil: 'A local geographer in the fifteenth century … stated that 200 mule loads of oil were exported daily from the pits near Baku' (Altstadt 1992: 10). In the late nineteenth and early twentieth centuries, oil was to become the source of wealth and the reason for foreign intervention in the area, causing rapid development as well as major population and economic changes in the whole of Azerbaijan.

The Russian Colonisation of Western Azerbaijan

Historical sources on Azerbaijan refer to the Russian conquest of the southern Caucasus as having taken place in stages, the routes of conquest following the region's geographical contours. After tsarist Russia conquered Vladikavkaz, opening the corridor to the Caucasus Mountains, it co-opted the Georgian nobles and princes and found its way into the lowlands of Georgia and modern-day Azerbaijan (Auch 2001: 2). One by one the mountainous areas were conquered. Georgia was incorporated into the Russian hegemony in 1801, and the khanate of Gəncə, in western Azerbaijan, in 1804, after a siege that lasted a month (see *Gəncə Tarixi Oçerk* 1994; Baddeley 1999 [1908]: 67; Auch 2001; *Gəncə Şəhərinin Tarixi* 2004).[39] After the conquest the city was given first to Tbilisi for administration (Auch 2001: 3). Later, when General Tsitsianov, the Russian commander, was

---

[39] Even the details of the fall of Gəncə are disputed by Azerbaijani historians. The authors of *Gəncə Şəhəri Tarixi* describe the heroic fight of Djavad Khan, the ruler of Gəncə, against General Tsitsianov, the Russian commander-in-chief, and how the khan refused any offer by the Russian commander. In contrast, the authors of the edited volume *Azerbaycan Tarixi* (vol. 4, 2000: 19) claim that the khan of Gəncə did not reject the offer of his becoming a suzerain of the Russian Empire; they write that he had maintained diplomatic relations with the empire since the 1790s. They note that Tsitsianov was rude to the khan, boastful, and vain (*yekəxana*), and that was why the situation came to a bloody war. For another account of Djavad Khan's connection to the Russian commanders, of Tsitsianov's style in exchanges with him and with other khans, and of how the capture of Gəncə set an example for the Russian conquest of Muslim lands, see Mostashari (2006: 14–16).

assassinated outside Baku, the conquered khanates became rebellious once again (Mostashari 2006: 16).

In the years that followed, wars between the Russian and Ottoman Empires continued to affect the region. The Russian presence and dominance in the southern Caucasus was challenged not only by the Ottomans but also by the Persian Empire. After the penetration of Russian forces into Azerbaijan, the first war between the empires lasted about nine years. In 1813, Russia and Persia signed the treaty of Gulistan, according to which Persia accepted the submission of many khanates, including Gəncə, to the Russian Empire. The treaty did not hold for long. Another war broke out between Persia and Russia in 1826 and lasted until 1828. Following the Russians' victory over the Persians in a battle in the area of Şəmkir, they re-entered Gəncə (Baddeley 1999 [1908]: 158). Ultimately, the remaining provinces, Yerevan and Nakhjivan, also fell to Russia. This marked the beginning of settlement by Armenians, most of whom arrived from Persia, in the newly annexed Yerevan (Auch 2001: 4).

Even if historians agree about the Russians' final penetration into the Muslim areas of the Caucasus, their interpretations of Russian colonial history and the nature of colonisation in the Caucasus vary. Audrey Altstadt (1992), for instance, claimed that the Russians were never fully accepted and that resistance to them was enduring. In contrast to Eva-Maria Auch's arguments (2001), Altstadt wrote that the khans resisted the Russian forces:

> Contrary to contemporary Russian and later Soviet accounts, the population and the khans strenuously resisted the Russian conquest, which was less a matter of Russo-Iranian armed conflict than of battles between khans and Russian forces. Initially, some khans thought to use the Russo-Iranian War to improve their own positions and supported the Russians because they seemed far away or because some traditional rival supported the Qajars [of Iran]. But contact with the Russians changed their minds. During the war Russians profaned mosques and forced their way into private homes. As the Russian forces neared a town or settlement, people would flee south. After the Russian victory, many khans and their families took refuge in Iran (Altstadt 1992: 17).

Firozeh Mostashari (2006) underlined another dimension of Russian colonisation at this early stage, writing that the personality, political, and strategy differences between military commanders of the Caucasus campaigns and the Russian tsar were important in shaping the ambivalence of Russian colonial policies. For example, by the spring of 1805,

> [Commander] Tsitsianov had intimidated the khans of Karabagh, Shusha, Sheki and Shirvan into accepting Russian suzerainty. Tsit-

sianov typically wrote the letters of capitulation, addressed to the
tsar, and forced the khans to sign the terms. In his reports to [Tsar]
Alexander, Tsitsianov distorted the events and suggested that the
khans had willingly joined the empire and were asking for Russian
protection. In return for their evinced desire to serve the crown with
'zeal', the tsar accepted the khans as subjects, conferred military titles upon them (typically the rank of lieutenant-general) and gave
them a yearly salary in silver (Mostashari 2006: 16).

The complexity of the relations, interests, and ambitions of Russian
and local actors allowed for different interpretations of the colonial conquest
and rule, depending on which part of the relationship was to be highlighted
and which aspect of the background was to take eminence. Although the
leading historians of the Academy of Sciences of Azerbaijan, who published
numerous volumes on Azerbaijan's history, retained in large part the Soviet
interpretation, describing the khans and *begs* as feudal rulers who sought
only their own self-interest, they elaborated their post-independence interpretation to note that the local people had always been against occupation,
whether Iranian or Russian:

> The local inhabitants of Azerbaijan did not relate to the Russian-
> Iranian war in similar ways. Some feudal rulers in Azerbaijan, espe-
> cially some among them who were afraid of losing their autonomy,
> approached the battle as their salvation and helped the warring par-
> ties to this end. The endless wars, which were caused by local and
> outside forces, forced sections of the local population to seek ways
> out and hence to support the Russian forces. On the whole, however,
> the people did not want either the Russian or the Iranian occupation;
> they supported their own khans against the occupiers and promised
> to help the khans in every way (*Azərbaycan Tarixi*, vol. 4, 2000: 2,
> my translation; see also Auch 2001: 5).

The inconsistencies and fluctuations of Russian colonial policy have
been analysed not only by Mostashari (2006: chap. 2) but also by Eva-Maria
Auch:

> No stable pattern of Tsarist policy concerning subjugated 'foreign
> peoples' was implemented until the second half of the nineteenth
> century. Policy oscillated rather between the establishment of he-
> gemony through repressive regulations intended to accelerate inte-
> gration and assimilation and consolidation of power through the rec-
> ognition of a certain status quo and a readiness for cooperation with
> local elites. The Russian monopoly on initiating action remained re-
> stricted insofar as parts of the local population demonstrated open
> resistance. Hence, this policy had an 'amorphous' character [and]

fluctuated between 'colony and fusion into the Empire' (Auch 2001: 5).

Tadeusz Swietochowski (1995), another prominent historian of Azerbaijan, illuminated the struggle between the competing schools of colonial administration, which continued after the 1840s. First, the khanate system was undermined as the reformed administrative system divided the territory into new districts (*uezd*s) and 'ended the age-old fragmentation of Azerbaijan in one stroke'. Later, the reforms were stopped for having gone too far. All military and civil responsibilities were then given to the Russian viceroy, who was to report directly to the tsar:

> The preferred policy of the first viceroy of the Caucasus, Vorontsov, was co-optation of the native elites to Russification and integration. In Azerbaijan, where the impoverished beys and aghas had seen their social status eroding, he favoured, in effect, creation of a new elite by upgrading their legal status to the level of the Russian *dvorianie* (gentry). On Vorontsov's recommendation, Nicholas I issued the December Rescript of 1846, which formally bestowed hereditary and inalienable rights on the Muslim holders of the *tül* lands.[40] A centuries-old institution, legal state ownership of most land, came to an end with the massive transfer of property titles into private hands[41] (Swietochowski 1995: 14–15).

After Vorontsov, Russian colonial policy began to fluctuate again, and his accommodating policies were reversed. As a result of administrative reforms made after Vorontsov retired, the imperial policy of centralisation and Russification re-emerged in the 1860s, followed by the rearrangement of administrative divisions such as *uezd*s and *uchastek*s (the smallest territorial units, which replaced neighbourhood settlements). There was 'a drastic reduction of native personnel at the lowest levels of bureaucracy, with most of the positions in territorial administration ending up in the hands of the Russians and Armenians' (Swietochowski 1995: 16). When Tsar Alexander III (r. 1881–1894) came to the throne, he 'denied the special status of Transcaucasia by replacing the office of viceroy with that of a simple governor-general, while at the same time restoring the authority of central government departments over the local affairs of the region' (Swietochowski 1995: 16).

---

[40] *Tül*, or *tiyul*, denotes a grant of land in the old Persian land tenure system; the *tiyul* holder had to support the khan with military service. See Lambton (2000); also Lambton (1991: 475); *Azərbaycan Tarixi*, vol. 4, 2000: 79–80.

[41] Regional differences existed, however. The contrast between the regions of Baku and Gəncə and the rest of the khanates is supported by Swietochowski (1995: 13), who wrote that the outright abolishment of the khanate – as in the case of Gəncə – was an exception. On variations in Russian colonial policy during the nineteenth century, see also *Azərbaycan Tarixi*, vol. 4, pp. 82–83.

Administrative Reforms and the Application of Law

The logic of the Russian administrative reforms and their consequences have been dealt with at length by Auch (2001) and Mostashari (2006). Auch emphasised that collecting taxes in the region and integrating it into the Russian Empire required the establishment of an effective bureaucracy. Efforts were made to reproduce an educated Russian bureaucracy in Azerbaijan (Auch 2001: 16–17), but difficulties and misunderstandings persisted. The Russians had difficulty finding the right people to be administrators, and the local elites perceived the Russians as wanting to intervene in their autonomy. The coexistence of a binary power structure opened the doors to misuses of power (Auch 2001: 16–20).

A chronology of the complex changes in administrative units in Azerbaijan after the Russian conquest (Auch 2001: 12) shows that the inclusion of the Caucasus regions in the Russian Empire was completed around 1860 and was followed by a range of reforms. The most important of these were the abolishment of serfdom and the creation of self-governing units (*zemstva*, in Russian) in the countryside (1864) and in cities (1870), along with reforms involving the justice, education, and the military systems. Auch (2001: 13) noted that these reforms were carried out at different speeds and with differing effectiveness, but the Russian state was nevertheless deeply committed to the integration of the periphery into the Russian centre. Liberal institutions such as independent courts, institutions of self-government, and a milder system of censorship were introduced with the abolishment of serfdom, paving the way for the transition from an autocratic state to a modern one and to a new notion of citizenship for regulating the relationship between state and society (Auch 2001: 13).

Mostashari, in evaluating the 'Great Reforms', pointed out that they were introduced with delays and implemented by half-measures. Although the introduction of the *zemstva* system, for example, was discussed for a long time, 'the tsarist officials never felt comfortable allowing this region to have self-government' (Mostashari 2006: 65). The implementation of the self-government reforms, Mostashari observed, revealed the colonial mentality by disqualifying those who did not understand Russian and giving more votes to Russian peasants than to Muslims. Regarding the introduction of an independent judiciary, she wrote that unlike in Russia proper, 'in Transcaucasia and Azerbaijan in particular, judicial reform was introduced without first freeing the peasantry from bondage' (p. 66). The delays, poor implementation, poor quality of officials, and slow processing of laws all contributed to the disappointment local people felt over the ineffectiveness of the reforms in the region. Russian prejudices were fed by the belief that the 'failure of the judicial reforms' had to do with the 'deep cultural differences

that separated Russia from the Caucasus' (p. 67). In the villages, the ineffectiveness of the reforms 'led the peasantry, whose rights to the land and to the
water supply were yet ambiguous, to take matters into their own hands when
land disputes arose' (p. 67). As a consequence, they seized *bek* lands, refused to pay dues, cut timber illegally, stole other people's cattle, and even
engaged in armed uprisings and arson. The latter, according to Mostashari,
was a popular form of protest that 'led to a vicious cycle of punitive expedi-
tions and repression' (p. 67).

Economic Effects of the Colonisation

Until the mid-nineteenth century, the political economy in the Caucasus
pertained mainly to gathering taxes and other payments and controlling the
customs from trade with Persia. Although Russian colonisation meant that
trade with Russia became profitable as customs rates fell, Russian traders
and goods had privileges over their Caucasian counterparts (Auch 2001: 9).
Some European goods, such as textiles, became more expensive for Cauca-
sians, relative to goods from central Russia. A ban on goods in transit trade
led to the flourishing of black markets, and in 1846 the transit trade was
allowed again (Auch 2001: 8–10).

The internal borders between the khanates, which were used to control
and tax trade and to channel the income from it directly to the state treasury,
were maintained until 1851, when a new customs tariff system was introduced. Foreign and local currencies, which were used in the region until the
1830s, were replaced by the Russian rouble, and thereafter significant steps
were taken to integrate the region directly into the Russian markets. Muslims, Armenians, and Greeks were the most important regional and international traders (Auch 2001: 10).

The first systematic plans to regulate and coordinate agriculture and
manufacturing, as well as trade, came with the colonisation of the Azerbaijani khanates. Historians of the Azerbaijan Academy of Sciences have
written that in 1833, a plan existed to exert these very controls (*Azərbaycan
Tarixi*, vol. 4, 2000: 58).

In keeping with the fiscal and infrastructural reforms in Azerbaijan
during the Russian colonial period, an oil boom from 1870 to 1900 was a
major economic development. It primarily affected Baku (Altstadt 1992: 22).
The banking system, which was already in place in 1880, and infrastructural
developments such as transport for facilitating the oil industry and commerce expanded rapidly thereafter:

> Railroad construction responded to the needs of the oil industry and
> had an impact beyond it. Baku's oldest rail line was built in 1880 to
> connect the city with the oil districts. ... The Transcaucasian Rail-

way was built to transport oil to the Black sea ... [and] was completed in 1884.[42] It ran from Baku to Batum via Ganje (Elizavetpol) and Tiflis. ... The railway drew the agricultural hinterland closer to industrial markets in Baku. A communication network enhanced their relationship. Telegraph lines connected Baku to Tbilisi via Ganje in the 1860s (Altstadt 1992: 23).

Although these infrastructural developments were aimed mainly at the major cities, their effects were felt in the regions around Gəncə and Şəmkir (see *Azərbaycan Tarixi*, vol. 4, pp. 244–245). Newly built railroads carried oil to neighbouring countries and ports and connected the region to the major cities of Tbilisi and Baku. Primarily because of developments in Baku, other regions began growing produce for consumers in that burgeoning city. This led increasingly to specialisation of production – silks in Shemaki, Nukha, and Sheki; wheat on the Mugan steppe – which further integrated the region, via Baku, with larger markets. 'Under tsarist orders cotton was planted at the expense of food crops. Loss of American cotton imports in the 1860s led to increases in the hated crop: Ganje guberniia cotton output rose from 1,500 puds in 1870 to 62,200 puds in 1894' (Altstadt 1992: 24).[43]

According to Altstadt (1992: 20), trade relations with the Russian Empire grew even before the rapid industrialisation of the 1870s, because of Azerbaijan's (particularly Baku's) transit location relative to Russia and because Azerbaijan was already becoming Russia's agricultural hinterland. These observations are particularly relevant to the history of trade and agriculture in western Azerbaijan: 'Trade in food and other agricultural products, perhaps more than in any other area of economic activity, linked the hinterland to Baku and other cities and towns. One reason Azerbaijani Turks were numerous in agricultural trade throughout the area was that the merchants were often friends, partners, or members of the rural families who produced the food' (Altstadt 1992: 24). Such patterns of networking among friends, kin, and neighbours for trade in agricultural produce remain conspicuous today, as I discuss in chapter 6.

Agrarian and Land Tenure Reforms in the Nineteenth Century

Historians of the Azerbaijan Academy of Sciences state that agricultural production in Azerbaijan in the first half of the nineteenth century was

---

[42] Auch (2001: 210) gave the date for the completion of the Baku-Tbilisi railway as 1883. For comparative purposes, note that the first European railway, between Fürth and Nürnberg, was opened in 1835.
[43] One *pud* equals about 16 kilograms.

dominated by feudal relationships (*Azərbaycan Tarixi*, vol. 4, 2000: 59).[44] The Iran-Russian war and the divisions among the feudal lords imposed a heavy burden on the agrarian structure. In the first three decades of the nineteenth century, Azerbaijan was invaded three times and was subjected to pillage, plunder (*qarət*), and destruction (*Azərbaycan Tarixi*, vol. 4, 2000: 59). Nevertheless, the production of wheat, rice, saffron, dried fruit, silk, and cattle was sufficient that those products continued to be sold to Russia and, to a lesser degree, in local markets and in Georgia and Iran. According to the academy historians (*Azərbaycan Tarixi*, vol. 4, 2000: 60), 'even if agrarian production units were still weak, they were drawn into cash crop and commodity relations'.[45] They add that despite Azerbaijan's becoming a Russian colony, some developments took place in the agricultural sector, because internal strife came to an end ('*daxili müharibələrə son qoyuldu*').[46] Some commodity production of agricultural items seems to have developed during the nineteenth century; not only did raw silk become a commodity for Russian markets, but so did tobacco and madder (*qızılboya*) for dying rugs (*Azərbaycan Tarixi*, vol. 4, 2000: 62–63).

Historians summarise the two main kinds of property after Russian colonisation as state land (*xəzinə/divan torpaqları*, in Azerbaijani) and privately owned land (*xüsusi sahibkar torpağı/mülk*). After the Russian conquest, state land included the land of former khans and *bəg*s as well as the village commons (*icma torpağı*) (*Azərbaycan Tarixi*, vol. 4, 2000: 79–80, 82–83). Peasants living on state land were called state peasants (*dövlət kəndliləri*), and they suffered most from land shortages (p. 83).[47] Privately owned land is described as having been the private (and feudal) property of the former khans. Some of the khans and beys were allowed to retain this property, even though they lost the right to rule the estates. Azerbaijani historians include the property of religious foundations (*vəqf*) and church

---

[44] The khanate system was designated 'feudal' in Soviet historiography, and interestingly, no critical evaluation of the term seems to have take place after 1991 (Shahin Mustafayev, Department of History and Oriental Studies, Azerbaijani Academy of Sciences, personal communication).

[45] '*Kəndli təsərrüfatları zəif olsa da, əmtəə-pul münasibətlərinə cəlb olunurdu*'; my translation.

[46] Again, this is contrary to the arguments made by Altstadt (1992).

[47] According to the historians of *Azərbaycan Tarixi* (vol. 4, 2000: 83), on average the tax-paying peasants (*rəiyyət*), who lived on state land, owned their own production equipment, paid taxes to the state, and each had 3.0 to 3.5 *desiatin* of arable land, although mere survival for a peasant household required a minimum of 5 *desiatin*. One *desiatin* equalled approximately one hectare.

property (*monastırlar*) in the category of private property but add that it did not amount to much in total area (p. 81).[48]

Among the major agrarian reforms in nineteenth-century Russia, which applied to Azerbaijan, were laws passed in 1861 that abolished serfdom and in 1866 that concerned peasants on state-owned land (Auch 2001: 13; see also Mostashari 2006: 67–69).[49] None of the most elementary preconditions for carrying out these reforms existed in Azerbaijan. The relationship between dependency, property, and estates was unclear; no cadastral work had been done; and there was no system for measuring land (Auch 2001: 13). Auch (2001: 13) summarized the way the landed nobility was incorporated into Russia after the reforms:

> Already in 1860 the landed nobility in Muslim provinces (*beg*s, *agalar*, *sultan*s and *melik*s) of the Russian Empire was divided into three categories. The first category consisted of all those who possessed a document from either the Ottoman or Persian Empire or who were recognised by the hereditary khans prior to the Russian annexation. These received hereditary noble titles for service to the state (in German, *Dienstadel*), and as such they could be commissioned as officers after four years of military service. The second category, the '*agalar*', consisted of those who had been registered in 1846 in the lists of the Commission for Agalar and had documents that attested to their pre-colonial title of *alişan*, and this status had to be substantiated by the separate testimonies of twelve people. This group of individual nobles could also be commissioned as officers, after six years of military service. The third category included the relatives of those agalar and begs who had documents from the provincial administration which exempted them from paying taxes, and they had the same duties towards the state as the *meşçane* [*meshchane*, in Russian, 'townspeople', e.g. shopkeepers and professionals].

In June 1861 a decision was taken to establish institutions for carrying out the measurement of land under the rule of the Trans-Caucasian administration (*Zakavkaskaia mezhevaia palata*), as a result of which the sale of land became easier, notwithstanding new claims to land made by the state (see also *Azərbaycan Tarixi*, vol. 4, 2000: 180–183). Auch (2001: 14) wrote

---

[48] On variations in state and privately owned land, use rights, the role of traditions, household plots and commons, and the use of water and irrigation systems, see *Azərbaycan Tarixi*, vol. 4, 2000: 261–270.

[49] State land (*xəzinə torpaqları*) covered nearly 83 per cent of all land in Azerbaijan, and land used by private owners came to 16 per cent of the total (*Azərbaycan Tarixi*, vol. 4, 2000: 261–262).

that the gradual introduction of such laws and regulations in the southern Caucasus first affected the Muslim peasants of eastern Georgia, who were freed along with Christian serfs in 1864 (see also *Azərbaycan Tarixi*, vol. 4, 2000: 181).

The agrarian reforms were fully implemented in 1870 in the provinces of Gəncə, Baku, and Yerevan, although in the beginning the regulations did not apply to peasants who voluntarily stayed on the land of Muslim or Armenian landowners (Auch 2001: 14–15).[50] The last group of peasants who voluntarily stayed on landlords' property was included in regulations passed in 1877–1887, and thenceforth their dependency on the landlords was declared to be annulled. The land on which the peasants had toiled was eventually to become their property, upon payment of a certain sum for the land share (*nadel'*) in question (see *Azərbaycan Tarixi*, vol. 4, 2000: 183). Each adult male (over 15 years of age) was entitled to receive from the landlord five *desiatin*s of land, or approximately 5.45 hectares. The landlord was allowed to retain at least one-third of his estate as private property, and in some provinces the original landowner secured as much as half the estate (Auch 2001: 15; Mostashari 2006: 68). According to Auch, this led to the fragmentation of the land, such that peasants acquired fewer than five *desiatins*. The consequences, amplified by the limited availability of fertile land and by population increase, were disastrous. The freed peasants could not afford to buy land from its former owners, nor did the Russian state make it possible for them to obtain cheap credit. They had to pay high rents or interest to money lenders, and tensions in the countryside increased (Auch 2001: 15; see also *Azərbaycan Tarixi*, vol. 4, 2000: 184–85).

Swietochowski (1995: 18) offered a similarly critical view of the effects of the agrarian reform of 1870, writing that it

> did not unleash a torrent of social and economic transformations. In Eastern Transcaucasia close to 70 percent of the peasantry lived on lands the Russian crown had taken from the khanates and thus had been exempt from the obligations that the reform abolished. Otherwise, the peasants were allotted … an amount of land so small that an average villager had to rent an additional one third of the acreage from either the crown or the local landlord. Unlike in central Russia, the government did not extend credits to the peasants for purchasing their plots of land. As for the beys and aghas, the great majority owned plots averaging 6.3 *desiatin*s and lived an existence hardly distinguishable from their peasant neighbors, even though they con-

---

[50] See also *Azərbaycan Tarixi*, vol. 4, 2000: 182–187. According to its authors, in the Gəncə (then Elizavetpol) administrative region, some 65,000 people in 200 villages stayed on voluntarily.

tinued to exercise their leadership through village assemblies and elective courts. Barely 4 percent of landlords possessed estates averaging 1,500 *desiatins*, from which was drawn the pool of land available for leasing. Overall, the Azerbaijani countryside remained unshaken in its tradition-bound way of life, and there was little social stratification and mobility.

Auch (2001: 15) wrote that the mismatch between the Russian agrarian reforms and their application in the Muslim colonies might be explained by the existence of different social and economic structures in those countries. She pointed out that even though serfdom never existed in the Muslim parts of the Caucasus, certain personalised dependency relations – often prescribed on the basis of old traditions and considered (primarily by the colonisers) to be old-fashioned – nevertheless existed. Colonial policies forced the Muslim dependents into a legal category comparable to that of Russian serfs, with the additional levelling out of dependency relations in legal but not real terms.[51]

Auch and Swietochowski agree that nearly 70 percent of the peasantry was exempt from the agrarian reforms because they lived on state land and not on that of feudal lords. These facts are valid for western Azerbaijan as well; only 20 percent of the peasantry in the provinces of Gəncə and Baku lived on the estates of feudal landlords (Auch 2001: 15). By employing various strategies of annexation and selectively recognizing some of the landed nobility, the tsarist Russian state managed to become the most important landowner. Not until after the turn of the twentieth century did the state granted inheritable use rights to peasants who worked state-owned land in the administrative regions of Baku, Gəncə, Yerevan, and Tbilisi. Auch (2001: 16) concluded that although the agrarian reforms had mixed acceptance and effectiveness in terms of ownership relations, one of their consequences was the acceleration of scientific and organised agricultural productivity, which stemmed from the establishment by the colonial administration of offices to look after land and production systems as well as the settlement of agricultural areas.

German and Other European Colonists in Western Azerbaijan

Apart from imperial Russia's general colonial policies concerning the southern Caucasus, the settlement of German colonists in western Azerbaijan and

---

[51] The authors of *Azərbaycan Tarixi* (vol. 4, 2000: 88) also point out the differences between the Azerbaijani system and that of Russia and Georgia in terms of dependency and feudal relations. In the Azerbaijani case, peasants dependent on landlords or feudal lords, as they called them, were not bonded to the land. They could leave a landlord and become state peasants or seek the protection and live on the land of another landlord.

eastern Georgia has particular relevance for my research sites, Təzəkənd and Şəmkir. The existence of these colonies in pre-Soviet western Azerbaijan necessarily influenced notions of property and changes in property regimes, even into the early Soviet period.

As evidenced by the memoirs of the German traveller Emil Rösler, written in 1901, European travellers saw the German colonies in the area of Gəncə as examples of European modernity, even if, at the turn of the twentieth century, they already lay in the shadow of large, rapidly modernising, Europeanised cities such as Baku and Tbilisi. Rösler wrote that Helenendorf, a small settlement of German colonists south of Gəncə, had amenities such as a school, a church, a reading room, newspapers, and a musical club. He reported technological and economic developments, too: a mill powered by electricity, a beer brewery, mineral water and cognac factories, and the well-known wine cellars of the wine trader brothers Vohrer and Hummel (Rösler, cited in Auch 2001: 20). The colonists developed agricultural production systems, especially for vineyards and for making wine and cognac[52], that were comparable to European systems of the time, and these seem to have carried over into early Soviet times.

The big property- and business-owning colonist families were liquidated during the early Soviet period. Many German colonist families of the lower social strata stayed on until they were deported to Central Asia in 1941 as part of Stalin's World War II strategy regarding so-called enemy populations, particularly in areas close to the war front. The fate of these families and the elimination of their rural activities changed the character of villages and of agriculture, and the fact that they could be so arbitrarily liquidated and deported greatly affected people's perception of the relationship between the state and land. The state came to be seen as holding ultimate power over people's lives and livelihoods, a perception that was corroborated by Stalin's collectivisation policy.

Auch (2001: 67–68) explained that German colonists were settled in the areas to the north of the Black Sea and the southern Caucasus at the end of the wars against the Ottomans, when the Russian Empire conquered the region and Catherine the Great made provision for foreign settlements. The colonists included heterodox religious groups from different parts of Germany, Holland, and Württemberg, the latter fearing religious persecution after Friedrich II came into power (1797) and later became king of Württemberg. Subsequently, Alexander I (1801–1825) instituted a new wave of immigration for more purely economic reasons:

---

[52] The historians of *Azərbaycan Tarixi* (vol. 4, 2000: 246), for instance, cite the vine business of the Vohrer brothers as having used primarily wage labour (*muzdlu əmək*).

Among other things, the government demanded that the newcomers be good farmers, specialists in viniculture, silk production and animal husbandry, or village artisans, own a minimum of property, as well as have a wife and children. The number of immigrants was limited to 200 families per year, before the mass migration was completely halted in 1819. The colonists were to receive 60 desiatin of land (6555 Ar = 65.55 hectare) and a settlement credit of 300 roubles, were permanently exempt from military and civil service while their tax exemption was limited to 10 years. At this time, primarily families from Baden and Württemberg decided to immigrate (Auch 2001: 68).

The reasons why the German colonists immigrated are still debated. Some say they were drawn because of kinship relations with preceding immigrants; others maintain that the Russian imperial policy of economic improvement in these areas was a crucial factor. The determining factors also included the political, economic, agricultural, and religious difficulties in Württemberg after the Napoleonic wars.

Whatever the inducements, the administration in Tbilisi was swamped by the number of people arriving, and organising their settlement was not easy.[53] The chronicles of a colonist in 1818 describe rebellions among the Muslim population against tsarist rule and how some 500 German families had to be escorted by Cossacks to the six designated settlements around the city of Gəncə. One of these settlements, Annenfeld – a village neighbouring Təzəkənd, known after 1941 as Leninkənd and today renamed Çınarlı – was settled by 84 families, a total of 600 people. According to archival records, 91 families had received approximately 3,479 hectares of land in Annenfeld by 1820 (see map 2).[54]

Land was apportioned to settlers after a reallocation of state and private property made it possible to distribute contiguous parcels. The archives state that German settlers received about 15 hectares of land per person. Notwithstanding the inducements, for some time the colonists apparently faced many difficulties and were not very successful. In addition to climatic disasters and epidemics, they were the victims of robbery and kidnapping for slavery. Their situation did not improve until the middle of the nineteenth century. Auch, who documented in detail the development of the population and wealth of the colonists in the region, observed that the breakthrough in

---

[53] The following passage, describing the settlement of German peasant colonists and the Vohrer and Hummel brothers in western Azerbaijan, relies primarily on Auch (2001: 69–98).

[54] Auch (2001: 72) referred to Annenfeld-Leninkənd-Çınarlı as being the centre of Shemkir (Şəmkir) *rayon*, which is not quite correct; it is a village or small town directly in the neighbourhood of the city of Şəmkir.

their economic situation came only with the introduction of vineyards and the production of wine.[55] Viniculture and wine production and trade were developed by some of the leading colonial families and improved the overall economy of the region. At the same time, it increased economic differentiation, not only among the colonists but also between the colonists and the local rural producers. Various kinds of economic relationships emerged between the two groups, involving agrarian production, sharecropping, and services. These developments accelerated the opening up of new markets and the introduction of new products for and from the region, with links to central Russia and thus as far as Siberia and Turkistan.

Auch wrote that the success of the colonists was also due to further measures taken by the Russian regime for their economic and administrative support. For example, during the Ottoman-Russian wars, the colonists were exempt from military service; they supported the Russians by maintaining production, transportation, and commerce during times of war. Because the sons of the colonists could inherit only use rights to land, the families developed the production of small crafts, agricultural goods, and wine, which served the Russian army billeted in the area during the long war years. At the same time, the colonies stayed relatively self-sufficient and developed agricultural and other forms of small production and trade. According to Auch (2001: 80):

> Tied to the area of settlement with its specific inheritance rights and regulations about the division of property, the settler families acquired a certain amount of security but at the same time the compulsion of productivity, which only proved to culminate in increased personal property when use rights to arable lands could be acquired. Although the inheritable use rights of individual families were balanced and levelled out by the rights of the youngest son to inherit the family property without the right to sell or mortgage it for a long time, in the course of the 1850s the use of kinship relations to create large economic units was made possible.

The colonists seem to have especially profited from the agrarian reforms of 1870 and the accompanying availability of free labour, from improvements in taxation, and from technological developments that followed from these changes. The settlers' efforts to improve their knowledge of viniculture, to more effectively control horticultural diseases, and to mechanise the cultivation of vineyards were enhanced by having their sons educated and maintaining contacts with Germany, as well as with other Ger-

---

[55] The authors of *Azərbaycan Tarixi* (vol. 4, 2000: 173) write that grapes had already become a cash crop in Gəncə in the late nineteenth century.

mans in the Caucasus. Ultimately, all this led to the export of village products to Russian and western European markets.

One of the most important of the family enterprises was that of the
Vohrer brothers, which Auch documented at some length. These men extended their family business by building an underground spring-water irrigation system (*kəhriz*), which enabled them to cultivate vineyards in agricultural areas that were formerly too dry. The irrigation system had the added
benefit of making drinking water available to the local population. The
Vohrer brothers enlarged their property holdings by leasing extra land,
sometimes already planted in vineyards, often from Armenian owners who
had moved to the cities to engage in real estate or trade. If the land produced
well, or if the owners had liquidity problems, then the Vohrers might purchase the land (Auch 2001: 83). What remains unclear is why they bought
land primarily from Armenians. One explanation might be that Armenians
enjoyed greater upward mobility under Russian rule, so that they integrated
more easily into the urban centres than did Muslims, who continued to live
on the land as peasants. It is plausible, then, that Armenians were more
inclined to sell their rural property than were Muslim landowners.

Between 1847 and 1910 the Vohrer brothers enlarged their landed
property from 35 *desiatin* (about 38 hectares) to 4,300 *desiatin* (about 4,698
hectares). By making wise technological investments and improving their
vines, they doubled the productivity of their vineyards over those of their
Armenian and Muslim neighbours. They followed this up by investing in
proper storage and refinement areas and building wine cellars. By 1910 they
had 30 cellars, some of them as much as three storeys high, with the capacity
to store more than 9 million litres of wine. The development of rapid transport by rail meant that profits could be made throughout the region, and the
Vohrers significantly extended their trade network. By 1913 they had
branches in Gəncə, Tbilisi, and Baku and further sales centres in Batumi,
Ashkabad, Merv, Kars, Aleksandropol', Tomsk, and Krasnovodsk.

The Hummel brothers were another German colonist family that established a successful business in western Azerbaijan. Auch wrote that
although their enterprise was more modest than that of the Vohrer brothers,
the four Hummel brothers bought up land for vineyards to the west and east
of Gəncə and invested in wine and cognac production, including factories
and cellars. Their business began to flourish after the turn of the twentieth
century, when they stepped up their land acquisition. By 1909 they had
purchased approximately 450 *desiatin* (about 492 hectares) of land close to
Annenfeld. After setting up irrigation systems in 1914, they were cultivating
vineyards on 85 *desiatin* (about 93 hectares) of it and orchards on 20 *desiatin*
(about 22 hectares). They also bought the vines of Azeri and Armenian

producers in places as far away as Göyçay and Şamaxı and started producing wine and cognac of high quality, which won prizes in international wine competitions. Much like the Vohrer brothers, the Hummel brothers sold wine and cognac in 39 provinces of the Russian Empire. In 1913 their products amounted to 34 percent of the total export from the province of Gəncə.

Plate 2. Memorial plaque for the Hummel brothers.

The Hummel family's successful wine and cognac enterprise became a model for cooperatives formed in the years leading up to the First World War, some of which, such as Konkordia, survived sovietisation in Azerbaijan. With the outbreak of World War I and the introduction of new laws liquidating the property of German subjects of the Russian Empire, most of the property belonging to German colonists was confiscated, and the leading businessmen were killed. The cooperatives that survived the early Soviet period allowed the remaining German colonists to engage in the wine business up until their deportation in October 1941. Today, only some elderly Azeri residents in Təzəkənd remember the German families who lived there before 1941.[56]

---

[56] Unlike some other ethnic groups displaced from the Caucasus during the post-Stalin period, the survivors of the deported German families have stayed on in Kazakhstan. Eva Maria Auch

With the outbreak of World War I, German colonists in the Russian Empire began to be seen as the 'internal enemy'. The liquidation of German property throughout the empire, including the Caucasus, followed a pattern described by Auch (2001).[57] First, the liquidation laws required all ethnic German residents in the border regions of the Russian Empire to be identified, in order to clarify their citizenship status. Initially, land given to the colonists was exempted from liquidation, but when the laws were implemented, little difference was observed between ethnic Germans who had assumed citizenship and those who remained German nationals. In 1916 the German settlements around Gǝncǝ were renamed (the names were changed again in the early Soviet period). The liquidation laws affected three categories of German colonist property: lease and collective property of the colonies (in German, *Pacht- und Gemeindeeigentum der Kolonien*); property of the colonists' cooperatives (*Eigentum von Gesellschaften der Kolonisten – Genossenschaften*); and real estate of individual colonists (*Immobilien einzelner Kolonisten*). Although colonist families protested that their sons were still serving in the Russian imperial army and had been decorated for their service or taken prisoner by Austrian forces, their pleas appear to have had little effect.

Throughout the liquidation of the land ownership of German colonists, newspapers covered the debate and reported on the auctioning of property. Auch wrote that the conditions of the sale of property amounted to expropriation, because of the drastic fall in prices that resulted from the forced nature of the sales and the undervaluation of buildings and equipment. After the Russian Revolution of 1917, some of the production and agrarian structures of the colonists, especially the most successful wineries, were spared, but with the Stalinist period and the deportations of 1941, German settlement in the region came to an end.

Consequences of the Russian Colonisation of Azerbaijan

Historians have evaluated the effects of Russian colonisation on Azerbaijan differently, depending on their level of generalisation – whether for a certain locality or for the entire region – and on individual stance. Some writers have viewed reforms in the legal and administrative structure of Azerbaijan as progressive; others have seen them as 'reaffirming imperial authority over the colonies'. Some have emphasised the uneven industrialisation, urbanisation, and social change that took place in the whole of the country. Altstadt

---

(personal communication) reports that the descendents of the colonist families maintain networks and attend get-togethers in Germany.

[57] The following pages rely primarily on Auch (2001: 195–202).

(1992: 28, 67, 78), for instance, interpreted differences between Baku and other cities and the rural hinterland as having contributed to Baku's being more influenced by socialism, whereas Gəncə retained a more national character. This point has some relevance for contemporary debates over contrasts between Baku and the countryside and between Baku and Gəncə. People say that Gəncə is 'nationalist', whereas Baku is either cosmopolitan or corrupt and filled with rich, self-interested, Russianised elites.[58]

Swietochowski (1995: 17), too, commented on the unevenness of economic integration in Azerbaijan: 'Despite the access to the Russian market, agricultural production in this land of southern climate remained stagnant, apparently because of the ineffectiveness of alien rule'.

On the whole, Russian colonisation had two predominantly positive long-term effects. One was the transition to a money economy, which was stimulated by the requirement that peasants pay rents in cash rather than in kind for land leased formerly from khans and later from the Russian treasury. The other was the break-up of the khanates, which initiated the integration of Russian-held Azerbaijan into the imperial economy. That integration gained momentum with the replacement of diverse local currencies by the rouble in the 1830s. Despite such advances, Swietochowski (1995: 18) concluded 'that the Azerbaijani economy was overwhelmingly agricultural, and that agriculture methods remained primitive'.

The seeds of unevenness in the structures of regional development and between the sectors of Azerbaijan's economy seem to have been sown by the end of the nineteenth century. Swietochowski (1995: 20) remarked that Azerbaijan at that time displayed 'a dichotomy not uncommon in a colonial situation: a generally traditional but lopsided economy, with a single rapidly growing industry based on mineral resources [oil] rather than on manufacturing, geared to external markets, owned largely by foreign investors, and operated by non-native skilled labor. Typical also was the contrast between the city rising out of the industrialization and the countryside unshaken from its timeless pattern of existence'.

The Russian state retained large land holdings dating from the overthrow of the khanates' monopoly on orchards, vineyards, and forests, when the large majority of peasants became state peasants. Contrary to the claims of socialist ideologues at the time of the establishment of the USSR, in Azerbaijan the socialist revolution – to the extent that it is understood – did not nationalise the privately owned land of kulaks but took it from the tsarist state and gave it to the socialist state. Hence, at the turn of the twentieth

---

[58] Altstadt (1992: 79) added that the population of Gəncə had begun to call itself 'Azerbaijani Turk' by 1897. However, in the city itself, 'though Azerbaijanis were over 60 percent of the population, they held less than one-third of the posts' (Altstadt 1992: 31).

century, peasants were paying increasingly less to landowners and more to the state for the use of land, animals, and water. They also paid taxes to the state, including an opt-out fee in place of military service. 'A law of 1 May 1900 permitted "continuous use" but not possession of land with payment of *obrok* (quitrent) to the state treasury. Lenin called it "state feudalism"' (Altstadt 1992: 35).

Chapter 3
Rural Economy and Property: From Socialist Structures to Postsocialist Reforms

At the centre of Təzəkənd stands a rundown building of the former state farm (sovkhoz) for vineyards and wine production, named after Əzizbəyov, a Bolshevik leader of Baku commune who was killed before the establishment of the Soviet Republic of Azerbaijan in 1920 (see Suny 1972; Swietochowski and Collins 1999: 33). The building was built by German colonists, and local people say it was once part of the wine production company that belonged to the Hummel brothers, who built the underground irrigation and spring system (kəhriz) still in use and other houses next to the sovkhoz building. After 1993 the sovkhoz liquidation committee used this building, and since 2000 it has housed the newly established local administrative body (bələdiyyə).

Not far from the former sovkhoz building, where the railway passes through the centre of the settlement, crossing the road north out of town, one sees several orchards where mulberry trees have been chopped down and a deserted building that at one time was the central depot for the collection and distribution of silkworm cocoons. In the garden of the deserted centre, a placard displays the socialist slogan 'Glory to labour' (eşq olsun əməyə). A bit farther down the road lie newly distributed private parcels of land, some of them recently enclosed. Adjacent to them are former vineyards, unused, the cement posts that held up the vines left behind. The used and the unused, the pre-Soviet, the Soviet, and the post-Soviet – all interspersed and side by side.

A stroll through the settlement reveals layers of history of property regimes and systems of administration. Although no records exist that show clearly when Təzəkənd was founded, it is plausible to assume that the village was first a dependent of the settlement of German colonists in today's Leninkənd (Annenfeld), where the Hummel brothers built the housing and administrative buildings and later added the wine factory – one of the first collectivised agrarian industries in Azerbaijan. The original sovkhoz remained in the area until the mid-1990s, and throughout the socialist period it incorporated both nearby and distant land into its agrarian administrative structures. The adjacent kolkhoz, or collective farm, also went through various phases, sometimes joining with other kolkhozes and sometimes giving up some of its land to the sovkhoz. The structural changes in the agrarian economy were mirrored by changes in the crops produced and the technologies used: from vineyards to cotton, then back to vineyards, and finally to the contemporary production of grain and potatoes.

In this chapter I highlight economic and structural changes that took place in the Şəmkir region during Soviet times and then discuss the agrarian reforms and privatisation of agrarian land of the mid-1990s. Throughout the chapter I examine the political, economic, and normative layers of property in Azerbaijan and the area around Şəmkir over the last 90 years.

The Integration of Azerbaijan into the Soviet System

The Soviet Republic of Azerbaijan was established in 1920, soon after World War I, at a time when the Caucasus region was going through one of many periods of turbulence. This included military interventions by the Ottoman and British Empires and the founding of the independent Caucasus republics between 1918 and 1920, the years of the struggle between the Bolsheviks and the Mensheviks. The region witnessed the simultaneous collapse of the Ottoman and Russian Empires immediately following World War I, which brought economic chaos and great physical destruction.

From 1920 onwards, the new Soviet regime implemented measures to consolidate the Azerbaijan republic into the socialist union.[59] One policy of consolidation and assimilation – indigenisation (*korenizatsiia*) – was intended to break up the legacy of the Russian Empire. During the early years of the Soviet regime, this policy 'amounted to more than simply promoting the natives into high positions in the Party and government. The *korenizatsiia* also called for the full equality of non-Russian languages with Russian and attempted to reconcile the nationalities to the Soviet rule. It sought to legitimize an urban-based revolution in a predominantly agricultural and multiethnic state by encouraging the development of distinct national identities' (Swietochowski 1995: 110).

These measures seem to have aroused some reaction among non-Azerbaijani urban dwellers, who were required to take instruction in the

---

[59] In this section I rely primarily on the discussions and works of Ələsgərov and Qasımov (1972); Allahverdiyev (1980, 1986); Mamedov (1985); Orucov (1990); Swietochowski (1995); Əliyev (1997); Məmmədov (1998); Baberowski (2003, 2004); and *Azərbaycan Tarixi*, vol. 7, 2003.

Azerbaijani language, but such irritations were probably absent in rural areas, where language and educational policies became effective only gradually and where the majority of the population was Azerbaijani-speaking anyway. The indigenisation policy was successful in 'Turkifying' higher learning, in that Azeri became the language of instruction at the university level. By 1930, 70 per cent of students and about 75 per cent of instructors were Azeris (Swietochowski 1995: 112). It is likely that this policy made it possible for many young people from the countryside to be educated at universities and technical colleges such as those in Gəncə, where Azerbaijani dominated both teaching and publishing in the branches of rural economy and agrarian sciences, as is still the case today.

Tadeusz Swietochowski (1995: 125–126) argued that in the years following the great purges of the 1930s, the Stalinist policy of promoting local particularisms was aimed at 'splitting [up] cultural, linguistic, or regional entities' and allowing only for vertical relations with the centre, discouraging horizontal links among the national republics, as 'a prelude to the process of forging a new Soviet nation', which 'would go hand in hand with Russification'. The historian Jörg Baberowski (2003, 2004) took up this view in his writings on the Stalinist regime, its purges, and particularly the case of Azerbaijan. He argued (Baberowski 2004: 22–23) that the indigenisation policy of the Soviet revolution in Azerbaijan led to local reactions against communist ideas such as class solidarity, according to which poor peasants should be against the rich landlord class. He pointed out that the peasants were bound to the landlords and *bəy*s through kinship and patronage (*tayfa-bazlıq*), and they neither understood nor concurred with the call to rise up against them. Instead, they got together with their local leaders and, on the basis of old enmities between clans and religious communities, eliminated their rivals by calling them kulaks. According to Baberowski, this amounted to feuding rather than class struggle; what was reported as kulaks and bandits resisting the Soviet authorities in the countryside was just peasants who had fled and were resisting rival peasants.

Ultimately, the central authority clamped down harshly, carrying out show trials with committees in the villages, and many people were executed. According to Baberowski (2004: 23–24), however, when the agents of the central authority withdrew from the countryside, everything went back to the older ways of everyday life, 'as if nothing had happened [*als ob nichts gewesen wäre*]', in the words of a local party chief. With the start of collectivisation, terror returned to the village. On the whole, Baberowski saw Stalin's great purges and pro-collectivisation and anti-religion policies in Azerbaijan as having reinforced existing networks and structures in Azerbaijani society, which chose to hold onto local ties and loyalties as resistance to the cultural revolution of the Soviet system.[60] This mobilisation of local forces replaced 'the stigma of backwardness with a matter of national honour' (Baberowski 2004: 27).[61]

Official records claim that there were 70,000 Azerbaijani fatalities during the great purges: 'the Great Terror of 1937, in Azerbaijan and Georgia, is described as "probably worse than in any other republic, barring the Ukraine"' (Swietochowski 1995: 127).[62] Swietochowski's analysis converges to some degree with Baberowski's; the latter, too, saw the parochial nature of the nationalism created during this period, relative to the national ideals of independent Azerbaijan in 1918–1920: 'The purges turned out to be more than a bloody political and bureaucratic shake-up. They were also a cultural reorientation. Its essence was the ascendance of parochial, ethnic, and secular nationalism, hostile to any broader vision such as Turkism and indifferent to the mirage of Azerbaijani unity. ... it now appealed to the instincts of peasants uprooted by industrialization' (Baberowski 2004: 127–128).

Another historical landmark relevant for the local population in Şəmkir involved the relationship of Soviet Azerbaijan to Iranian Azerbaijan (see Nissman 1987; Swietochowski 1995; Atabaki 2000 [1993]; Shaffer 2002). In 1941 the Soviet Union and Great Britain occupied Iran in order to prevent it from supporting Germany during the Second World War and also

---

[60] See Bruce Grant (2004), who offers a fine analysis of a historical uprising in the mountainous region of Sheki. He illustrates how cultural idioms of rebellion, of power and authority, and of magical mobility in the mountains were equally important, and he presents a much more complex reading than that of local rural networks versus communist forces for understanding these rural uprisings.

[61] 'So gelang es den Bolschewiki am Ende, den öffentlichen Raum zu besetzen und den offiziellen Islam zu marginalisieren. Sie schnitten die Muslime vom schriftlichen Erbe des Islam ab, aber es misslang ihnen, die konkurrierenden Auslegungen der Welt zum Schweigen zu bringen. Im Widerstand gegen die Kulturrevolution erwarb die Bevölkerung eine Kommunikations- und Organisationsfähigkeit, die sie unter normalen Umständen gar nicht aufgebracht hätte. So gesehen führte der Kulturimperialismus der Bolschewiki widerstrebende Kräfte zusammen, überwand Gegensätze zwischen Stämmen und Clans. Das Stigma der Rückständigkeit verwandelte sich in einen nationalen Ehrentitel' (Baberowski 2004: 27).

[62] In both Təzəkənd and the locality I heard of only one person of kulak ancestry, whose father was a bəy, owned large land holdings, and was killed during Stalin's purges. An elderly man remembered his uncle's fleeing to Turkey because he was a molla (Muslim priest); mollas were equally in danger of being labelled 'enemies of the people'. My host in the village claimed that his father was able to keep private property in the form of a sizable herd of sheep because of the toleration of local party officials, who respected his status as village elder (aqsaqqal) and his ancestry. He came from a seyid lineage and was addressed as seyid himself. Apart from such occasional cases, there was no common memory of any large landowners who were persecuted and their property taken away. I suspect this had already happened early on, in 1920, with the liquidation of German colonist landlords in the region.

to put pressure on Turkey. Most of the Soviet occupation forces in northern Iran were Azeris from the Soviet Socialist Republic of Azerbaijan (Swieto-chowski 1995: 135–162; Atabaki 2000 [1993]; Shaffer 2002). During the subsequent experiment in autonomy for Iranian Azerbaijan in 1945–1946, the influence of Soviet ideas and strategies, as well as those of the Azerbai-jani communist leaders in Baku, seems to have been significant. This brief episode came to an end in May 1946 when Soviet troops left Iran, partly as a result of negotiations between Iran and Moscow concerning concessions to Russia for oil extraction in Iran. At the end of December 1946 the Iranian Azerbaijani autonomous government collapsed, and the Iranian army marched in. After the demise of the regime, nearly 15,000 people fled to Soviet Azerbaijan.

Many of those who came from Iranian Azerbaijan and were not di-rectly involved in the political project there kept their passports and became known as 'Demokrats' – followers of the Democratic Party. The newcomers were dispersed throughout the country. In Şəmkir there are still many villag-ers with Iranian Azerbaijani origins. They are referred to locally as Demok-rats, even if few people are now aware of the exact meaning of the term.

The Socialist Economy in Azerbaijan: General Trends

Azerbaijan is depicted as having experienced rapid modernisation and de-velopment with the oil boom at the end of the nineteenth and beginning of the twentieth century. This period was characterised by substantial urbanisa-tion, ethnic diversification and in-migrations of non-Azeri population groups, the building of technological and strategic infrastructure, and the rise of both nationalist political ideas and their socialist rivals. As early as 1920 the newly established Soviet government decreed that all agricultural land was to be nationalised. The *rayon* of Şəmkir was immediately affected, and some of the first sovkhozes were established there.

The Soviet government was concerned primarily with rapid economic development: 'In the years before 1950, industrial growth in Georgia and Armenia exceeded that for the USSR as a whole, and agricultural output in all three republics [Georgia, Armenia, and Azerbaijan] far outpaced the national average growth. Characteristically, rapid economic growth was fuelled by large infusions of investment and labour. In Azerbaijan, well over half of total investment was allocated to industry' (Schroeder 1996: 461). This was the case even though more than half the labour force in these Transcaucasian republics was still engaged in agriculture; substantial agri-cultural development could be observed only in the post–World War II years.

The oil industry, however – the motor of economic development – began lagging behind soon after the formation of the Soviet Union, because the
available technology became outdated and the investment needed to upgrade
it came in too slowly to keep pace with rapid developments:

> As decade after decade of the Soviet epoch wore on, the golden age
> of Baku oil receded into memory, a result of the steady depletion of
> the oil fields through overexploitation and even more – underin-
> vestment in exploration efforts. After World War II the center of So-
> viet oil extraction shifted from the Caspian coast to the Volga basin
> and the Ural Mountains. ... For Azerbaijan, the shift had cascading
> effects and their impact was exponential. By the 1980s Baku's oil
> output would dwindle to a meagre 3 per cent of the Soviet total
> (Swietochowski 1995: 179; see also Schroeder 1996: 466).

Consequently, during the years from 1950 to 1978 Azerbaijan had the
lowest rate of industrial growth among all the Soviet republics (Swietochowski 1995: 179). After assessing industrial growth in the three Transcaucasian republics and comparing them with one another and with the whole of
the USSR, Gertrude Schroeder (1996: 462) concluded that for the period
from 1950 to 1990, gross industrial output rose 'at an average annual rate of
6.8 percent in Georgia, 8.1 percent in Armenia, and 6.2 percent in Azerbaijan, [while] on a per capita basis, industrial growth in all three republics was
well below the average for the USSR as a whole'. As for the growth of total
and per capita national income for 1960–1990, she pointed out that although
the other two Caucasian republics, Armenia and Georgia, exceeded the
national average, Azerbaijan lagged behind in both measures (Schroeder
1996: 462; see also Swietochowski 1995: 179).[63] The standard of living in
these republics was another point of comparison; the record showed that
Armenia and Georgia were 10 per cent and 15 per cent below the USSR
median, respectively, but 'the figure for Azerbaijan was as much as one-third
below. ... In this respect, Armenia and Georgia ranked with the western
republics of the USSR while Azerbaijan was closer to the impoverished
Central Asia' (Swietochowski 1995: 180).

Unlike industrial growth, agricultural production more than tripled by
1990 in all three of the southern Caucasus republics, each of which was
more agriculturally oriented than average for the Soviet Union. Rapid population growth, however, 'reduced the gains markedly on a per capita basis'
(Schroeder 1996: 462, 464).[64] Particularly in the early years of Soviet Azer-

---

[63] For an overview of the economic situation in Azerbaijan during the last decade of Soviet
rule and the early 1990s, see Wiesner 1997: 142–164.

[64] Swietochowski (1995: 181) also underlined population growth as one of the reasons for
stagnation despite economic development in Azerbaijan. He also noted that Azerbaijanis were

baijan, economic development in urban areas encouraged agricultural labourers to leave the land for the cities. As the pace of industrial transformation eased, 'the number of labourers leaving the agricultural sector slowed down; by 1970 about two-fifths of the work force was still engaged in agriculture and related occupations' (Swietochowski 1995: 179).

Another characteristic of rural production in the southern Caucasus was its relatively diversified agriculture. All three countries produced a variety of vegetables, fruit, potatoes, and some grains and maintained a significant livestock sector while also cultivating specialised agricultural products such as cotton in Azerbaijan and tea in Georgia. One-third of the grapes in the Soviet Union were produced in the southern Caucasus (Schroeder 1996: 467). The relatively large role of the private sector in agriculture is another marker of Transcaucasia. For the years 1986–1988, total farm output of the private sector for Georgia was 46 per cent, and for Azerbaijan, 26 per cent (Schroeder 1996: 467). Schroeder also indicates, however, that the statistics for production on private plots were inadequately reported, and actual production might have been much higher (see also Humphrey 1998 for Buryat rural households). Azerbaijan specialised in cotton, which could not be produced extensively on private plots, whereas the production of products such as tea and grapes, which did take place in Azerbaijan in the 1980s, was more suitable for such plots.

The overall assessment of the Soviet experience and economic dependency between Azerbaijan and the Soviet Union evoked many debates among academicians and politicians at the time and continues to do so today. Swietochowski (1995: 180–181), for instance, summarised one argument concerning the overall benefits of Azerbaijan's incorporation into the Soviet economy: 'Western writings in the post-Stalinist and pre-perestroika period inclined toward a view that the Soviet Middle East benefited from its association with a large centralized economy, at a cost to the USSR as a whole: "The Soviet ideological commitment to creating a native proletariat and combating backwardness in the national republics caused a diversion of capital to these areas, which, on strictly economic grounds, would have provided a higher return elsewhere"'.[65] Swietochowski expressed the belief that such a view fell short for understanding conditions in Azerbaijan, much less for accounting for the decline of the oil industry there. He argued that Azerbaijan could not defend its national interests because it could not resist the unfair pricing of oil by the central Soviet authorities and lacked alterna-

---

less inclined to migrate than, for instance, the Azeris of Iran. It was only in the 1980s that Azerbaijanis began to migrate in great numbers (see also Derlugian 2002).

[65] Swietochowski quotes Alec Nove and J. A. Newth, *The Soviet Middle East: A Communist Model for Development* (New York: Praeger, 1966), p. 122.

tive industries. Other Middle Eastern countries, he wrote, were better able to use their oil wealth once they gained independence. The centralized Soviet economy simply failed to reinvest enough money in sustaining Azerbaijani oil production. 'Apparently, Russia had reached the point beyond which colonialism brought more liabilities than assets' (Swietochowski 1995: 181).

Swietochowski's assessment, therefore, is that Azerbaijan, relative to Armenia and Georgia, contributed more to the Soviet economy than it received, not only in respect of the oil economy but also in the agricultural sector. The reason for this unequal exchange was its having 'a product mix based on oil and cotton, which suffered from arbitrary pricing' (Swietochowski 1995: 180).[66]

The assessment of the assets and liabilities of the Azerbaijani economy vis-à-vis the former Soviet Union remains an ongoing, central debate in Azerbaijan (Hanke 1998: 31–39; Quliyev 2002, 2004; Derlugian 2005: chap. 5). The more nationalist and anti-colonialist arguments, agreeing with Swietochowski's view, emphasise that the Soviet centre extracted more from Azerbaijan than it invested in it. Other political interpretations tend to focus on the complexity of the Soviet economic system and the interdependency among all the republics. Schroeder (1996: 475) summarised the Azerbaijani economy of the post-Soviet period as having inherited moderate industrialisation encumbered by a large trade dependency. This dependency was caused by the Soviet Union's having promoted specialisation rather than diversification, a system that rendered the republics interdependent on one another while all were dependent on the economic centre. The trade dependencies were apparently so large that the three Transcaucasian republics 'conducted 93–98 percent of their trade with other republics'.

A highly centralised administrative structure is often considered to be a further Soviet legacy to the now independent Transcaucasian states, such that in 1990 'all-union ministries controlled firms accounting for about half of industrial production and employment in Azerbaijan' (Schroeder 1996: 475). Schroeder noted that although business people in Transcaucasia had almost no experience of producing and purchasing in competitive markets, those states had skilled and well-educated labour forces, and their 'flourishing underground economies gave evidence of abundant entrepreneurial talents' (Schroeder 1996: 476). Because many writers have claimed that these underground economies were heirs to the 'second economy' of the Soviet period and that the second economy was particularly strong in the Caucasus, Schroeder warned against what she viewed as a misinterpretation

---

[66] 'Comparisons with Azerbaijan's non-Soviet neighbours, risky and unreliable statistical exercises as they are, indicate that in 1977 Iran's GNP was $2,160 per capita while estimates for Azerbaijani SSR are $1,825, or 11 percent less' (Swietochowski 1995: 180).

of this flourishing economy. She wrote that the Transcaucasian countries had no monopoly on the practice of an extensive second economy. In Transcaucasia, the second economy took 'a variety of forms – illegal production, theft from the state, black market sales, bribery, extortion, cheating, and abuse of public office' (Schroeder 1996: 474). As such, it helped only to 'redistribute existing goods and incomes and raise prices' rather than add to the supply of goods and services. Although it did not necessarily lead to a better life for the local population (Schroeder 1996: 475), it did result in better distribution of available goods and services. This perceptive assessment throws light on the widespread networks that competed to control the redistribution of resources. I come back to the issues of bribery, black market sales, and abuse of public office when I discuss comparisons between the Soviet period and contemporary times made by people whom I talked with.

Another issue in the assessment of the role and place of the Azerbaijani economy within the former USSR relates to differences in scale and space. For instance, people in the Şəmkir region primarily remember some phases, such as the 1970s, as times of affluence and growth. Villagers in Təzəkənd refer to the late 1970s and early 1980s as years of relative prosperity, a time when they were able to trade surpluses from household plots in neighbouring markets and cities and when they began to substantially renovate existing houses and build solid new stone houses (see chapter 4).[67]

The period between 1969 and 1982, when Heydər Əliyev was the first secretary of the Communist Party of Azerbaijan, is one of the most enigmatic times in Azerbaijan's Soviet history with regard to economic and political developments. These years were crucial for Azerbaijan because of changes in bureaucratic cadres, in economic indicators, and in Əliyev's policy towards the political power centre in Moscow. The difficulty lies in knowing how to evaluate the procedural changes and in attributing ex post facto intentionality to the policies; many political analysts seem to want to distance the events and processes from their historical context and instead evaluate particular decisions from the perspective of contemporary considerations. The other difficulty in assessing this period relates to Heydər Əliyev's return to Azerbaijani politics in 1993 as a leading authoritarian figure and as president during the crucial years of independence. He remained in this position until his death in 2003, when his son Ilham Əliyev succeeded him after some changes were made to the Azerbaijani constitution and presidential elections were held. During Heydər Əliyev's regime and presidency, neither his political party nor the role of the KGB during the

---

[67] Grant (2009: 127) quoted a school teacher in Sheki, in north Azerbaijan, who pointed out the relativity of such positive memories of the 1970s. The teacher reminded him that 'it took 50 years to buy fish again in a seaside republic or eggs in a state store'.

Soviet period could be impartially discussed, and certainly no one could attempt to criticise or offer a balanced evaluation of his presidency after independence.[68]

Western scholars such as Swietochowski (1995: 182–184) and Swietochowski and Collins (1999: 14–15) state that Heydər Əliyev concentrated on cleaning up government corruption and cracking down on networks and nepotism by introducing a 'frequent cadre rotation' (Swietochowski 1995: 183). Similarly, such sources evaluate his economic performance positively: 'The Azeri party boss seemed to be proving that despite adverse conditions and structural weakness in the economy, essential improvement through proper cadre policies, discipline, and legality was not only possible, it could actually reverse the trend' (Swietochowski 1995: 183). Swietochowski added that 'by 1974 Azerbaijan had risen to fourth position among union republics in industrial labour productivity and national income growth, ranking sixth in overall industrial productivity'. Accordingly, Əliyev's most obvious success was his cadre policy, but it was applied like another version of indigenisation (*korenizatsiia*), resulting in the consolidation of the native *nomenklatura* and its upgrading through an infusion of technocracy (Swietochowski 1995: 183; see also Hegaard 1977).[69] Even if this was true at the beginning of Əliyev's term and at a general macro level, in the late 1970s it was Əliyev's cadres who organised and were involved in a scandal over fraud in cotton production, which I discuss later.

Another period that is subject to various interpretations is the Gorbachev years. Swietochowski's evaluation runs counter to the popular local interpretation in Azerbaijan. He analysed the Soviet system basically as an empire that came to a structural crisis through overextension, which Gorbachev's perestroika brought into focus (Swietochowski 1995: 193). He identified decolonisation as the turning point in the disintegration of the Soviet Union, because of 'diminished returns from the conquered lands, economic stagnation combined with the pressures of rapid population growth, and the consolidation of native elites with their rising expectations for a greater share of power, a problem compounded by the specifically Soviet condition of bureaucratic over-centralization' (1995: 193).

The crucial difference of interpretation between Swietochowski and popular opinion in Azerbaijan lies in evaluations of the local effects of Gorbachev's reforms. Without further discussion of other, conflicting expla-

---

[68] Even the historians of the Azerbaijan Academy of Sciences use very partial language when documenting and evaluating recent Azerbaijani history of the Əliyev period (see *Azərbaycan Tarixi*, vol. 7).

[69] *Nomenklatura* refers to the system in the former Soviet Union whereby influential posts in government and industry were filled by party appointees.

nations of the end of the Soviet Union, which have been abundantly supplied by Sovietologists and transitologists (see Gleason 1992; Motyl 1992; Orlovsky 1995), I turn to local Azerbaijani interpretations and recollections of the Gorbachev period and the end of the Soviet Union. Local memory recalls this as a time when some free political thought was allowed and trade possibilities were expanding, but also as a time of unreasonable economic restrictions that had detrimental effects on the local economy. An example of this was Gorbachev's anti-alcohol campaign, which led to the destruction of vineyards in Azerbaijan and, in the first decade after independence, to the complete destruction of viniculture there.[70]

The political events of the early 1990s, when Azerbaijan became independent and the People's Front of Azerbaijan (PFA) was formed, present a complex picture. Other than touching on some highlights of recent social memory concerning those years, I limit my comments in order to focus on historical and economic developments as they affected my specific place of research. People remembered the final years of the Soviet Union and the first years of the new Azerbaijani Republic with uneasiness. This was a time of chaos, confusion, and political turmoil (*qalmaqal*), not only because of the Karabakh movement and the following war against Armenia but also because law and order broke down throughout the countryside. Unlike residents of the capital city, Baku, rural people did not reminisce about independence rallies or share memories of Soviet Army tanks rolling down the streets on what came to be known as Black January 1990 (see Swietochowski 1995: 202–210; also Goltz 1998; de Waal 2003: 92–95). Instead they recalled general chaos and young people bearing arms and roaming around in cars and trucks, shooting in the air and harassing anyone thought to oppose them. Although people referred to the Bozkurts, followers of certain national factions of the PFA, they were reluctant to name them or say what they had been after. A likely reason for this reluctance was that those people were still around. People identified deceased Bozkurts, but not those who were alive and had taken part in the political and military clashes of the times.

Swietochowski (1995: 202) explained how the divisions that developed within the PFA movement illustrated 'the age-old and deepening divide between the intelligentsia, urban, and educated elements on one side and the bulk of tradition-bound, mainly rural, and often Shi'ite population on the

---

[70] Mehman Necmeddinov, who was the head of the vine production unit of the Ministry of Agriculture, said that in 1985 there were 250,000 hectares of vineyards in Azerbaijan, of which approximately 100,000 hectares had been destroyed by 1993, primarily because of the anti-alcohol campaign of the perestroika years (*Azərbaycan* [daily newspaper], 8 January 1993).

other'; the question of unity with southern Azerbaijan was another point of disagreement within the movement. But these issues were not, apparently, central to the political clashes and other events taking place in the countryside. Rather, the conflict over the status of the Nagorno-Karabakh Autonomous Region had a more direct effect in the countryside as families were called upon to send their sons and husbands to war. In the beginning some went willingly, but as time passed, willingness diminished. All families had vivid memories of trying to buy their sons out of front-line military service or of privately buying food and clothing for their poorly provisioned family members in military service.

Swietochowski (1995: 221) described the political situation following the brief presidency of the first non-communist leader, Elçibəy, as the demise of post-colonial society:

> The usual characteristics were all in place: 47,000 troops of the Russian Fourth Army were stationed at various points in the country; interdependence upon the imperial economy meant that the country lacked economic self-sufficiency; there was a sizable settler population in the cities; and disputes over state borders and inter-communal strife were turning into full-fledged warfare. Over this situation presided the newly emerging power elite, who lacked sufficient political or administrative experience and were dependent on assistance from the ancient régime's personnel.

This picture could be elaborated on with stories that emerged around this time from the countryside. They tell how rural people neither followed what the struggle was about nor identified with many of the lofty ideals of independence or new politics of openness and freedom, except during the earliest days of the conflict.

Between 1991 and 1994 Azerbaijan waged war against Armenian forces in Karabakh and lost nearly one-fifth of its territory (de Waal 2003; Derlugian 2005: chap. 6). The political turmoil of these years forced the elected president, Elçibəy, to resign his presidency and set the stage for Heydər Əliyev to re-enter the political scene in 1993. Following his election as president, Əliyev brought political stability to the country, first by effecting a ceasefire in Karabakh and then by initiating peace negotiations (which still have not reached a conclusion) and by drawing up the famous 'hundred years' contract' with international partner companies for oil production and the Baku-Tbilisi-Ceyhan pipeline project. Although the pipeline project has begun to bring in huge revenues for the state from the international oil markets, creating trade surpluses, the country still struggles to establish transparency, develop democracy, and improve production and product quality in non-oil sectors (Bertelsmann Stiftung 2007; Economist Intelligence Unit, Azerbaijan Country Profile 2008).

Təzəkənd and Şəmkir in the 1980s

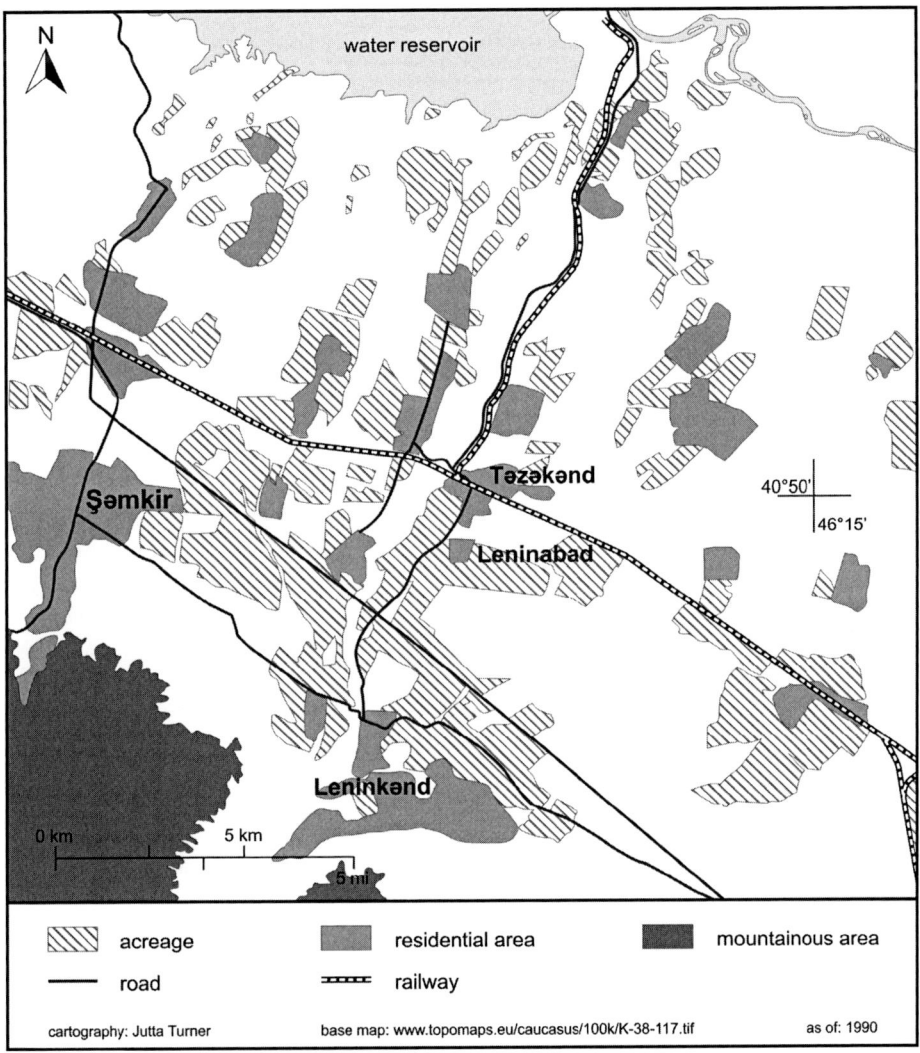

Map 2. Şəmkir, Təzəkənd, and the surrounding agricultural area.

The *rayon* of Şəmkir is situated on lower mountain slopes in a landscape suitable for cultivation twice a year (map 2).[71] Two major rivers, the Kür (Kura) and the Şəmkir, and the power plant (*Şəmkir Su Elektrik Stansiyası*) on the Kür provide enough water and electricity for irrigated agriculture.[72] The region is noted for having relatively good transportation infrastructure. The main motorway runs through it, a railway connects Baku and Tbilisi, and Gəncə has an airport. According to Rəcəbli (n.d.), before the agrarian reforms of 1996 the *rayon* had 9 kolkhozes, 38 sovkhozes, a complex for rearing animals for agrarian use, a poultry factory, a meat provision centre, a centre for slaughtering animals, a dairy factory, a firm producing construction materials, a centre for providing chemical products, and a firm for veterinary and zoological services.[73]

Plate 3. A private heated greenhouse for growing tomatoes and cucumbers.

The most common agricultural products were grapes and wine, but people also grew potatoes, vegetables (tomatoes, cucumbers, and onions,

[71] For general agricultural production and structures in the *rayon,* I rely on Rəcəbli (n.d.) and the entry 'Şamxor' (Şəmkir) in *Azerbaijan Soviet Encyclopaedia* 1987: 462–464.
[72] See the entry for 'Şamxor Su Elektrik Stansiyası' in *Azerbaijan Soviet Encyclopaedia* 1987: 464. The power station commenced operating in 1983.
[73] In the entry 'Şamxor rayonu' in *Azerbaijan Soviet Encyclopaedia*, 1987: 464, the number of kolkhozes in the *rayon* in 1987 is given as 13, and the number of sovkhozes as 29.

among others), grains (wheat, barley, maize), and fruits (melons, watermelons, apples, pears, *xurma, gilas*) and raised animals, especially cattle, sheep, and poultry. Eight factories produced wine, and one, cognac, which was produced for foreign markets as well.[74] When the *rayon* was connected to the natural gas distribution system, the production of flowers (especially carnations) for both the internal market and socialist countries was lucrative. Once gas provision was reduced and then terminated, flower-growing declined.

The entry 'Şamxor rayonu' in the *Azerbaijani Soviet Encyclopaedia* (1987: 464) gives the amount of arable land (*kənd təsərrüfatına yararlı torpaqlar*) in Şəmkir *rayon* as 98,600 hectares, more than half of which (56,300 hectares, in Azerbaijani, *otlaq*) is said to be pastures. The entry has only one sentence about cotton production, saying that cotton was cultivated in the *rayon* until 1984. This is a cryptic reference to the fact that cotton production ended in the *rayon* because of the cotton scandal, also known as the *pripiska* scandal[75], in the early 1980s, when many kolkhoz and sovkhoz directors and other officials such as bookkeepers were put on trial and sentenced to years in prison, many serving their sentences in Moscow. The Communist Party head of the *rayon* is said to have committed suicide out of fear of the court case.

My local sources described how *pripiska* worked in the area. People paid money to the sovkhoz so that they could be recorded as having sold cotton to it, and then the sovkhoz declared that it had produced a much larger amount of cotton that year than it actually had. It received money from the state for the larger, fraudulent quantity and distributed the surplus money among those who had 'invested' at the beginning. The extra cotton that was supposed to have been produced either never materialised or was purchased from Uzbekistan. The fraud was organised at the highest national and intra-Soviet levels of the production and control structures.[76]

The second most important crop, grapes, is said to have been cultivated on 5,200 hectares out of a total 22,900 hectares in cultivated area (*umumi əkin sahəsi*) (*Azerbaijani Soviet Encyclopaedia* 1987: 464). According to local accounts, there was *pripiska* in grape cultivation as well. My neighbour Naima explained how it worked. The sovkhoz had to fulfil ever

---

[74] The entry 'Şamxor konyak zavodu [cognac factory]' in *Azerbaijan Soviet Encyclopaedia* 1987: 463 says that the factory was founded in 1923, whereas local people say it was founded by German colonists. It is likely that this factory, like the wine factory in Təzəkənd, had simply been taken over from the liquidated property of the Hummel brothers.

[75] *Pripiska*, meaning 'addition', was the term used to describe fraudulent 'additions' made to cotton production figures.

[76] For the Uzbek side of the cotton scandal and its post-Soviet repercussions, see Trevisani (2010).

increasing production plans for grape cultivation, so the villagers were asked to show their private, household garden plots (məhləs) as areas for growing grapevines. They had to state their number of grapevines and were paid money for that number. At the end of the cultivation season, they received more than they had 'invested' for having 'sold' a certain quantity of grapes to the sovkhoz. The sovkhoz had either to falsify its documentation for the quantity of grapes received or buy grapes through illegal means from another sovkhoz. Apparently, the *pripiska* in wine production did not become publicly talked about as widely as that for cotton. Probably this rather low-key *pripiska* went 'unnoticed' by the Soviet centre because of the anti-alcohol campaigns that immediately followed the *pripiska* period, which drastically reduced the area under cultivation anyway.

Two other important activities in the agricultural sector pertain to the pre-independence decade in Təzəkənd. First, people began using greenhouses for cultivating household plots at that time. Subsidised state gas was still available, and new markets were emerging in the region and in Russia for selling fruits and vegetables grown in greenhouses. Second, the sovkhoz for grapes and wine production was being transformed. Some privatised cultivation was introduced in the late 1980s, and control mechanisms were weakened such that some sovkhoz workers and officials were able to organise illegal sales of wine and cognac on a large scale. Under Gorbachev's regime, the sale of alcohol in the Soviet Union was rigidly controlled, and alcohol production went underground. Some wine producers in Azerbaijan took advantage of the situation to illegally transport alcohol into Russia by train. This activity involved local sovkhoz workers and agricultural technicians and some people in higher positions. The illegal train transport of wine continued until about the beginning of the war over Karabakh, allegedly making some families and individuals in Təzəkənd very rich. For some, this was also their first experience of illegal, organised trade in Russia and the beginning of substantial trade and migratory movements from Azerbaijani villages to Russian, Ukrainian, and Kazakh cities.

Agrarian Reforms

Agrarian changes have been taking place in Azerbaijan since the mid-1980s. In the wake of perestroika and the *pripiska* scandals of the early 1980s, agricultural production systems came under scrutiny. Towards the end of the 1980s, for instance, kolkhoz workers and brigadiers were being allowed to sharecrop land belonging to the socialist agricultural structures and to establish themselves as individual farmers (*fermerler*) or as members of cooperatives to cultivate land as enterprises independent of the kolkhoz or sovkhoz

(Ibrahimov 1998: 9).[77] A considerable spirit of private enterprise seems to have been engendered during this period. Many villagers in Təzəkənd said they began cultivating their private plots in greenhouses at this time, growing vegetables and herbs that they sold at both local and faraway markets. The greenhouses seem to have functioned because the state was still providing cheap, subsidised natural gas for heating. Once the gas supply was cut off in the early 1990s, growers had to resort to other sources of energy. Some changed to liquid gas for heating, buying it privately. Some stopped producing early vegetables in heated greenhouses altogether, shifting to the open-air production of vegetables and herbs.

One nine-person household that I visited for my survey exemplified households' earnings from selling vegetables during the 1980s. Its members explained that by selling extra cucumbers, beans, tomatoes, and aubergines from their household plot (məhlə) in the markets of Şəmkir and Gəncə, they had been able to earn approximately 1,000 manat (the Azerbaijani equivalent of the rouble) yearly during that period. By comparison, in 1985 kolkhoz workers in Şəmkir earned an average of 59 manat per month, and in 1990, 103 manat per month. Sovkhoz workers earned an average of 108 manat per month in 1985, and in 1990, 122 manat per month.[78]

It is clear that agrarian reforms and privatisation were being discussed and planned during these transformational years. Privatisation and liberalisation of consumer and producer prices had already occurred in the early 1990s (Wiesner 1997: 144; Hanke 1998: 146–148). In an interview I conducted in 2000 with İrşad Əliyev, then minister of agriculture, he explained that the reforms had necessarily arisen as a consequence of changing from the socialist system to the capitalist one[79]: 'Azerbaijan was a part of a whole. It lost the whole. And there was nothing to substitute for it. The produce did not go to Russia any more [SSR əlaqələri kırıldı; Rusya'ya məhsul gedməyib]'. The quality of Azerbaijan's agricultural products was already

---

[77] Islam Ibrahimov (1998: 9) mentioned democratisation, voluntarism, entrepreneurship, and the creation of a new, efficient relationship to property as the main motives behind the new regulations and rules at the beginnings of the new independent states. On 1 January 1990, *Ulduz*, a local newspaper in Şəmkir, reported that 88 per cent of the vineyards in the *rayon* (7,861 hectares out of a total of 8,892 hectares) was already under cultivation by sharecroppers (*icarə podratı*). In the spirit of self-criticism typical of the time, the author of the article complained that production was declining in all branches: in vine cultivation, only 87.4 per cent of the plan was fulfilled, and even wheat production had dropped from 23 *sentner* to 18 *sentner* per hectare (1 *sentner* = 100 kg). Note the difference with the 'doubling the plans' of the early 1980s.

[78] *Kolxoz, Sovxoz və Təsərrüfətlararası Kənd Təsərrüfatı Müəssisələrinin Əsas İqtisadi Göstəricilərı 1985–1990 cu İllər* 1991: 13–14.

[79] The interview, held on 20 September 2000, was not recorded, so quotations from the former minister are taken from my handwritten notes.

low, he said, referring mainly to wine, and so they were 'not competitive enough [rəqabət edəməyən məhsul]'.[80] In order to improve production, Azerbaijan 'had to establish contact with broader world markets [dünya bazarına əlaqə başladı]'.

The minister explained that privatisation went through a difficult phase: 'Ninety-five per cent of the people were against privatisation. There were many talks, debates, discussions; people accepted this afterwards; they saw that there was no alternative'. In the former system, there was a major discrepancy between large subsidies and the poor work morale that resulted from low productivity and disappointing returns. As the minister put it:

> Two billion manat was spent yearly for subsidies in agricultural production. People were used to working less and gaining more. In the villages, thirty people worked but one hundred people lived from it [100 nəfərdən 30'u işi aparırdı]. The productivity of land was low. When the produce was high, its costs were high too. ... People wanted to work less and earn and accumulate lots [Məhsul yüksək, mali dəyəri də yüksəkti ... İnsanlar az işləyib, çox yığsınlar istərlərdi].[81]

The reforms came in stages. First, committees for liquidation (called reform committees, islahat komissiyası) were established to decide what needed to be distributed, its value, and how to distribute it. These committees were set up in local settings as well as hierarchically at the rayon and national levels.[82] There were also plans for some support after recipients had received their land shares, so that they could begin some cultivation activities. For instance, the minister of agriculture whom I interviewed said that in 1995–1997, people who had recently received land shares were given

---

[80] The minister suggested that Azerbaijan could revive its vineyard production and produce high-quality spirits (araq) from grapes, as much as 400,000 to 500,000 decilitres a year, if markets for it existed.

[81] See also Wiesner (1997), who studied privatisation in Azerbaijan in 1991–1994. Among other problems of the Azerbaijani economy immediately following independence, she mentioned 'the crumbling of controls in the years which led to the breakup of the Soviet Union and its aftermath [which] paved the way to far-reaching asset stripping, and theft of resources and final goods in all branches of industry and the economy as a whole' (1997: 146).

[82] There were three bureaucratic levels of hierarchy. The merkez agrar islahat komissiyası was composed of ministers, high bureaucrats, and academicians and was led by a minister, deputy to the prime minister. The next level, rayon agrar islahat komissiyası, was composed of rayon-level technical experts, kolkhoz and sovkhoz directors, agrarian economists, and other relevant bureaucrats. Finally, the yerli agrar islahat komissiyası had 13 to 17 members who were village-level bureaucrats and former officials and technicians of the agrarian structures, such as kolkhoz and sovkhoz directors, economists, agronomists, technicians, and the like. Agrar islahat komissiyası were set up in 1995. See also Hanke (1998: 172) and Ibrahimov (1998).

cheaper petrol for agricultural machinery and were exempt from the land tax. After 1997, this was stopped.

On the whole the minister was optimistic about the results of the reforms. He believed that the innovative character of the people would be the moving principle behind improved agricultural production: 'The nation's entrepreneurial spirit is crucial [*millətin aparıcı gücü əsasdır*]'. As an example of the creativity and entrepreneurship of the people, he explained that they were using every means possible to access markets intelligently:

> People should learn how the market economy works and how they should function in it and make it stronger [*Bazar iqtisadiyyatı bərk etməli*]. People have access to knowledge through their own connections. They learn about prices and trade conditions almost daily from one another by asking one another [*Bazar konusunda canlı enformasiya var*]. There are three railroad and motorway connections. Along all these one could see people travelling almost daily, coming to Baku for the day and trading at the market.[83]

The minister was confident that rural producers were being economically active in a reasonable and efficient way and that the government should focus on non-intervention in its efforts to promote free-market activity.[84] As examples of the success of privatisation measures in the agrarian sector he cited statistics showing that almost all mills were now privately owned and that numbers of livestock were increasing. He had seen a TV film on rural production in the *rayon* of Tovuz, in the west of the country, where a farmer had 10,000 sheep, which clearly indicated to him that the entrepreneurial spirit was developing in the countryside. Finally, the minister underscored one aim of the agrarian reforms, that of creating suitable living conditions in the countryside so that people would stay there ('*Kəndə şərait yaradmak lazım ki orda kalsınlar*'). This was not a new vision – it had been one of the primary concerns of Soviet-period agrarian policy – and it is difficult to say conclusively how successfully it has been realized. So far, contemporary

---

[83] Until 2002 Baku still had spontaneous markets and traders of local agricultural and other products all over the streets. Then the city administration introduced restrictions that limited the areas where traders could set up their stalls. Consequently, the dynamism and openness of access to Baku markets about which the minister spoke are already gone.

[84] The minister described an ambitious programme that was being developed to gather and disseminate knowledge about agriculture and optimal production methods within it. The information would flow between the Institute for Economics (*Iktisadiyyat Enstitüsü*), the Information Bank (*Bank enformasyonu*), and the information centres (*enformasya merkez*) in 6 *rayon*s. There would be 5 regional centres and 31 information centres in *rayon*s. All ministry decisions (*qanunlar, fermanlar, qararlar*) would be pooled in these centres and then posted on the Internet so that people could look up information for themselves on subjects such as the quality of seeds and how to plant them. Services to the rural sector would aim to get people interested and informed (*alakalandırıcı*).

trends indicate the opposite – that people are leaving the countryside not only for Baku but also for temporary or permanent out-migration to the Russian Federation.

In September 2000, Həsən Həsənov, an agricultural expert and agrarian economist then working under the state minister, described the implementation of the agrarian reforms in Azerbaijan as follows:[85]

> The process of privatisation went like this: first the animals were divided [*paylandı*]. Later on the land was distributed. Various buildings that had to do with sovkhoz and kolkhoz organisations with animal production were still not privatised; they remained state property. The technical equipment that was left behind was given to only a few people. This equipment, however, was very old and needed to be renewed. So all this procedure led to some problems in privatisation [*özəlləştirmədə uygunsuzluqlar olub*].

Discussions among experts at the time and by the public in newspapers revealed that people had different proposals and opinions about how the land should be divided among the residents of rural settlements.[86] The minister of agriculture, İrşad Əliyev, gave fear of rural unrest as the reason for including all rural residents and not giving agrarian land solely to, for example, agrarian workers and cultivators, as had been the case in Ukraine (see Kaneff and Yalçın-Heckmann 2003). 'There would be disputes and fights [*Dava olur*]', he claimed. It is remarkable that no appreciable fights broke out when some people were excluded from the land allocations, especially in light of the obvious irregularities and favouritism that attended the distribution. Həsən Həsənov was critical of the corruption and misuse (*yaranmaq oldu*) in the initial agrarian credit cooperatives that were established with support from the World Bank. He attributed the termination of the credit programme in 2000 to its corruption (*proje hələ dayanmış*).

The division of privatised land differed according to family size and the amount of land available in each locality. Families in the form of households received land together as units, and each unit's allocation equalled the standard per capita plot for their locality times household size. Sometimes

---

[85] Həsən Həsənov is a pseudonym for a state official whom I interviewed on various occasions. The quotations from these interviews, too, are from handwritten notes taken during the interviews.

[86] See Wiesner (1997) for a discussion of the methods of privatisation in previously centrally planned economies (pp. 63–123) and of privatisation as carried out in Azerbaijan (pp. 231–253). The method used for agrarian land in Azerbaijan partly followed what is described as 'free transfer to citizens' (pp. 97–100), although recipient citizens or residents received direct deeds to land instead of vouchers. For the processes of agrarian reform and the laws and regulations concerning agricultural structures and property that were passed in the first half of the decade, see also Hanke (1998: 165–175).

the standard allotment was 1 hectare per person, and sometimes only 0.01 hectare, which is 1 *sotka*, the measure used for land parcels. Həsənov claimed that 95 per cent of rural people received land deeds (*torpaq aktı*). He also pointed out that associations such as the wheat union (*tahıl birliği*) were set up in all *rayons*. Their purpose was to provide consultation and control as well as to disseminate information on matters of production and marketing (*istihsal və ihraçda, nəzaret və informasiya*).

Ilham Ismailov, another bureaucrat high up in the ministry's Office for Agrarian Reforms, was also critical of the way the reforms were taking place, although he was careful in the way he formulated his critique. Unlike the minister, he thought villagers had little knowledge of how to improve their production and lacked money for either manure or fertiliser.

The organisation of relevant new agrarian structures and the mainte-nance of bureaucratic positions to deal with land and agriculture depended on the availability of personnel in the countryside. Because the state no longer provided a system of control and administration, suitable people for new systems had to be found within the ranks of knowledgeable people in the rural sector. During our interview, the minister suggested who the new actors and knowledgeable persons might be, advising me to talk to former kolkhoz leaders (*geçmiş kolxoz rehberleri*). He said they would now all be working properly, implying that those who had not followed instructions from the political centre had already been replaced.

My interlocutors on the whole believed that positions were not filled exclusively on the basis of candidates' education, experience, and capabili-ties, but were filled according to the networks maintained by powerful people who had personal connections to the presidential apparatus.[87] The higher one's access and connections reached, the more powerful one was thought to be (see also Willerton 1992). Because the governor (*icra hakimi*) – the head of the *rayon* administration – was appointed by the presidential office, he was considered the highest authority and thus the most powerful person in the *rayon*. Having access to the governor was seen as the key to accessing local power.

The general belief was that even villagers' pettiest concerns could be resolved if the governor personally interceded in them. He was expected to intervene in the decisions and implementations of almost all other offices and bureaucrats in the *rayon*. Even if a particular governor possessed no special qualifications, people found him powerful partly because of his

---

[87] Trevisani (2010) offers a sensitive ethnography of the complex structures of local power holders in post-Soviet Uzbekistan. He argues that centre-periphery or patronage models of relations between states and rural societies are not always helpful for explaining individual actors' multiple strategies for mediating and challenging state power.

habitus (Bourdieu 1977) as a power-holding person – for example, humiliating his inferiors, bestowing arbitrary favours, and showing the right demeanour in front of people of higher position and authority. He was said to exercise strict control over his inferiors and administrators, who were expected to report to him and seek his permission for certain decisions.

For example, for almost any information I wanted to collect from official persons concerning the *rayon*, such as production figures, administrative decisions, and maps of sovkhoz and kolkhoz land, I was referred to the governor for his permission or recommendation (*tapşırık almak*), even though I had already given him my letter of reference from the Academy of Sciences in Baku and he had instructed his assistants to support my research. On one occasion I had to confront him for withholding information from me that was available otherwise. I wanted a copy of the map that showed how privatised land was to be divided in Təzəkənd, from which rural residents learned the location of the plots they were to receive. The governor accused me of wanting access to a 'state secret' (*dövlət sırrı*) and ordered the Bureau of the Cadastre to show me the map but not give me copies of it.

Local people saw such habitus of intentional and imagined ultimate control as an essential part of their relationship to scarce resources such as jobs and access to pasture land. The career of Cəmil Rüstemov, a former sovkhoz director, illustrates the way people in high local positions seemed to be concerned more about their informal links to other power holders, especially those in the political centres, than about possessing the right education and professional experience.

Rüstemov was the director of the Əzizbəyov sovkhoz in Təzəkənd during the 1980s. Born in Armenia in 1938, he had come to Azerbaijan with his relatives in 1948 as a refugee (*qaçqın*) and was sent directly to a neighbouring village where the Əzizbəyov sovkhoz had some land. He finished his secondary education in 1957 and then attended the technical college for agriculture in Gəncə, where he studied fruit and vegetable cultivation. In 1961 he joined the Əzizbəyov vineyard (*üzümçülük*) sovkhoz as a brigadier, looking after 30 to 35 workers. His job was to document their labour time and keep track of who did not work. He stayed in this job until 1974.

In 1975 Rüstemov became the Communist Party committee member (*partkom*) for the sovkhoz, a position he held until 1979. His duty was to 'look after the quality and running of the sovkhoz [*işin kəyfiyyatına, təsərrufata bakardı*]'. In 1979 he became sovkhoz director after the *rayon* party committee (*raykom*) recommended him and the ministry chose him. (The *raykom* director at the time later killed himself in prison because of the cotton scandal.) Rüstemov remained sovkhoz director until independence and left at the time of the People's Front of Azerbaijan, knowing he would soon be laid off.

From 1993 to 1995 he directed the chemical union (*kimye birliği*) in another town; it provided state firms with chemical products such as fertilisers and pesticides for agriculture. From the end of 1995 until about the end of 1998 he was director of another sovkhoz, in a village in the same vicinity, and in 1998 he was elected the first secretary of the district *agroprom*, the state unit for coordinating agrarian production. *Agroproms* remained in existence until 2000.

In September 1999 Rüstemov became president (*sədr*) of the reform committee (*ıslahat komissiyası*) in his village, and in December 1999 he was elected the new mayor for the *bələdiyyə*, the local administrative body. He said the reason he wanted to become the *bələdiyyə sədri* was that he needed a job.

Rüstemov's career in agriculture typifies the possibilities and restrictions characteristic of the Soviet and early post-Soviet periods. The Soviet system made it possible for someone like Rüstemov, a refugee from Armenia, to acquire an education and to be upwardly mobile under the Communist Party promotion system. His biography also illustrates the way local networks and knowledge could be used as resources in such a career. Rüstemov managed to retain his career throughout crises such as the cotton scandal, the anti-alcohol campaign, the turn of the regime from socialism to independence, and the Nagorno-Karabakh war. What is remarkable is that he was able to be a sovkhoz director, then a director of the liquidation (reform) committee, and finally the mayor of a rural settlement – positions that might seem incompatible with one another because each was designed to re-structure and change the former position. Yet Rüstemov used his social capital and local networks efficiently enough to secure himself continuous employment.

Another sovkhoz director whom I interviewed had been prosecuted for *pripiska* in cotton and spent some time in jail, although he maintained his innocence. The delicacy of balancing local power positions with available government jobs, together with the scarcity of jobs in private enterprise that offered secure, stable salaries, put severe strains on people as production systems were re-structured. The aforementioned directors were interested primarily in securing administrative jobs, and their background allowed them to maintain networks connected to the local administrative power centre of the governor and to hold on as local actors by strategic use of knowledge and networks.

Implementation of Land Reforms

Land reform in Azerbaijan was implemented in the field of laws and legal regulations, on the one hand, and in the workings of local power holders, on the other. In some places the distribution of land titles and privatising of property of the former agrarian structures was still going on in 2000–2002, although this was an exception. In most places, I was told, the procedures had come to a close. During my fieldwork I was able to observe people who went to the newly elected head of the new local administration in Təzəkənd – the *bələdiyyə sədri*, who was in charge of showing people where their piece of land was on the map – so that they could then go to the land committee, ask to have their land measured exactly, and have the boundaries marked on the ground. Conflicts and quarrels arose frequently when people found out the location of their share of the privatised land. The mayor was embarrassed to have me around, observing disputes between land recipients and the administrators who had to explain why a share happened to be in a particular (often unfavourable) location.

The disputes I observed appeared to concern the least powerful members of the local society, mostly single and elderly women or impoverished households with few working adult men, who came to make complaints to the mayor. Their complaints were about the location of the land or about not being allowed to use it, in cases where someone else had taken the deed and was claiming use of the land. In one exemplary case, Cəmile, an old, single woman who lived in my host family's neighbourhood on the main road, told me that she could not get her *pay* deed because someone else was apparently using her land. To find out and make a complaint, she went to the representatives of the central administration (*selsovet*), who informed her that her title had been taken by a journalist who was a brother of certain political and economic power holders in the area. She wanted to fight for the land but did not know how to pursue her case. Living alone with her teenage grandson, she had no close relatives in the village to back up her claim.

The point of Cəmile's story is that people who have neither the means nor the confidence to make formal complaints to the authorities and to fight for their rights may lose their land title or use rights to others who knowingly collect the deeds of such people precisely because they know they will not make much trouble. As I show in chapter 5, Cəmile's case was the opposite of that of a woman I call Mila, who, although she was unwilling and unable to cultivate her land herself, did everything necessary to rent it and obtain money from it.

Plate 4. Cash crop herbs being prepared for sale.

Large Landowners

How did one become a large landowner during and after the agrarian reforms? What trends can be observed in people's strategies for gaining access
to and cultivating land? One way to gain access to land was by becoming a
fermer in the early 1990s, when new laws and regulations made it possible
for formations such as cooperatives and independent farmers to take root.[88]
The cases of Əli and Mahir, which I describe next, offer good examples.

Before the 1996 reform laws, Əli, who was the accountant (*buğaltır*)
for the Əzizbəyov wine factory, had taken 45 hectares of land from the
sovkhoz in order to become a *fermer*. At the time, he used the names of
relatives and neighbours to claim this land. With the 1996 agrarian reforms,
he was required to return 35 hectares because the people whose names he
had used for the first arrangement could now claim land as individual households with ownership rights. Əli retained 10 hectares for a family of 60
people (he had 10 children, as did his brother Tarıq), and he managed to
keep his holdings together in the same place. To my knowledge, no special
provision existed for allocating land to such units of collective users, so I
infer that Əli resorted to using private connections, as did a woman named

---

[88] See the Law for Rural Farmer Households (Kəndli fermer təsərrufatı haqqında Azərbaycan
Respublikası Qanunu), 8 April 1992, cited in Hanke (1998: 167 note 111).

Sədaqət, who told me she had paid a bribe to keep the same piece of land she had had as a *fermer*. Əli also managed to acquire private plots (*məhlə*s) for his four sons, right next to his own, so in the end he had 53 *sotka* (about 0.53 hectare) of *məhlə* land, with each of his sons having a separate house in a *məhlə* adjacent to his. Some villagers suspected that Əli's position as the former *buğaltır* of the sovkhoz had given him an unfair advantage. He was entitled to accumulate a large amount of land because of the large size of his kin group, but it could not have been purely down to luck that the *pay* share he received was in the former vineyard, where irrigation was no problem.

Mahir, too, had acquired a large amount of land by becoming a *fermer* before 1996, but he was unable to retain it for reasons very different from Əli's. Mahir took some 30 hectares of land in 1992–1993 and cultivated it until 1994. Then he had a car accident and became an invalid needing expensive medical treatment. Around the same time, his sons and their families left for migratory work and trade in Russia. In the end, Mahir returned all the land he originally had. In 2001 he primarily cultivated *məhlə*s for herbs and received some financial support from his sons abroad. His and Əli's cases illustrate that access to large pieces of land was already possible before the agrarian reforms, but keeping it or acquiring new, large areas of cultivable land after the reforms required special skills, connections, and financial resources for bribes, in addition to suitable household and kin groups to support such investment and production.[89]

The new large landowners in Təzəkənd were either people like Əli, who had taken land from the sovkhoz before 1996 and managed to keep it, or people who had connections to the village administration or to the former sovkhoz. Interestingly, one of the larger land users – not an owner but a sharecropper on many families' privatised shares – was one of the newly elected mayors, the *bələdiyyə sədri* Məhman. In one of my talks with Məhman he mentioned the work the *bələdiyyə* had done up to that time. Among other things, it was cultivating the land of people who were willing to give it over to sharecropping. He said that in 2002 the *bələdiyyə* cultivated 17 hectares belonging to people who could not cultivate it themselves. Məhman, with two partners, cultivated 75 hectares belonging to 150 families. They grew wheat and barley and got about 3,000 kilograms per hectare, which they sold to mills for 400–420 manat (then worth about US$0.08) per kilogram. They paid 200 kilograms per hectare to the families whose land they were sharecropping.

Apart from himself and the village administration, Məhman could think of only six people as big landowners. Seymur, a policeman, had 114

---

[89] Of the two cases known to me, besides Əli's and Mahir's, one person had taken 100 *sotka* (1 hectare), and the other one had 40 hectares.

hectares, and Salman, the assistant to the central administrator of the village, had 100. Asker, an agronomist and a former member of the reform committee for the Rüstəməliyev kolkhoz, had more than 50 hectares. Kemal, a restaurant owner, had 26 hectares; Asım, a teacher, 6; and Qubad, the former head of the sales department of the sovkhoz, 8. In the whole village Məhman named only one person as owning a combine, although he remarked that that year (2002), the landowners had been able to hire enough combines from other areas to harvest their crops. He named four people who owned tractors, all of whom had been tractor drivers for the sovkhoz before privatisation.

In short, large landowners were few in the vicinity of Təzəkənd. Significantly, the people who were cultivating large land shares were those who held governmental positions either formerly or at the time of my research. Indeed, people such as the policeman, the restaurant owner, and the teacher had not previously been involved in agriculture at all; their success was due to their strategic use of their social status and access to networks and information.

Of the people Məhman named, I knew Salman, Seymur, and Asker. Salman had been helping me work through the village registry list when I needed to select names for my survey. Through his position as assistant to the central administrator of the village, he knew exactly which households and individuals were unable to cultivate their privatised shares because they were poor, lacked a household labour force, had no useful network, or were simply away in migration. He had approached these households about sharecropping their land and convinced many of them to hand over their deeds to him.

I knew the policeman, Seymur, less well. He lived in the neighbourhood of my host family and was known as one of the newly rich, having built himself a big, ostentatious house with private electricity and water connections. It was common knowledge that his wealth could not have come from his policeman's salary alone and that all police officers at the higher level of the hierarchy took bribes. Seymur's wealth, however, was due not solely to his position but also to the overall influence of his family. All his brothers either had governmental jobs in the *rayon* or were involved in trade and business, so the family had the reputation of being wealthy and influential. This social capital probably facilitated Seymur's access to land that would otherwise have gone uncultivated, helping him to convince land holders to give their deeds to him.

Asker, as agronomist for the former kolkhoz, was the only one on Məhman's list who had expertise and experience in agricultural production and had been a member of the agrarian reform committee. Like Məhman and Salman, he must have had access to information about the availability of land shares that would probably not be used by their new owners. Furthermore, he belonged to a big family that included quite a few influential and educated people, as well as migrant businessmen. Thus, he benefited from the support of his kin group.

Not only did the large landowners and cultivators have to develop strategies to gain access to land shares, but they also had to use their networks and financial resources to organise the cultivation of their land. Big farmers faced considerable structural limitations, as is shown by the case of Şəhriyar, in the neighbouring village of Karaca. His situation exemplifies large land ownership by families pooling together as sharecroppers as well as using political links to local power holders to rent grazing areas for another profitable agro-business, the raising of cattle and sheep. Şəhriyar's case demonstrates the structural limitations of big farming.

I met Şəhriyar after I asked some leading men and women in Karaca about farmer households (*fermer təsərrüfatı*). They disagreed over whether there were still *fermer təsərrüfatı* in Karaca, and some of them wanted to introduce me to people whom they said were *fermer*s. One such person was Şəhriyar, the brother of the mayor (*bələdiyyə sədri*) in Karaca, who had been a member of the reform committee of the kolkhoz. Şəhriyar was keen to meet me and soon took me to see his land. On the way there in his car, he told me that he needed technical equipment (*texnika*) and asked if I knew people at the ministry who could help him get credit. He explained that he had obtained 50 hectares of land from 27 families, including that of his brother, and he cultivated wheat and cloves. He worked with his three sons and lived with his wife, Zübeyde, in a wagon in the middle of a field. Together with a man at the governor's office who was in charge of rural production in the *rayon*, he had taken 250 hectares for pasture, on which he grazed about 200 sheep. When I asked Şəhriyar why he could not obtain credit for himself, he said that only people who had *adam* (literally, 'person', i.e. connections) in the ministry could get credit. Although he attended training courses (*fermer kursları*) in Gəncə and made business plans, he had not succeeded.[90] When he realised that I could not help him, he was visibly disappointed.

Şəhriyar's story is significant because, unlike the big farmers mentioned earlier, he actually engaged in production, even living in the middle of a field in order to care for his sheep and crops. He had successfully acquired a large area for cultivation, thanks to his own capabilities, the fact that his brother was the mayor, and his links to governmental bodies and offi-

---

[90] *Fermer kursları* are courses, mostly organised by NGOs with the financial support of foreign aid institutions such as the World Bank, that train people in making business plans and then applying for credit for farming.

cials. Yet his prospects for success were limited by the restricted availability of technology and credit. Even though he had good local contacts, it seems that his network did not reach high enough to ensure his sustainable success, and so he was vulnerable.

Another example of large a landowner-farmer in Karaca was Maya. I was told that she was a 'socialist hero of labour' (əməq kahramanı) and, with 12 children, a 'socialist hero–mother of many children' (kahraman ana). She had worked as a milk woman (sağıcı) at the sovkhoz for 30 years. In 1998, before the distribution of privatised land, she took 7.5 hectares for 15 people, all members of her family, and became a fermer. At the time I met her, she was cultivating wheat and cloves on this land and kept 50 sheep. She, too, complained about the lack of texnika; she particularly needed a combine harvester. She had been looking for one urgently because her wheat was ripe and had to be harvested. She pointed out that there were only four combines in Karaca, and they were not enough. In former times, the kolkhoz had received help from the mountain rayons, because their harvest time came later than that on the plains. Now there were fewer combines and they had all been privatised, so their owners had to travel long distances and did not get around to everyone in need. Maya begged me to write about this problem.

Maya's case exemplifies the way people could have access to large shares of land through the use of social capital – in this case, her reputation as a hard-working person – that derived from the former Soviet system. Yet as an elderly woman, she was more vulnerable than Şəhriyar. Her connections to both old and new local elites and power holders were limited, and she probably relied heavily on gifts of cash earned in Russia by her son, who had been gone for some 11 years.

Concluding Remarks

The seeds of the continuities and discontinuities between the socialist and postsocialist periods in Azerbaijan in terms of agrarian and land tenure systems lay in the ruptures and destruction of the early decades of the Soviet Union. In the locality of Şəmkir, those years saw the liquidation of the rich German entrepreneur families, such as the Hummel brothers, the abolition of private property in 1920, the rush to collectivise the land, the establishment of the first sovkhoz in 1929, and the deportation of the remaining German families in 1941. Neither Stalin's great purges nor collectivisation was strongly inscribed in the memories of contemporary Azerbaijani families, because there were no significant large land-owning families in the region. The settlement of political refugees from Iranian Azerbaijan and of deported

Azeris from Armenia at the end of the 1940s, however, had a strong effect on settlement patterns and the composition of the population.

Most of the time, Soviet agricultural policies determined rural production patterns. Sovkhoz and kolkhoz land holdings were merged into one another, new land was opened up for cultivation, and crops were cultivated or removed from production according to the central plans of the Soviet economy. Local power holders – the party *nomenklatura* and agrarian experts and officials – seem to have followed the nation-wide strategy of modifying the agrarian policies dictated from centre to suit their own needs. Insofar as these modifications brought the local power holders wealth and privilege and were supported by local producers, people remembered the socialist years as a time of abundance and well-being. The moment existing patronage networks failed to prevent persecution from the top, however, as in the case of the *pripiska* scandal in the mid-1980s, local power holders of various ranks (party officials, sovkhoz leaders, bookkeepers, etc.) suffered substantially. They seem to have become even more cautious in the way they managed their dependency and patronage relations with those at the top, especially immediately following independence, when those at the top themselves were often jockeying for position, sometimes violently.

Land was nationalised in the Soviet Union in 1920, but regardless of the ideological argument behind doing so, the majority of land had already been state land under tsarist Russia. Collectivisation and infrastructural development led to gradual agrarian development and the creation of new agricultural jobs everywhere in the Soviet Union. Vineyards and cotton production were subsidised by the socialist state, and many former *sovkhozniki* and *kolkhozniki* remembered the last decades of the Soviet Union as a time of stable income from state jobs and extra benefits from trade and the sale of produce in regional markets.

The 'end' came with crisis and war. Confusing changes took place in Azerbaijani politics, and some of them had local ramifications. People referred to Heydər Əliyev's return to political leadership in 1993 as the beginning of some stability. Under his leadership the oil industry became a successful enterprise for the whole of the country, concomitantly reducing the significance of non-oil production, especially that of rural agriculture. The agrarian reforms of 1996 distributed the available land to residents free of charge, creating incentives for rural people to remain on and work the land. Other than free access to land, however, these residents received hardly any incentives or resources for rural production. The depletion of local jobs, devaluation of rural production, and dissolution of former markets for rural produce such as wine all contributed to detrimental developments in the countryside. Local structures of patronage and networks still affected access to land and other resources. Nevertheless, it is difficult to talk of privatised land shares being accumulated by a few power holders, because production on these shares still suffers from structural problems of deficits in technical equipment, credit, transportation, and markets. As I show in the following chapters, it is the cultivation of formerly 'owned' household plots, which have better irrigation facilities and sometimes better soil, that has become important for rural production.

Chapter 4
Village Households and Agricultural Economy: Survey Data and Analysis

In this chapter I look at the economic activities of households in the village of Təzəkənd. I examine the way different types of households have access to and manage land, labour, and other economic resources with different degrees of success, such that some households seem to have better chances of economic survival and economic mobility than others.[91]

The discussion is based on the results of the household survey I carried out in Təzəkənd in 2001, through which I collected data on immovable property such as houses, household plots (in Azerbaijani, *məhlə* or *həyətyanı*), and privatised land shares (*pay torpağı* or, for short, *pay*) and on sources of income such as salaries, pensions, and remittances from migrants. My aim is to examine the structural links between agricultural production (on household plots and privatised shares), households' economic surpluses (achieved through salaries, remittances, and income from agriculture), households' economic capital (land and houses), and certain demographic and social factors, such as household composition, occupation of the head of household (*təsərrüfatın başçısı*)[92], household size, and availability of other kin in the village. Ultimately, I deal with questions such as whether households with large economic surpluses tend not to cultivate their land and whether households with labour shortages (small household size) have less tendency to engage in agriculture. More generally, the issue of economic rationality and households' choices about using land is at stake.

---

[91] In writing this chapter, I profited considerably from discussions with and readings by Patrick Heady, as well as substantial support for the statistical analyses by Tuba Bircan. I thank them sincerely, although any mistakes are my responsibility.

[92] For consistency, I have followed the Azerbaijan government's formal definition of household head (*təsərrüfatın başçısı*) as the person in whose name the household plot is registered in the village registry and who is administratively accepted as the head of the household. During interviews I discovered that the actual household head was sometimes someone different. Although I have noted this, I follow this formal principle for making my comparative assumptions.

Although notions and relations of kinship are entangled in all household matters, I focus in this chapter primarily on the unit of the household
rather than on the individual or the kin group. The primary reason is that
privatised land shares have been given to individuals only insofar as they are
registered members of households. From the perspective of Azerbaijan's
agrarian reforms of 1996, the household is the unit of agricultural land
management.[93] The sociological reason for choosing the household as the
unit of analysis is that the rural economy and patterns of settlement and
administration are organised and based on it. The more anthropological
reason is that households are referred to by more than one term and reflect
different shades of meaning, and the physical and social existence of households enables individuals and kin groups to be related to one another. The
village family is composed of households; the physical structure of dwellings is designed to accommodate households; and economic resources are
exploited by households.[94]

The Azerbaijani term for a household is *təsərrüfat*, meaning '(unit of)
economy'. *Halq təsərrüfatı* refers to the science of economics (similar to
Volkswirtschaft in German), and *kənd təsərrüfatı* refers to agriculture.
Təsərrüfat is the term villagers use when they want to make it clear that their
household is an administrative unit, as in conversations with official persons
and in claims to be allocated a household plot of the sort formerly distributed
by the kolkhoz, sovkhoz, or village council (*selsovet*) and today distributed
by the local administrative body (*bələdiyyə*). When they want to refer to
becoming a separate household, as when a son separates his family from the
parental one, people say *ayrıldıq* ('we have separated') or *ayrı evik* ('we are

---

[93] National statistical sources reporting on the rate of privatisation of agrarian land cite the
number of families (*ailə sayı*) who received privatised land, rather than using the term
təsərrüfat (household). I assume that the term *ailə* (family) in these sources has been treated
synonymously with *təsərrüfat*. Accordingly, 830,000 families were to receive 1,327,700
hectares of land altogether. *Azərbaycan Respublikasında 1–i Sentyabr 2000–ci İl Vəziyyətinə
Aqrar İslahatın Gedişi Haqqında* 2000: 2.
[94] I am aware of the long history of discussions concerning the household as a social unit and
the problems involved with taking the household as a social unit. Both feminist critiques and
developmental studies are critical of the use of the household as an economic unit. For
instance, see Dwyer and Bruce (1988) for a collection of anthropological critiques in which
women's roles in household economies are comparatively and critically discussed, with
examples from different parts of the world and different economic settings. My aim is not to
advocate a return to an uncritical usage of the term; I understand the inherent problems of
differential decision-making within the household and the fact that households may be
divided through migration and differential access to resources (see also Smith, Wallerstein,
and Evers 1984). But given that the household is favoured as the unit that receives privatised
rural property in Azerbaijan, I am forced to stick to this unit and live with its problems of
analysis.

a separate family/house'). Hence, the term *ev* could mean house, family, or household.[95]

These variations in meaning become evident when one looks at how the members of a household may form one residential unit but be registered as two *təsərrüfat*s in the village registry, particularly if one member of the residential unit (household) has applied to attain a separate household plot in order to build a separate house. Alternatively, a residential unit might consider itself to be one *ev* but not one family (*ailə*), as when an unmarried adult sister or a widowed sister has been incorporated into the household.[96] In that case, *təsərrüfat* is the common term used in conjunction with claims to property; the household that is to receive privatised land shares (*pay*) is a collective unit on the ground. In all these variations, the meaning of household as an economic unit is central. The household is where resources are pooled to some degree and where there is an internal, socially and traditionally accepted yet often contested structure of decision-making, distribution, and consumption.[97]

Statistical analyses of my survey findings allow me to highlight significant data concerning the differentiated use of household plots and privatised land shares in Təzəkənd. On the basis of these data, I suggest some explanations for why certain households use household plots more than others and how this usage might be connected to cash crop production, household structure, remittances from abroad, and the use or non-use of privatised land shares. Although the quantitative data allow useful conclusions to be drawn about the use of land and agricultural resources in post–agrarian reform rural Azerbaijan, I offer further insights into household strategies in the following chapter, where case studies of chosen households

---

[95] Ingrid Pfluger-Schindlbeck (2005: 12–13) drew attention to the use of the word *məhlə* for referring to a family's genealogical group, the minimal lineage, all of whom come from one *məhlə*, one plot of land on which the parental house is built. *Məhlə*, however, is primarily a physical space, the courtyard and the land, whereas *ev* has a more abstract meaning as house, not only the physical space but also the group, as in 'house of Windsor'.

[96] During my household survey I came upon discrepancies between the residential unit and the unit registered as *təsərrüfat* in several cases when I sought a household with a specific registration number but found two households living there, when I found the person registered as household head living in another household, or something similar. The problems of treating households as single residential and family units on the basis of the way they were registered in the Soviet registry system and have continued to be counted have been discussed by Kandiyoti (1999).

[97] Discussions of the development and structure of households and their relationship to kinship and other domestic and economic groups have long appeared in historical studies and in economic and social anthropology. See, for example, the contributions to Netting, Wilk, and Arnould (1984). For earlier discussions in classic anthropological studies, see Fortes (1967 [1949]), Goody (1971 [1958]), and Firth (1983 [1936]).

illustrate why some have better chances of survival or economic upward mobility than others.

Household Size and Composition

To what degree do the members of a household act together as a unit? The answer to this question depends primarily on intra-household relations. Even if the household is treated as a residential unit within which members have certain rights and certain obligations towards one another – some of them legally articulated – actual social relations within a household depend on many factors. A primary factor on which I focus here is demographics: the size of the household, the number of generations living together, and household composition, or the number of married couples and unmarried adults living in the same unit and their relationships to one another. In what follows, I present various distributions of the households in my survey according to household size, number of generations, and sex and age of the household head.

Within the total sample of 77 households, mean household size was 5.3 persons, and the median was 5.0. The smallest household size was 1 (n = 5), and the largest, 13 (n = 2) (fig. 4.1). When household sizes are grouped, the largest group, 4–6 people per household, amounts to 42 per cent of the total. Nearly one-third of the households comprised 7 or more people, from which I conclude that Təzəkənd has significantly large households. It also has a large percentage of multi-generational households: 43 per cent of the survey households (n = 33) encompassed three or more generations, and another 44 per cent was two-generational (n = 34).

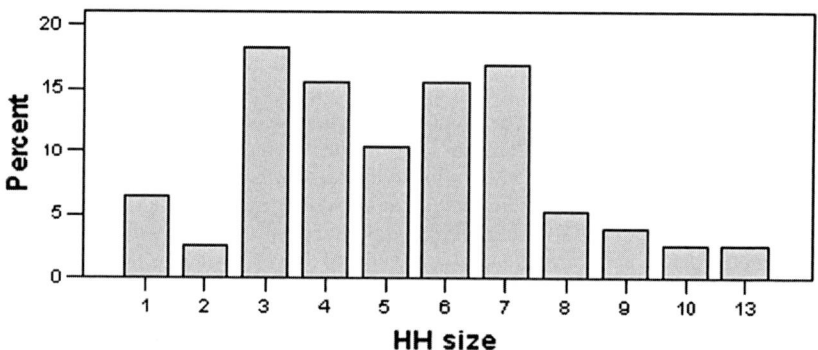

Figure 4.1. Household (HH) size among 77 surveyed households in Təzəkənd.

Nearly one-third of the households (25 of 77) were led by female heads of household (HHHs).[98] Female HHHs were found more often in average-size households than in larger ones; only 4 of 25 female-headed households consisted of 7 or more persons, whereas 20 of 52 male-headed households were of that size.[99] Nearly half of all female-headed households were three-generational. Furthermore, in 12 of the 33 three-generational households, the HHH was a woman; commonly, these households were led by a widowed mother living together with her married son or sons and grandchildren.[100]

The mean age of HHHs was 53, which can be explained by the administrative as well as the social definition of a household head (təsərrüfatın başçısı) and by the fact that acquiring the status of HHH implies receiving a household plot from the local authorities. These issues are dependent on the developmental cycle of the household, the availability of economic resources and accumulated capital for starting a household, and the politics of the allocation of household plots by the local authorities. All these factors seem to have a delaying effect on a person's becoming a household head, such that 56 per cent of HHHs were in the age groups of 51 and older.

The occupations of HHHs varied to some degree. I grouped these occupations into six categories (see table 4.1). Pensioners made up the largest group in the sample, at 39 per cent ($n = 30$) of all HHHs. The majority of the pensioners had been employed as kolkhozniki (in Azerbaijani, kolxozcu) or sovkhozniki (sovxozcu) and so had worked in the agricultural sector. The second largest group was HHHs currently working in the agricultural sector (18 per cent, $n = 14$). The 'unemployed' category (12 per cent, $n = 9$) included household heads who also had worked in the sovkhoz or kolkhoz but considered themselves unemployed because these structures had been dissolved before they reached the usual pension age.[101] Among these three

---

[98] This figure represents the socially and emically defined household head and not necessarily the officially designated one. For this figure I counted 'real' household heads and ignored the village registry.

[99] My prediction that there might be a correlation between households led by women and a particular size or number of generations in them was not met.

[100] See chapter 5 for case studies of households led by women.

[101] Indeed, the reason these HHHs called themselves 'unemployed' (bekar) was that this was the official label for people who had been employed in the sovkhoz until its dissolution. Those who said they were pensioners were older and had already begun receiving their pensions before the sovkhoz came to an end. This observation is corroborated by other anthropologists, such as Nora Dudwick and colleagues (2003: 12–13), who worked in poverty assessment programmes for the World Bank in several former Soviet countries, including Armenia and Georgia, and who point out how being unemployed was understood as having 'no "real" employment', such as a job in the state sector, even if respondents were engaged in informal or private-sector activities.

categories together, nearly 60 per cent of all household heads in the sample had been or continued to be involved in agriculture.

Distribution of Household Variables by Location of Settlement

Household sizes in Təzəkənd differed among parts of the village that I call 'settlements', or neighbourhoods (see map 2). I surveyed households in four settlements: Leninabad, Düzqışlaq, Demiryolu üstü, and Demiryolu altı. For statistical purposes, I grouped the four settlements into two sets. Leninabad and Düzqışlaq, which form one set, were both settlements of former *kol-khozniki* and *sovkhozniki*, a factor that accounted their having relatively large household plots. The two settlements in the other set, Demiryolu üstü and Demiryolu altı, were both in the central part of the village, to the east and west of the railway, respectively, and were densely and heterogeneously populated. In these settlements, household plots were smaller and less used for growing cash crops.

I surveyed 39 households in Leninabad and Düzqışlaq together, and 38 in Demiryolu altı and Demiryolu üstü together. Mean household size in the first set was 5.90 persons (standard deviation [SD] 2.817), and in the second set, 4.66 persons (SD 2.044), for an average household size of 5.29 persons (SD 2.528) among all settlements in the survey.

Not only was mean household size larger in Leninabad-Düzqışlaq than in the Demiryolu settlements, but also the distribution of household sizes in the two sets differed. In Leninabad-Düzqışlaq, the smallest house-holds (1–3 people) amounted to 23 per cent of all households, whereas in the Demiryolu group, 32 per cent of households were of that size. Conversely, there were more large households in Leninabad-Düzqışlaq: 46 per cent of households there (18 of 39) consisted of 7 or more persons, whereas the comparable figure for Demiryolu altı and üstü was 16 per cent (6 of 38 households). More than half the households in the latter group (20 of 38) had a size of 4–6 persons.

Table 4.1 shows the number of household heads in each occupation group by settlement. Agriculture was the predominant occupation in Lenina-bad, whereas pensioners predominated in the central village settlements of Demiryolu altı and üstü. Interestingly, no one among the random sample in Leninabad, the settlement of former sovkhoz workers and agriculturalists, was employed in the state sector (for example, as teachers or doctors).

Table 4.1. Numbers of Heads of Household in Six Occupations in Təzəkənd, by Settlement.

| Settlement | Occupational Category | | | | | | Total |
	Pen-sioner	State Sector	Agricul-tural Sector	Self-Em-ployed	Pri-vate Sector	Unem-ployed	
Leninabad	11	0	13	3	5	3	35
Düzqışlaq	3	0	0	0	0	1	4
Demiryolu altı	7	1	0	3	4	2	17
Demiryolu üstü	9	4	1	4	0	3	21
Total	30	5	14	10	9	9	77

Looking at the settlements again in two sets, some relationship can be seen between occupation of household head and household size. In the primarily agricultural settlements, Leninabad and Düzqışlaq, 6 of the 13 HHHs working in the agricultural sector had 7 or more persons in their households. Half of households led by pensioners in Leninabad-Düzqışlaq (7 of 14) consisted of 7 or more persons, whereas in Demiryolu altı and üstü only 2 of 16 pensioner-headed households were of this size, and 14 of the 16 consisted of 1–6 persons. I discuss the relevance of household size for agricultural occupation and activity later, when I look at the contrast between cultivating household plots and cultivating privatised land shares.

Household Networks

Many households had kin in Təzəkənd, either in the settlement where the household lived or in other parts of the village. Eighty-three per cent of all HHHs and nearly 50 per cent of their partners reported having such kin relations. These kin included parents, married sons and daughters, brothers, sisters, cousins, uncles, aunts, nieces, and nephews. On the whole, kin relations were important for rural residents; they provided the potential for social, economic, and political relations, which needed to be cultivated and shaped.[102] The existence of kin did not imply unquestioned support and solidarity. The case studies in the following chapters show that even if the HHH had siblings in the same neighbourhood, relations of daily support and exchange might be limited. Kin relationships might be restricted to what Bourdieu (1977) called those of 'official kin', who support the household mainly on ritual and ceremonial occasions.

---

[102] For a fine discussion of kin, affinal, and other networks among families and households in a northern Azerbaijani village, and of associated strategies and processes of alliance and conflict, see Pfluger-Schindlbeck (2005).

In terms of access to property, kinship relations were significant, according to the quantitative data, especially in the areas of inheritance and access to housing. Inheriting one's parents' house and *məhlə*, as well as sharing these with siblings, formed the basis of access to property, as I discuss later. It was expected that sons would be provided with houses once they married and established their own families. Parents felt social pressure to provide each son with a dwelling, much as they had previously supported their education and occupational training. Although providing daughters with houses was not the rule, giving them an adequate trousseau was the expected and fairly expensive practice (see Yalçın-Heckmann 2001).

Houses and Household Plots

Household plots were shares of land given to people who wanted to build a house and use the plot for a subsidiary garden. They were given primarily to *kolkhozniki* and were called 'subsidiary gardens for *kolkhozniki*' (*kolxozcuların yardımcı həyətyanı təsərrüfatı*) (Allahverdiyev 1980: 18).[103] Apparently the *selsovet* also gave such plots to other rural residents for starting new households. In everyday Azerbaijani they are referred to as *həyətyanı* or *məhlə*. Households in Təzəkənd had received plots of different sizes, depending on when and in which neighbourhood their house was built, but 97 per cent of my sample households had *məhlə*s. Because the neighbourhoods of Leninabad and Düzqışlaq had been settled mostly by former kolkhoz and sovkhoz workers, household plots there were relatively large, ranging from 20 to 25 *sotka* (about 0.20 to 0.25 hectare). Houses built in the centre of the village, close to the train station, sometimes had no *məhlə* at all.

Because household plots were given primarily for the building of a house, 87 per cent of the houses inhabited by the sample households had been built by the present inhabitants. Only 5 per cent of the houses had been inherited from the respondents' parental generation – the generation that was no longer alive. Houses were crucial for providing not only shelter but also the initial capital with which a person could set up a household. Young men, especially when they got married, came under social pressure from their age-mates to achieve the ownership of a house by either building or buying one as soon as possible. Houses also functioned as factors of stability in the economic and psychological senses, especially if men were forced to earn their living abroad through migration. The house demonstrated both concretely and symbolically a sense of belonging to the community and the locality. I illustrate this point with case studies in the next chapter.

---

[103] On the same agricultural organisation in Soviet central Russia, see Dunn and Dunn (1967: 41–45), and on collective farms in Buryatia, see Humphrey (1983).

In my sample of 77 heads of household, 59 of them (77 per cent) owned the house in which they lived at the time of the survey. Of these 59 HHHs, 30 (51 per cent) had built the house themselves, and 24 (41 per cent) had inherited it. Only 4 HHHs had purchased the house in which they lived. Hence, there was a strong correlation (Pearson's correlation = .847) between HHHs' owning their houses and their having acquired them by building the houses themselves or through inheritance. Among the 17 HHHs who did not own the houses they were living in, 10 (56 per cent) lived in houses owned by their parents. Only one HHH among the non-owners lived in the house belonging to his or her partner.

Another way for family and kin to provide access to housing was for close kin to provide financial support for building a house. Among the HHHs who had built the house they lived in (67 out of 77) – even if they did not own the house, which might be legally owned by a parent still living in the household – nearly 39 per cent had financed the construction themselves, and 24 per cent had received financial support from their fathers. This followed the well-known tradition in which, for married sons who want to separate their household from the parental one, the father is expected to build or finance the building of a separate house. Further evidence of financial support for male members of the household emerged when HHHs were asked if they had built a house for one or more sons or other members of the household. Out of 77 HHHs, 15 responded positively. When I asked HHHs who would inherit the family house, 32 (42 per cent) said they had a plan, and within this group, 13 (40 per cent) had decided for the youngest son, again following tradition in Azerbaijan (see Quliyeva 1997; Pfluger-Schindlbeck 2005). The remaining respondents had not yet decided who would inherit the house, because they had only daughters, because their children were still very young, or because their sons were migrants abroad.

Family could also be crucial for acquiring land on which to build a house in the first place. Of the 73 HHHS who owned the *məhlə* on which they had built the house in which they lived, 29 (40 per cent) said they had inherited the land from their parents.[104] Twenty-six of the 73 (36 per cent) – the second largest proportion – had received land for building a house from the *selsovet*, sovkhoz, or kolkhoz administration. Among the 35 households

---

[104] When asked directly how households had acquired their present *məhlə*, 56 per cent of the 73 HHHs said they had inherited it, 18 per cent had been given it by the *selsovet*, and 20 per cent had purchased it. The difference between this figure of 56 per cent for inheritance and the figure of 40 per cent given in the text may be explained by the different uses *məhlə*s may have, by the time lapse between acquiring a *məhlə* and building a house on it, and by the involvement of different people and generations in inheriting and acquiring land and building a house on it. In any case, *məhlə*s were more often inherited than purchased or received from the *selsovet*.

in Leninabad alone, by far the largest number, 18, had received *məhlə*s through inheritance. Nine had purchased their land, 7 had received land from the *selsovet*, kolkhoz, or sovkhoz administration, and 1 fell into none of those categories.[105]

Almost all the houses in the sample were separate dwellings; only one family lived in what is called a *zdanya* in Russian, referring to a flat in the block building that formerly belonged to the sovkhoz and was now privatised. A large number of the individual houses (77 per cent) were built of stone, unlike the older style of mud bricks (*kerpiç*) that was used until the late 1960s.

As for available living space, more than 70 per cent of the houses had 2 to 4 rooms, and 22 per cent had 5 or more rooms. Although one might expect the number of rooms in a house to be proportional to the number of people in the household, I found no such correlation. Instead, 22 per cent of the houses had 5 or more rooms, whereas 57 per cent of households had 5 or more people, meaning that the rate of increase in the number of rooms in houses did not correspond to the rate of increase in household size. This is the reverse of what one would assume for western Europe, where wealth and family size would be reflected in size of living space.[106]

A final characteristic for assessing the quality of housing was whether or not houses had been renovated. Of the 77 HHHs, 53 per cent said they had made some renovations to their houses since they had built or begun occupying them. Altogether, the houses in which respondents lived were fairly homogeneous in size and quality of construction and presented no strong contrasts in terms of wealth and status.

Sizes and Cultivation of *Məhlə*s

The mean size of household plots surveyed for my sample ($n = 75$) was 14.25 *sotka*, or about 0.14 hectare. Among the village settlements, however, mean sizes differed considerably. In the more agricultural neighbourhoods of Leninabad and Düzqışlaq together, the mean for 39 plots was 19.33 *sotka* (about 0.19 hectare). In Demiryolu altı and üstü, where HHHs represented

---

[105] There was a strong correlation between the way households had acquired their present *məhlə* (whether for building a house or not) and where they lived in the village (Pearson's correlation = .247).

[106] Although I did not ask whether or when HHHs increased the living space available to them, in general people said that during the Soviet period it was not easy to alter a house, because it could be interpreted as conspicuous consumption or as having used illegally acquired building materials. This could in part explain why houses remained more or less the same size and why well-off people managed to expand their living space only after independence.

many different occupational backgrounds, including railroad worker, trader, functionary of the kolkhoz, sovkhoz, or machinery and tractor station, white collar and semi-skilled worker, and self-employed, the mean for 36 plots was 8.75 *sotka* (about 0.09 hectare). In the entire sample, 28 households had *məhlə*s in the size range of 6 to 12 *sotka* (0.06–0.12 hectare), and 25 households had *məhlə*s in the range of 20 to 29 *sotka* (0.20–0.29 hectare) (see Appendix, table 1). *Məhlə*s of 20 to 29 *sotka* were found primarily in Leninabad and Düzqışlaq (19 of 25 cases). *Məhlə*s larger than that – 30 *sotka* (0.30 hectare) or more (2 cases) – were found only in that settlement group.

Comparing the occupations of HHHs with their access to *məhlə*s also yielded interesting results. Not only were pensioners a large group within the sample, but they were also by far the largest group among those who inherited their *məhlə*s: 18 of 43 inheritors altogether were pensioners, and 18 of 30 pensioners were inheritors. This pattern reflects the time dimension involved in accessing *məhlə*s through inheritance, and it is one of the clearest signs of the de facto existence of private ownership of household plots – important sources of income and subsistence during the Soviet period – through inheritance. Such plots are evidence of the origins of family- and household-orientated individualism in inheritance and cultivation practices.

Although *məhlə*s could increase or decrease in size over households' developmental cycles, on the whole respondents reported that *məhlə*s remained stable: 77 per cent of household plots had not changed in size. Among the 8 cases in which plots had decreased in size, 6 had done so because the property had been divided through inheritance. Only 7 households reported having increased the size of their *məhlə*, mostly by purchasing a neighbouring plot. There was no apparent correlation between size of household and size of *məhlə*, but 30 per cent of households reported having more than one *məhlə*. The settlement group of Leninabad-Düzqışlaq was significant in this category: 64 per cent of households with more than one *məhlə* were in Leninabad alone, and 14 of 39 households in this settlement group had one or more extra *məhlə*s.

Within my survey sample, 65 of the 75 households with *məhlə*s (87 per cent) had cultivated their household plots during the previous year, 2000. Furthermore, 44 of the 65 households that had had cultivated their *məhlə*s (68 per cent) had grown cash crops.

Size of *məhlə* played a crucial role in promoting cash crop cultivation. The larger the size of the *məhlə*, the more likely a household was to have produced a cash crop during the preceding year (see Appendix, table 2). In addition, households in the 6–12 and 14–19 *sotka* groups were nearly twice as likely to have produced a cash crop as to have grown only subsistence foods, and those with *məhlə*s of 20–29 *sotka* were five times as likely to have done so.

The next variable I examined that might have affected the cultivation of household plots was household size – that is, the availability of labour. Table 3 in the Appendix shows, by size of household plot and size of household, whether or not households engaged in cultivating cash crops. Because households with *məhlə*s of 6–12 and 20–29 *sotka* tended strongly to engage in cash crop production (Appendix, table 2), I looked at whether or not household size in those two groups resulted in any other differences. Appendix table 3 shows that in the *məhlə* group of 6–12 *sotka*, more than 50 per cent of cultivators (15 of 26) grew cash crops, and household size made no great difference in whether they did or not. For *məhlə*s of 20–29 *sotka*, fully 80 per cent of households (20 of 25) produced cash crops, and the larger the household, the greater the likelihood that it did so. Households of 7 or more persons with *məhlə*s of 20–29 *sotka* exhibited the strongest tendency to engage in cash crop cultivation; 11 of 12 such households did so.

I also looked at *məhlə* use in Soviet times relative to that in the post-socialist period. Among the sample households, 77 per cent (59 of 77) had cultivated household plots during the Soviet period. Of those 59, 75 per cent grew vegetables, alone or in combination with fruit trees; 60 per cent sold at least some of their produce; and nearly 40 per cent consumed all of it. More than half of producers consumed 50 per cent or less of their produce and distributed the rest of it among relatives and friends, as well as selling some. The most common practice ($n = 30$) was to sell some produce in neighbouring towns or city markets.

Since independence in 1991, the number of households engaged in production on *məhlə*s had increased, from 59 during the Soviet period to 72 in 2001. However, some variation appeared in intensity of cultivation and type of production. Forty per cent of respondents (29 of 72 households) said they had cultivated the same products since 1991 as in former times, whereas 36 per cent (26 of 72 households) said they had added new products to their cultivation (table 4.2).

Table 4.2. Changes in Production on *Məhlə*s since 1991.

Settlement Group	Number of Households Responding as Follows:					
	Continued to Grow Same Products	Grew Same and Some New Products	Culti-vated Little or Nothing	Changed Products	Other	Total
Leninabad-Düzqışlaq	10	23	2	0	3	38
Demiryolu altı and üstü	19	3	8	1	3	34
Total	29	26	10	1	6	72

Of the 26 households that had added new products to their mix, by far the greatest number – 23 households – were in the Leninabad-Düzqışlaq neighbourhood. The new produce in Leninabad since 1991 consisted of cash crops, primarily herbs, cucumbers, and tomatoes, grown in greenhouses and sold in Russian markets. Eighty-five per cent of respondents answered affirmatively to the question, 'Did the household cultivate its *məhlə* last year?'. This again confirms the importance of cultivating *məhlə*s.

I also looked at the way the previous year's *məhlə* produce had been used. Out of 64 households, 27 said they had sold some produce and con-sumed some, 21 households had sold all of it, and 16 households had con-sumed all of it. Of households who said they had sold their produce, 48 per cent had sold 90 per cent of it, and 32 per cent had sold 80 per cent of it, suggesting a strong dependence on income from produce. Of households who had sold their produce, nearly 80 per cent sold it to traders (*al-verci*) who came and bought produce directly from the household. In that year, three-quarters of *məhlə* cultivators had devoted the labour of their own household members to production.

Privatised Land Shares

Almost all households in my survey in Təzəkənd (74 of 77, or 96 per cent) had received privatised land shares (*pay torpağı*). Of households that had received shares, 43 per cent had received theirs together as one unit, and the shares were not dispersed in different locations. Households were able to enter the drawing of lots and receive their shares together with other kin who were not household members.

Table 4.3 shows the distribution of *pay* shares by size. The largest number of *pay* (35 per cent of the total) fell in the range of 40 to 79 *sotka*

(0.40–0.79 hectare). Only 5 per cent of recipients had received land shares larger than 200 *sotka* (2 hectares).

Table 4.3. Distribution of Privatised Land Shares (*Pay*) by Size.

Size of Land Share in *Sotka*	Number of households	Percentage
0–39	13	16.9
40–79	27	35.1
80–119	13	16.9
120–159	5	6.5
160–199	3	3.9
200–239	1	1.3
240+	3	3.9
No information	12	15.6
Total	77	100.0

Of households that had received *pay* shares, 39 per cent (*n* = 30) had not received their title as of the time of the survey. They knew they would be given privatised land but had not yet taken title it, for a variety of reasons. Nine out of 30 households, for instance, were interested in *pay* but were unable to use it, and 6 of the 30 were uninterested in it.

The general trends for *pay* cultivation were that 82 per cent of respondents (63 of 77) did not cultivate their own *pay* shares, and only 12 households out of 74 *pay* receivers had taken their land title and were also cultivating their share.[107] However, when I formulated the question to find out whether the *pay* share had been cultivated by anyone at all in the preceding year, 38 of 77 respondents (49 per cent) answered yes, versus 33 (43 per cent) who answered no. In other words, even if households were not personally cultivating their *pay* shares, those shares might well have been cultivated by others.

Of the 63 households that were not cultivating their own *pay* shares, 35 (56 per cent) had not given their *pay* share to anyone else, whereas 28 (44 per cent) had done so. Among the 28 households that had given their *pay* share to others, nearly a quarter had given it to a relative, and the rest, to neighbours, friends, the municipality, or a larger cultivator. Among the 28 households that had given their *pay* shares to someone else to cultivate, 37

---

[107] Another observation that underscores the difficulty of cultivating *pay* shares is that 4 of the 12 households who were cultivating their shares did so using non-kin hired labour, meaning that these were relatively well-to-do households that could afford to hire labour.

per cent said they received nothing in return, and 50 per cent said they received some payment in kind, in cash, or both.

Household Strategies and the Cultivation of *Məhlə*s and *Pay* Shares

One of my hypotheses concerning the relationship between the cultivation of household plots (*məhlə*s) and the cultivation of privatised land shares (*pay*) was that if households cultivated their *məhlə*s for cash crops, then they were less likely to cultivate their newly acquired *pay* shares. The reasoning is that if households invest their labour, time, and other resources in growing cash crops on their *məhlə*s, and if they earn enough from this land, then they are less motivated to cultivate any other piece of land and have fewer resources with which to do so. To test this hypothesis, I first consider the cultivation of *məhlə*s by my sample households during the year preceding my survey – the year 2000. Because my two sets of neighbourhoods differed in sizes of *məhlə*s and cash crop production, I look first at the Leninabad-Düzqışlaq group and then compare it with the Demiryolu altı–Demiryolu üstü group.

Leninabad and Düzqışlaq Households

As I described earlier, households in Leninabad and Düzqışlaq comprised mostly former kolkhoz and sovkhoz workers and employees. All but four heads of household among the 39 surveyed in this settlement group were involved in agriculture at the time of the survey or had been earlier.[108] All the households had *məhlə*s, and all but one household cultivated their *məhlə*s during the period of the survey, 2001–2002.[109] Of the 38 households that cultivated their *məhlə*s, all but one raised cash crops on them. The distribution of *məhlə* size among households that were cultivating their *məhlə*s in this settlement group is given in table 4.4.

---

[108] Of the four HHHs who had not been involved in agriculture, one was a teacher, one was a guard at a private firm, one was a driver, and the fourth was a small trader (*al-verci*) abroad.

[109] The HHH of the one non-cultivating household was the guard mentioned in note 18. He was the only adult man in his household. Two women in his family earned salaries as teachers. They seemed to be earning enough cash to cover the family's expenses and did not have time to cultivate the household's *məhlə*. When I visited the family in September 2005, they had begun cultivating their *məhlə* for cash crops of herbs, because three salaries were no longer enough and they needed to cover education costs for two children in the family.

Table 4.4. Households in Leninabad and Düzqışlaq Using *Məhlə*s and Producing Cash Crops, by Size of *Məhlə*.

Məhlə Size (in *Sotka*)	Number of Households Using *Məhlə*s in Preceding Year	Number of Households Producing Cash Crops
0–7	1	1
8–15	12	12
16–23	9	8
24–31	15	15
32+	1	1
Total	38	37

To what extent did these households also cultivate their *pay* land? It
might be argued that households already engaged in cultivation would be
more inclined to cultivate other types of land, because they had the knowledge, expertise, and networks. Alternatively, it might be argued that these
households had exhausted their resources of labour, time, and cash input into
cultivation, so they would *not* be interested in further cultivation.

The data for Leninabad-Düzqışlaq do not support the first argument.
Even though nearly all households in this group cultivated their *məhlə*s, and
95 per cent grew cash crops on the plots, 79 per cent of Leninabad-
Düzqışlaq households (31 of 39) *did not* cultivate their *pay* shares. Only 7 of
the 39 did so (with no information available for the last of the 39 cases).

Table 4 in the Appendix, showing cultivation of *məhlə* and *pay* land in
Leninabad-Düzqışlaq by occupation of head of household, offers an explanation for why this argument does not hold. HHHs in only two occupational
groups, pensioners and farmers, engaged in cultivating *pay* shares. Interviews revealed that all the pensioners in the sample from these two
neighbourhoods had some experience of agriculture, in either the sovkhoz or
the kolkhoz. Among the 14 pensioner-headed households in Leninabad-
Düzqışlaq, 3 were cultivating their *pay* shares, and they all had shares larger
than 100 *sotka* (1 hectare). One of them even had 1,000 *sotka* (10 hectares)
as a result of putting his large kin group together (married sons and daughters with their families, and the families of his brothers) and thereby receiving a large *pay* share as a collective kin unit. In other words, pensioners'
households had to rely more heavily on extra-household kinship relations
than on the labour of their own household. On the other hand, the families of
farmers who were cultivating their *pay* shares (4 out of 8 farmers in Leninabad-Düzqışlaq) had an average of 53 *sotka* (0.5 hectare) of *pay* land, which
means that these households had entered the *pay* distribution as single
households and relied primarily on their own household labour to cultivate

their shares. Knowledge of farming, therefore, was not the crucial factor for engaging in agriculture on *pay* land; what mattered was the size and composition of the household, along with the size of the *məhlə*.

Finally, households in Leninabad-Düzqışlaq that were cultivating their *pay* shares did not grow the same kinds of cash crops on them that they grew on their *məhləs*. Although produce from *pay* land might be for sale, it was destined primarily for local, not international, markets, unlike the herbs and tomatoes produced on irrigated *məhləs* and sold in Russia. The main crops grown on *pay* shares were wheat (only for local markets) and potatoes and onions (for local and national markets). Hence, even if the produce could be called a cash crop, the profit derived from it varied depending on the market for which it was destined.

Demiryolu Altı and Demiryolu Üstü Households

In Demiryolu altı and üstü, I surveyed 38 households, of which 28 (74 per cent) had cultivated their *məhləs* in the preceding year (table 4.5). Only one-fourth of those, however, or 7 households, had raised cash crops on their *məhləs*. Apparently, the relatively small sizes of *məhləs* in these neighbourhoods were not conducive to cash crop production. By comparison, in Leninabad-Düzqışlaq, where *məhlə* plots were generally larger, 95 per cent of households had grown cash crops on their *məhləs*.

Table 4.5. Households in Demiryolu altı and Demiryolu üstü Using *Məhləs* and Producing Cash Crops, by Size of *Məhlə*.

Məhlə Size (in *Sotka*)	Number of Households Using *Məhləs* in Preceding Year	Number of Households Producing Cash Crops
0–7	14	3
8–15	7	2
16–23	3	0
24–31	3	2
32+	0	0
No information	1	0
Total	28	7

It might be hypothesized that if the relatively small sizes of *məhləs* in Demiryolu altı and üstü discouraged people there from growing cash crops on their *məhləs*, then they might show stronger motivation to cultivate their *pay* shares. Data on the relationship between *məhlə* cultivation and *pay* cultivation in Demiryolu altı and üstü do not bear out this hypothesis (Ap-

pendix, table 5). Among the 38 households surveyed in these neighbourhoods, only 5 (13 per cent) cultivated *pay* shares, all of whom had also
cultivated their *məhlə*s during the preceding year. Those cultivating both pay
shares and *məhlə*s had relatively small *məhlə*s, but the number of these cases
was too small to allow for generalisations about causality.

Nor did the sizes of *pay* shares themselves seem to determine whether
or not the shares would be cultivated. In Demiryolu altı and üstü, 11 households had received *pay* shares larger than 100 *sotka*. Of those, only two
households were cultivating the shares themselves. Three did not cultivate
their shares at all, and six had given theirs to be cultivated by someone else.
Moreover, three households that had received pay shares smaller than 100
sotka were in fact cultivating them. Despite the small numbers involved,
there appears to be no correlation between *pay* size and *pay* cultivation in
Demiryolu altı and üstü.

Households in Demiryolu altı and üstü seem to have been somewhat
more inclined than households in Leninabad-Düzqışlaq to give their *pay*
shares to others for cultivation. In the latter group, the *pay* shares of 14
households out of 39 were being cultivated, and 9 of those shares (64 per
cent of cultivated shares and 23 per cent of all shares) were being cultivated
by people other than the owners. In Demiryolu altı and üstü, the *pay* shares
of 21 households out of 38 were under cultivation, and 16 of those shares (76
percent of cultivated shares and 42 per cent of all shares) had been given to
others for cultivation. Of course, few households in this group were cultivating cash crops on their *məhlə*s, either, so one might infer that people in
Demiryolu altı and üstü were less inclined to engage in cultivation at all. In
some cases, perhaps their need for income was met by lending their *pay*
shares to others. In Leninabad-Düzqışlaq, even when people did not cultivate
their own *pay* shares, they tended not to give them to others. Perhaps they
hoped to cultivate the plots themselves if they became able to finance the
necessary inputs.

Tables 4.6 and 4.7 show agricultural strategies for the 70 producers in
my survey of 77 households. The largest number of households raised cash
crops on their *məhlə*s but not on *pay* shares. The second largest group cultivated only subsistence crops on *məhlə*s. Households that one would expect
to have acquired the greatest wealth from agricultural production – those that
engaged in cash crop production on *məhlə*s in addition to *pay* cultivation –
made up only 12.8 per cent of agricultural producers. For households in
Leninabad-Düzqışlaq alone, 18 per cent (7 of 38 households) engaged in
both practices, three times the percentage in Demiryolu altı and üstü, where
6 per cent (2 of 32 households) did so.

Table 4.6. Strategies of Agricultural Production among Surveyed House-holds.

Strategy	Number of Households Practising Strategy	Percentage
No cash crop on *məhlə*	27	38.6
Cash crop on *məhlə* but no *pay* cultivation	34	48.6
Cash crop on *məhlə* and *pay* cultivation	9	12.9
Total	70	100.0

Note: No information was available for 7 of the 77 households in the survey.

Table 4.7. Strategies of Agricultural Production by Settlement Group.

Strategy	Leninabad-Düzqışlaq	Demiryolu altı and üstü	Total
No cash crop on *məhlə*	2	25	27
Cash crop on *məhlə* but no *pay* cultivation	29	5	34
Cash crop on *məhlə* and *pay* cultivation	7	2	9
Total	38	32	70

Household Income and Economic Well-being

In order to assess the economic well-being of the households I surveyed and augment my data on household agricultural activities, I asked questions about household property other than houses, *məhlə* plots, and *pay* shares, about household members' regular incomes, and about occasional income in the form of remittances from migrants abroad.[110] I asked for people's self-assessments of their household's present economic situation and for their projections for the future, and I asked how the head of household compared the contemporary economic situation with that of the Soviet period.

---

[110] I am aware of the problems of assessing income in surveys. Both Dudwick and colleagues (2003) and Perrotta (2002a: 170–171) have described the difficulties of collecting household income data in rural Ukraine, because of problems such as the uncertainty and irregularity of incomes, people's reluctance to reveal sources of income, and their tendency to exaggerate expenses relative to income.

Eighty-seven per cent of the sample households had no property other than the types listed earlier. Among the 77 households, 26 (34 per cent) said they owned vehicles: 23 owned a car, 2 owned tractors, and 1 had a truck.

Assessing income from agricultural produce for all sample households was difficult, because respondents could not effectively be asked to provide reliable information about what they earned from produce. Sixty-six households (86 per cent) received regular cash income. In 22 of those cases (39 per cent of income-receiving households), it was the HHH who had the regular income, and in 32 cases (49 per cent), more than one household member received regular income. Among household members other than the HHH who earned income were the HHH's partner (in 34 per cent of 66 cases) and the HHH's father or mother who lived in the same household (23 per cent). In all cases of regular income, a pension was the most common kind. Fifty-six per cent of HHHs were pension receivers, as were 17 per cent of the partners of HHHs and 83 per cent of the fathers and mothers of HHHs. Household members most often (27 per cent of HHHs and 23 per cent of HHHs' partners) had regular incomes of 5 şirvan (about US$11) monthly.[111] Household heads who received wages from a workplace amounted to only 10 per cent of those who received regular cash income (7 of 66).

The largest proportion of households receiving added cash income (n = 27) received 5–14 şirvan per month, equivalent to about US$11–31. Only 13 households (18 per cent of income-receiving households) earned more than 30 şirvan (about US$67) per month. Within this group, only four households earned more than 100 şirvan (US$222) per month, which could be classified as a good income in rural Azerbaijan in early 2001.

Of the 32 households with more than one income, 59 per cent comprised three generations. Calculating per capita amounts of cash income for the entire sample of 77 households produces the results shown in figure 4.2.[112] The largest number of households (n = 22, 30 per cent) fell into the per capita income range of 0–15,000 manat, the higher figure being equal to only US$3. Households with per capita income of up to 45,000 manat (US$10) per month amounted to 67 per cent of the total sample. Even though these figures show only regular cash income such as pensions and salaries, they reveal a strikingly low rate of per capita income.

---

[111] Five şirvan equalled 50,000 manat in the Azerbaijani currency of the time. In 2000, US$1 equalled 4,500 manat.
[112] Per capita income in Azerbaijan in 2001 was 2.2 million manat, or about US$492, for a per capita monthly income of about US$41 (*Azərbaycanın Statistik Göstəriciləri* 2001: 37).

Number of
Households

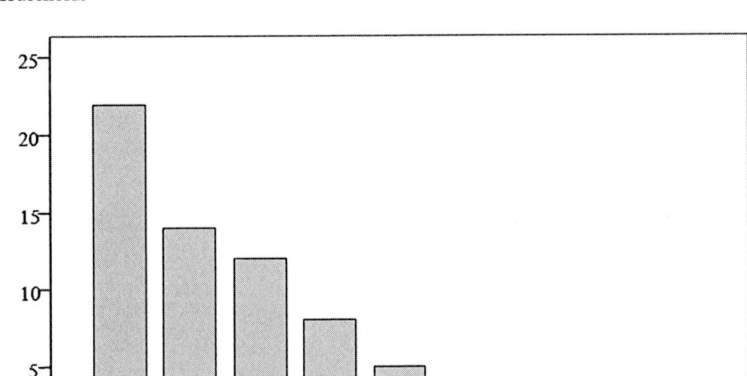

Figure 4.2. Per capita income per month (in manat) for the author's survey sample in
Təzəkənd.

Finally, some households had access to cash through migrants abroad.
Forty-two per cent of survey respondents (*n* = 32) said they had a family
member abroad. Table 4.8 shows that those migrants were predominantly
sons, with 19 out of 32 cases. Almost all the migrants in the sample were in
Russia (31 of 32).

Table 4.8. Identities of Migrants Abroad in Surveyed Households in
Təzəkənd.

Migrant or Migrants	Number of Households	Percentage, among House-holds with Migrants
Son 1	12	37.5
Several sons	7	21.9
Head of household (HHH)	4	12.5
HHH's partner	1	3.1
Another household member	4	12.5
Another relative, not a household member	4	12.5
Total	32	100.0

Fourteen respondents said that the migrant was still considered to be a member of the household. Considering the preponderance of sons among the migrants, it seems surprising that in only 12 of 32 households did the migrant member send money home regularly, and in 9 of 32 cases, the migrant sent home no money at all. This could be seen as potential grounds for strained intra-household and intra-kin relationships. Among the 20 cases in which I received a response to my question about how much money had been sent from abroad in the preceding year, 5 had received nothing, but 4 had received US$1,000.[113]

When it came to self-estimation of one's economic situation, 30 of 77 respondents (39 per cent) considered theirs bad or very bad, and only 10 respondents considered their present economic situation to be good (table 4.9).

Table 4.9. Households' Assessments of Their Economic Situation.

Assessment	Number of Households	Percentage
Very bad	6	7.8
Bad	24	31.2
Medium	23	29.9
Sufficient	14	18.2
Good	10	13.0
Total	77	100.0

When respondents were asked to compare their present economic situation with that during the Soviet period, only 10 found their situation to be better now, whereas 57 (74 per cent) thought for various reasons that they were economically better off in Soviet times. When asked how they saw their future, 20 respondents out of 65 answered with optimistic expectations. These expectations, however, were related more to the economic improvement of the whole country (for example, selling more oil and ending the war against Armenia) than to the direct economic improvement of their rural community.

People's self-assessments of their economic situation showed some relationship to strategies of agricultural production. All households that both cultivated cash crops on their *məhləs* and cultivated *pay* shares assessed their situation as medium or better, whereas among households that considered

---

[113] As with regular income, in order to assess economic support through remittances, one needs to look at the sizes of households receiving remittances from abroad.

their economic situation to be bad or very bad, none was cultivating *pay* land (table 4.10).

Table 4.10. Households' Assessments of Their Economic Situation in Relation to Strategies of Agricultural Production.

	Agricultural Production Strategy			
Assessment	No Cash Crop on *Məhlə*	Cash Crop on *Məhlə* but No *Pay* Cultivation	Cash Crop on *Məhlə* and *Pay* Cultivation	Total
Very bad	4	1	0	5
Bad	11	11	0	22
Medium	8	11	1	20
Sufficient	1	9	4	14
Good	3	2	4	9
Total	27	34	9	70

Self-assessment of economic situation proved to have no significant relationship with age of head of household, at least when HHHs were divided into two groups. Among HHHs aged 21 to 40, 41 per cent assessed their situation as bad or very bad, and 18 per cent assessed their situation as good. Among HHHs aged 41 or older, 38 per cent assessed their situation as bad or very bad, and 16 per cent assessed their situation as good – percentages very similar to those of the younger group.

Another variable that had no significant effect on assessment of economic situation was occupation of household head. Predictably, the unemployed largely assessed their situation as bad or very bad (6 of 9), but almost all HHHs in the state sector (4 of 5) and one-third of the pensioners (10 of 30) made the same assessment. The fewest assessments of bad or very bad were found among HHHs in the agricultural sector (3 of 14). Those who estimated their situation as good were found in all occupational groups except those in the state sector.

Household size, on the other hand, was found to be a significant factor bearing on self-assessment. Among small households (1–3 people), 62 per cent assessed their situation as bad or very bad, whereas only 30 per cent of households with 4 or more people felt that way. Conversely, 8 out of 10 households that assessed their economic situation as good fell in the size category of 4–6 persons.

Regular household added income seemed to be strongly related to self-assessment of economic situation. Nearly half of households with added income of 0–14 şirvan (up to US$31) per month assessed their situation as bad or very bad. Among households with incomes of 15 şirvan (US$33) or more per month, only one-third assessed their economic situation that way, and above about US$65 per month, very few households made a negative assessment.

The strongest relationship was found between gender of HHH and assessment of economic situation. More than half of households headed by women (13 of 25) assessed their economic situation as bad or very bad, whereas only one-third of male-headed households made the same assessment.

Summary

The results of my household survey in the village of Təzəkənd can be summarized as follows:

- Households in Təzəkənd were relatively large, with a mean of 5.3 persons per household. Forty-three per cent of them included three or more generations. Correspondingly, the ages of household heads (HHHs) were also high: more than half of HHHs were 51 or older.
- The sample showed pensioners to be the predominant occupational group among HHHs (39 per cent). But many of them were pensioners from the former sovkhoz or kolkhoz, and when they are added to HHHs who were still actively engaged in agriculture, agriculture becomes the major occupation in the sample.
- Household-related variables showed some correspondence to different areas of settlement in the village. Larger proportions of pensioners were found among the former kolkhoz and sovkhoz workers in Leninabad and Düzqışlaq than in other areas of settlement. Leninabad and Düzqışlaq also had more large households than the other settlement group, Demiryolu üstü and Demiryolu altı.
- A significant majority of households had other kin in the village. More than half of HHHs had such relations, and so did more than half of their partners. This suggests that a dense network of kin is available for social and economic relationships.
- Intergenerational relationships proved to be crucial for access to housing. Seventy-seven per cent of HHHs owned the houses they were living in, and 41 per cent of those owners had inherited their house. Moreover, more than half of HHHs who did not own the house were living in their parents' house. Kinship rela-

tions were also important in gaining support for building and renovating houses.

- Although access to housing came primarily through kinship, access to land on which to build a house and cultivate a household plot was provided by the local administrative and agricultural institutional structures, such as the former sovkhoz, kolkhoz, and *selsovet* and, more recently, the communal administration (*bələdiyyə*).

- Almost all households had household plots (*məhləs*). These were an important source of income and subsistence; 86 per cent of households had cultivated their *məhləs* in the year preceding the survey. However, *məhlə* sizes were not evenly distributed in the village. More than half of households in Leninabad and Düzqış-laq had *məhləs* larger than 20 *sotka* (0.2 hectare), whereas only 17 per cent of households in Demiryolu üstü and altı had *məhləs* of that size.

- *Məhləs* usage showed some continuity with that of the Soviet period, when 77 per cent of the sample households cultivated such plots and more than half sold produce from them. Nevertheless, the kinds of produce being grown on *məhləs* had changed somewhat since independence. Forty per cent of households were cultivating the same produce as before, but 36 per cent had added new products to their agricultural mix – mostly vegetables and fruits to be sold in national and international markets. Almost everyone who sold their produce sold it to petty traders (*al-verci*) who collected the produce directly from the plot.

- Almost all households (96 per cent) had received privatised land shares (*pay*). The largest proportion of the sample households (35 per cent) had received *pay* shares measuring 40–79 *sotka* (0.40–0.70 hectare). Although 82 per cent of households said they did not cultivate the *pay* land they had received, nearly half of those respondents said that their *pay* share was being culti-vated, meaning that someone else was doing so. Out of the total sample of 77 households, only 12 were cultivating their own *pay* shares.

- In a comparison of agricultural strategies, nearly all households in Leninabad and Düzqışlaq cultivated their *məhləs* and pro-duced cash crops on them, whereas 76 per cent of households in Demiryolu üstü and altı cultivated their *məhləs*, and only one-third of them raised cash crops on their plots. Twenty per cent of

Leninabad-Düzqışlaq households cultivated their *pay* shares, but only 13 per cent of households in Demiryolu üstü and altı did so.

- In Demiryolu üstü and altı, households were four times more likely to give their *pay* shares to someone else to cultivate than households in Leninabad-Düzqışlaq.

- Only 13 per cent of all households were cultivating both *məhlə*s and *pay* shares. Thirty-nine per cent were cultivating neither cash crops nor *pay*, which suggests that these households were particularly vulnerable economically.

- Nearly 40 per cent of heads of household assessed their economic situation as bad or very bad. Almost half of those who had no agricultural production (neither cash crops nor *pay* cultivation) assessed their situation that way. Among the few households that both produced cash crops and cultivated *pay* shares, none assessed their economic situation as bad or very bad.

- Small households (those of 1–3 people) and households led by female HHHs seemed to have the greatest vulnerability in terms of being unsatisfied and concerned about their economic situation.

Chapter 5
Collective Strategies for Managing Household and Property

The quantitative data presented in the previous chapter demonstrate the possibilities and limitations households experience for cultivating various kinds of land and for securing economic viability. In this chapter I look at households' strategies from a qualitative and ethnographic perspective, examining a number of households as case studies to show what kinds of strategies were available to them. I then discuss whether and why they follow the statistical average, and I present complex cases that require further analysis. My purpose is to explore the way households manage their property relations and what kinds of economic, moral, and social notions they display in their strategies (Bourdieu 1977). I construct households as social actors and explore how factors such as kinship, morality, and ideology may account for their social and economic actions.

I place this inquiry in the theoretical field between 'new institutionalism' and Bourdieu's type of analysis of symbolic and social context (Ensminger 1998: 786). As Jean Ensminger (1998) has rightly pointed out, causal explanations continue to be weak in social and cultural anthropology since the cultural and post-modern turns, and new institutionalism offers many insights that help anthropologists investigate social and economic phenomena by focusing on the question 'why?' and bringing out causality.[114] Yet as she also highlighted, seeking the causal role of institutions has not been the invention of new institutional economics alone; it was part of many social anthropological investigations in the 1960s and 1970s, especially those that looked at political institutions (Bailey 1969), entrepreneurship (Barth 1963), and the like.

---

[114] For other well-known 'new institutional' and economic anthropological studies, see North (1991), Acheson (1994, 1996), and Ensminger and Knight (1997). For a more recent example, see Finke (2004), and for a general overview of new institutional economics, see Ménard and Shirley (2005).

I view my approach as a continuation of these studies because I am concerned with the goal-driven behaviour (Ensminger 1998: 780) of individuals as members of households, kin groups, and larger social units. This need not be understood narrowly as economic maximising behaviour or simply as a question of rationality (see also Barth 1992: 21–22). I am equally interested in risk-reducing behaviour and relations of reciprocity and sharing, which have long been central themes in economic anthropology (Ortiz 1967; Sahlins 1972; Gudeman 1978; Cashdan 1990; Gambold-Miller and Heady 2003). Even if actors behave in a goal-driven way, Bourdieu's notions of rules and strategy are important for understanding why and how their behaviour may follow rules but produce unintended results and how rules are turned into strategies once the effect of time is taken into consideration (Bourdieu 1977: 9).

Bourdieu's approach also offers more analytical insight for explaining how individual goal-driven behaviour comes into being in a social context and how, in turn, this behaviour affects the social context rather than following the simple credo of methodological individualism, which holds that 'goal-driven behaviour still lies at the level of the individual' (Joyce and Winter 1996: 71, quoted in Ensminger 1998: 780). Hence, in the following I look at households' narratives of economic behaviour, including property management as well as individual and collective action, and seek answers to some of the questions raised by the village-level statistical data: Why do certain households engage in agriculture? How do they manage this? Where do they run into difficulties, and what limitations and obstacles do they face? Which households lack the means and do not employ the strategies of economic survival or accumulation, and why not?

Strategies of Kin Groups

Azerbaijan's postsocialist agrarian reform legislation designated the village household the property-holding and property-managing unit – that is, the group of people who were to hold property together at one location as a physical unit. But there were also kin groups who took action to obtain, hold, and manage property as a collective group of households. When using quantitative data, one issue that is difficult to cover efficiently is why and how such kin groups and collectives of households cooperate in managing property and what consequences their collective strategies have. In the rest of this section, I summarise the case of a household that operated as part of a kin group and managed large parts of its property collectively.

The kin group of Əli Şahverdi consisted of Əli's household and those of his four sons (fig. 5.1). At least two households in this kin group were co-resident, even though the father's and one son's households were entered as separate households in the village registry and the son had already received a plot on which to build a house. At the time of the survey, they had not yet separated their households from each another.

Kin group and household of Əli Şahverdi

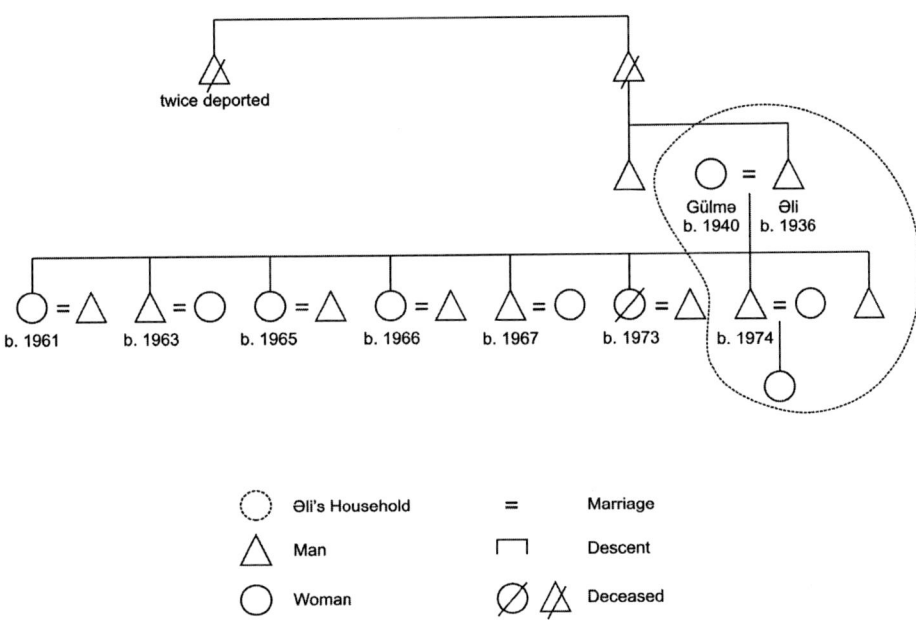

Figure 5.1. The kin group and household of Əli Şahverdi.

The family of Əli Şahverdi (b. 1936) came from Vedi, Armenia, near the Turkish border. Əli's father was killed in 1941, during World War II, and his father's brother (FB) was deported (officially re-settled) to Kazakhstan in 1937, returning to Vedi in 1947. The following year, when Əli was 12, his FB was deported a second time, and Əli and his brother, now orphans, went with him. The family went first to Salyan, in central Azerbaijan, where the climate is very dry and hot. Then, like many other Azerbaijanis deported from Armenia, they moved to Leninabad, a settlement now part of Təzəkənd. Many such families who were deported from Armenia during this period seem to have stayed together in their places of settlement.

As early as 1955 Əli bought from the sovkhoz the *məhlə* on which he still lived in 2001. That same year he built a mud brick (*kerpiç*) house, where he lived with his brother, separate from the household of his FB. It was not until 1975 that the family began building the larger stone house in which they lived in 2001. Such houses were signs of relative wealth in the 1970s and 1980s. Əli said that the size of the household's *məhlə* then was 40 *sotka* (0.40 hectare) and that in 1970 he and his brother divided it equally. In other words, from 1955 to 1970, Əli and his brother shared a single household.

Əli then bought *məhlə*s for three of his sons, each comprising 8 *sotka* (0.08 hectare). Two of the sons built houses on their *məhlə*s, with Əli's financial support. The first son separated his household in 1988 and built his house in 1989; the second separated his household in 2000. The third son, who was married, had children, and still lived with his father in 2001, hoped to build a house when he and Əli were able to meet the expenses. The fourth, who had not yet married at the time of our interview, was expected to stay with his parents and inherit their *məhlə* and house.

Əli and his wife, Gülmə, also had four daughters, all of whom had married within the Leninabad neighbourhood. Three of them were married to sons of families who also came from Armenia. Gülmə, too, had been born in Armenia and had come to a settlement near Təzəkənd as a child with her family in 1948.

Both Əli and his wife were employed until 1992–1993. Əli worked as a driver of a *zil*, a Russian-made truck used in construction work, in a *rayon* tractor station. Gülmə was employed in the local sovkhoz vineyard as an agricultural labourer (*fəhlə*). Both received pensions; in 2001 he received 9 şirvan (US$20) monthly, and she, 14 şirvan (about US$31), with extras because of the number of children she had. Əli and Gülmə said that despite their large household and many children, they had been able to feed their family well during the Soviet period ('*Ikisi işləyib herkəsi saxlayırdı*'). They were able to buy garden plots, build houses, and trade their own produce in neighbouring markets. They started producing vegetables in greenhouses as early as the late 1980s. Their sons were involved in trading the produce of their own and other local households – tomatoes, cucumbers, and herbs – in Russia during the 1990s, but they quit because of the high risks and insecurity involved: 'People were getting killed because of money, so they returned [*Pul üstünə adam öldürüblər; qayıtdılar*]'.

The parents and the separate families of their sons entered the lottery for privatised land jointly and were cultivating their shares together, the father pooling the income and dividing it among the sons and their households ('The father divides the money from the produce [*mehsulun pulunu ata paylayır*]'.). The sons also traded and worked for wages, bringing in income to the father's household, where he had the ultimate authority to decide what the major expenditures would be.[115]

---

[115] I do not have precise figures for consumption in Əli's household. He mentioned that his eldest son had to sell his car when he was separating his own household and had to finish his

The Şahverdi family's history and father Əli's biography illustrate, first, how the Soviet state and the global politics of World War II impinged on people's fates and livelihoods with vigour and violence. Əli's father's brother was only one of many Kurds and other Muslims from Vedi who were deported from Armenia, and it was the same Soviet state that finally settled them in Leninabad, where many such deported families were given land by the sovkhoz to start new lives. These families are still referred to as 'Yeraz' – Azeris who arrived from Yerevan, although they generally came from other parts of Armenia – and can be seen as a special regional or ethnic group, since they are thought to have certain characteristics and to maintain dense social contact with one another (see Sidikov 2007). Əli and his brother's households and family members are also referred to as Kurds, although they themselves do not use this identification.[116]

Although the Soviet state exerted arbitrary power over Əli's parental family, after settling in Leninabad the family seems increasingly to have experienced the state as provider. First they were given land to settle on; then Əli, at 19, was able to acquire a *məhlə* for himself and his brother and start their own household. He and Gülmə, on reflection, felt that they had been able to raise their family on their own, without extensive support from other kin. But although they had built a stone house and purchased *məhlə*s for their three of their four sons, the parents had so far managed to support the construction of only two houses for their sons. Their resources had been insufficient for the third. Changes in the economy and possibly in power structures in the locality had also affected their household. People were no longer able to receive relatively large *məhlə*s in the late 1980s, so the sons' plots were smaller than the parents', and after 2000 *məhlə*s could not be acquired without paying a substantial amount of money or a bribe to the local authorities.

Moreover, the scale of the market economies in the region had changed. Formerly, Əli and his wife could supplement the family budget by selling surplus produce from their household plot in local markets or sometimes as far away as Tbilisi. After independence, they were first lured by the emergence of lucrative new informal markets, especially across the borders in Russia and Kazakhstan. Like many other people in the area, Əli and his sons became engaged in the informal trade of vegetables and fruits in Russia. They wanted to cash in on the profitable but risky business of taking produce by truck to Russia and selling it in big cities such as Moscow or St. Peters-

---

house. When Əli's youngest son went to do his military service, the family had to sell all their sheep. All this suggests that for any major expense, they needed to sell property.

[116] For more on the secondary and implicit nature of Kurdish ethnic identification in contemporary Azerbaijan, see Müller and Yalçın-Heckmann (2004).

burg. But such trade arrangements were complicated, requiring stable credit facilities and skilful management of payments to producers, traders, dealers, border police, customs officials, and mafia groups. Əli claimed to have given up the trade when it became too risky for him and his sons. Əli's household was not alone in having tried this trade. Numerous others were successful and made good money, now lavishly displayed in the form of large villas and expensive cars. Other families suffered the loss of their sons in fights between mafia groups. They either got killed or, because they embezzled money from local producers or other local traders, had to disappear in some faraway Siberian settlement and could not return to live in the village again.

With his authoritarian, patriarchal style of managing his kin group's economic activities, Əli managed to get his sons out of the risky, informal international trade and turn them to cultivating privatised land shares as a group. Thus, risk reduction seems to have been a primary motive for his kin group and household management strategy. The whole family cultivated wheat on their joint land share, profiting from economies of scale by pooling their labour, land, and other resources. Əli's practice of pooling and re-distributing the family's profits seems to have been feasible because of the group's authoritarian parental structure and inter-generational interdependency. Very likely, the sons would have tried to start separate businesses on their own if they had possessed enough economic capital. Lacking this, they continued to be dependent on their parents for shares of the family's economic returns.

Finally, the kin group's ethnic and social background seems to have strengthened – or perhaps impelled – its group solidarity. Yeraz are usually met with scepticism and prejudice in Təzəkənd for being an introverted and self-supporting ethnic group. Non-Yeraz people suspect that Yeraz favour their own people over anyone else and thus make unreliable economic partners for anyone who is not also Yeraz. Bahodir Sidikov (2007: 315–319) highlighted these self and other identity ascriptions and attributed the identity markers to the Yeraz's collective experience as a minority in Armenia. Furthermore, being labelled Kurds, Əli's kin group was considered even more 'other' than the Yeraz.[117] During my stay in Təzəkənd, Əli's brother's household was involved in some scandalous adultery, an incestuous liaison that led to a suicide attempt. Əli had to be careful not to be drawn into the gossip concerning his brother's household and to maintain the image of being able to control his sons and their families.

---

[117] Sidikov (2007: 318) noted that Kurds had been a sub-stratum among the Yeraz, but this further specification of identity was not widely known and acknowledged in Təzəkənd. Hence, I suggest, it made families such as Əli's even more 'different' than others in the eyes of their co-villagers.

All in all, the many limitations of exclusion and structural differences, as well as the force of rules of shame and moral reputation, seem to have affected Əli's family's management of economic resources, including land, as a kin group. Nevertheless, even if Əli's large kin group held its land jointly, the returns from it were insufficient for them to be classified as wealthy landowners and agriculturalists in the village.

Female Household Heads as Petty Traders, Producers, and Money Lenders

One-third of the households I surveyed in Təzəkənd (25 out of 77) had female household heads, and half of those households (13) assessed their economic situation as bad or very bad. Only one-third of male-headed households made the same self-assessment.[118] In this section I explore some cases of female-headed households, looking at whether and why they had limited chances of economic sufficiency or of accumulating wealth.

Most of the female household heads in the survey sample had chosen to engage in full-time or part-time petty trade (al-ver). Such trade, especially in clothes, small household goods, and other consumer articles, was a prominent economic activity for sustaining these households (see also Bellér-Hann 1998; Heyat 2002; Yurkova 2004; Kaiser 2007). Accounts of some of these women and their households display the ways in which they managed their livelihood strategies and where they were successful, met limitations and restrictions, or seemed to be extremely vulnerable. The discussion also illustrates whether, how, and why land is a viable economic resource for these female-headed households, since the women and their households, like all others in the village, had received privatised land shares.

Case 1: The Household of Meliha

Meliha was a neighbour of my host family in Təzəkənd and the mother of Məhman, a good friend of the family's sons. She was a widow, and her family was poor, living in a single-room house in the central part of the village. Meliha had worked as a milk woman in the sovkhoz before becom-

---

[118] For cases of households headed by women being vulnerable and at risk of poverty in Tajikistan, see Gomart (2003: 61). She claimed that other than households headed by women, 'young parents with small children; families with many young children and no grown-up sons; ... [and] families whose male members were incapable of demanding physical work' were all at risk. Furthermore, as in the case of Təzəkənd, having a large number of adult men in the household seemed to ensure 'access to the market, access to activities with higher income potential ... and seasonal mobility to other former Soviet Republics'. On rural women's vulnerability in Uzbekistan, see Kandiyoti (2002).

ing unemployed. At the time of my fieldwork, she supported her household of two adult sons, a daughter, and herself with petty trade in clothing and other manufactured textiles, travelling with other women to the Baku airport and buying goods there cheaply.[119] She sold her goods through contacts in the village and in neighbouring settlements.[120] Her whole trade network functioned with no open sales facility, and she did not declare her work in public, much the way informal trade in textiles, small household goods, and luxury items was carried out during the Soviet period.[121]

Meliha had a shy and modest personality and was careful not to carry out her activities in public, unlike many other female traders on the market.[122] Her timidity about publicising her trading was related to her feeling of loss of social and economic status, her moral and social vulnerability as the widowed mother of unmarried adult sons and a daughter, and her dependency on kin and support from friends and neighbours. She had experienced several catastrophes: her house had once burned down, and later her in-laws claimed half the property – a house and half a məhlə – that she had inherited from her husband. Her conflict with her in-laws was acute during my stay, and she literally had to defend the walls of her house, which were being claimed by the brother-in-law living next door.[123] In the face of this conflict, she had somehow to survive through trade, meanwhile keeping her older son, Məhman's, temper under control; he had a tendency to get into fights

---

[119] This was a strenuous journey. A group composed almost exclusively of women, mostly from Təzəkənd and some from surrounding villages, took a bus to the Baku airport market together. The bus could not be driven fast, because it was one of the oldest vehicles in the village, and the roads were bad. The drive took eight to nine hours, and the traders left in the evening and slept on the bus. At the airport market they shopped and bargained for wholesale goods for some five to six hours and then, without sleeping, took the bus home again. Altogether they spent more than 24 hours on the road and in trading.

[120] For similar trade practices by women as 'flying traders' in informal economies, see Prodolliet (1995). On Uzbek female petty traders, see Yurkova (2004).

[121] I was told that because free trade was not allowed during the Soviet period but consumer goods of higher quality were available in some big cities like Moscow, women travelled there, bought such goods by going through the queue several times, then brought them back in suitcases and sold them by spreading the news among trusted friends. 'Middle-class' rural residents desired such goods and were eager to find out what items had arrived in the village when someone with the secret reputation of engaging in spekulasiya returned from Moscow. Considerable danger was involved, especially if the buyers and sellers had Communist Party functions, so the transactions were kept secret and took place within confidential networks. See also Heyat (2002: 23).

[122] On women who felt shame over getting involved in petty trade in Azerbaijan, see Heyat (2002). For similar moralities and markets in Bulgaria, see Kaneff (2002).

[123] The reason for this conflict was unclear to me. From my talks with Meliha, I got the impression that her deceased husband had had bad relations with his brother, and the conflict over property division might have dated back to his lifetime.

with neighbours and kin, in addition to being often drunk and jobless. Her younger son had recently gone to Russia to earn money in petty trade. He had sent no money home to date but seemed on the whole to be able to manage his economic situation on his own.

Meliha's survival strategy could be described as muddling through on the border of real poverty. She depended heavily on her genealogical kin and her neighbours (who, for instance, helped her rebuild and partly renovate her burnt-down, single-room dwelling), and she constantly sought resources to stabilise her household's income. For example, she sent (or rather allowed) Məhman to go to Russia in 2003 in spite of his alcohol problem and his having no knowledge of Russian. She saw no alternative way to guarantee her household's survival, lacking as she did sustainable support from kin and friends. She gave her small amount of *pay* land, about 0.46 hectare, to her brother to cultivate. In return, she received some flour to make her family's bread. She had neither the labour nor other input resources to cultivate the land herself; the small plot primarily allowed her to cultivate her kinship relationships with her paternal family and siblings. She considered her economic situation to be vulnerable and relied on support from her agnatic kin and from neighbours to prevent her household from losing any further social and economic status.

That was the situation in 2002–2003. During my visit to the village in September 2007, I found that Meliha's household had appreciably improved its economic situation. She had finished renovating the one room in which I had previously visited her and had enlarged the house to cover the whole space available on her tiny *məhlə*. She proudly told me that her two sons, who had by then been in Russia for four to five years, were building their own rooms on the house so that they could come back, get married, and bring in daughters-in-law (*gəlin*). Her daughter was still unmarried, but Meliha felt that her family was more economically stable and was hopeful that she would find a suitable husband for her daughter. More important, she told me that she no longer did petty trading, because she no longer needed the money. The sons' migration strategies seem to have saved the household's livelihood and given it economic security.

Case 2: Mila's Story

Mila, too, was a female head of household on the verge of poverty. I recall her as a tough fighter, especially over land holdings and her right to privatised land shares (*pay*) vis-à-vis other farmers who were trying to encroach on them. Moreover, she was one of the few women I knew in the village who had the entrepreneurial strategy to start a business – as a tailor – a plan that unfortunately went unrealised. What made her and her household special, so that she carried out this struggle?

Mila was born and had lived all her life in Təzəkənd. She was referred to as *Rus* (Russian) Mila, because her mother, despite having been born in the village, was of Russian origin. Mila's father was a local Azeri who had been a sovkhoz director and later a bookkeeper in the sovkhoz. At the time of my fieldwork, Mila was in her early fifties, had worked in the sovkhoz in her youth, and, after divorcing her drunken husband in 1970, had begun earning a living by sewing. She had borne three daughters, although the third had died as a young woman in 2000. Mila lived next to her other two daughters in one of the sovkhoz flats, which were poorly maintained and could have been considered among the worst lodgings in the village.

Mila's reputation and status in the village were controversial. As a divorced woman with a divorced daughter as well, and grandchildren living alone with their mother, she and her daughters were often subjects of gossip and were both implicitly and explicitly accused of prostitution. Mila had a sharp tongue and was known for her loud, furious, public confrontations with her detractors, during which she strategically and meticulously resorted to her memory of things past and present. She was one of the few women who dared to publicly challenge the newly elected mayor of the municipality for corruption, which she claimed took place during the mayor's former position as head of the sovkhoz liquidation committee. She also led a dispute against a relatively wealthy farmer to whom she had sold the land share her household received after privatisation. The farmer, Tahir, had not paid the money, and Mila was trying to use all her connections with the local authorities, as well as other strategies, to pressure him to pay his debt.

I often saw Mila on the bus during her almost daily trips to the district centre to try to gain an audience with the governor or one of the less influential authorities dealing with privatisation and land issues. She frequently used this travelling time to regale her fellow passengers with accounts of her disagreements with Tahir or to accuse the mayor of trying to prevent her from defending her rights and getting her payment. Such public slander and aggressive gossip can be damaging to the person employing this strategy as well as to its objects.[124] According to some villagers, Mila was shameless for making such accusations in public and visiting the authorities every day without showing the proper, restrained behaviour that an 'honourable' woman was expected to display. On the other hand, people generally agreed that her sharp tongue was effective and that she was successfully defending her rights by virtue of her sometimes shameless perseverance.

---

[124] See Gilsenan (1976) on the power and uses of gossip for honour and social standing.

What made Mila's case different from Meliha's was that Mila was able use her social status from the socialist past – referring, for instance, to her father's high standing during the Soviet period and strategically employing her knowledge and invocations of former leading socialist personalities – in order to benefit from the present system of favours and distribution of rights. I have described her use of public knowledge and memory elsewhere (Yalçın-Heckmann 2005). The point here is that although she was unable to cultivate her household's *pay* share on her own, it was in a fertile area, and she was determined to get her money for it by selling it at a good price to Tahir, who was already using it illegally. Social behaviour like Meliha's, in which women behave modestly and in a restrained manner in public, even if they engage in petty trade, did not suit Mila. She had little to lose, since her own and her daughters' reputations were already bad, so she employed an aggressive style that allowed her to publicly challenge men who were elaborately setting up their own networks to exploit remaining and new resources.[125] The lack of a supportive kin group made her vulnerable, for no kin were there to stand up for her. At the same time, she could turn that deficit into an asset because it left her enough social space to fight others on her own.

Case 3: The Story of Zarifə

Zarifə is someone whose biography I know in less depth, even though I visited in her home for my household survey. Otherwise, I regularly saw her trading at the weekly market, where she had a stand for the consumer household articles that she bought and sold as a petty trader. She was in her late sixties and had a reputation as a thrifty and hard-bargaining trader, having worked as an illegal trader in Soviet times. She was one of the few people in my survey who evaluated the postsocialist period positively, from the perspective of her trading experience: 'Earlier we had to do the trade secretly. They were constantly chasing us as if we were criminals. Now there is freedom [*indi sərbestlik var*]', she said. She had no typical family or kin group around her but lived with her aged sister, who helped with her trading activities. The sisters lived in one household, and judging from what I observed during my visit, they lived in poverty. Many people, however, believed that although they 'lived like beggars', they must have accumulated considerable wealth – often imagined as cash hidden at home, but most likely judged on the basis of the trade goods the sisters hoarded at home.

---

[125] As explained in chapter 3, some local men who formerly or still had administrative positions were privileged in finding out about unused land and sharecropping it. Often these plots belonged to single women or to female-headed households.

Zarifə had never married; her sister had married and then divorced. From that marriage the sister had a son, who died in an accident and left his own young son, who was being cared for by Zarifə and her sister. The three formed the household, although the grandson also stayed fairly regularly at his mother's household, in another part of the village. The sisters managed trade and household affairs together. They had not claimed their privatised land share and showed no interest in giving it to others for cultivation. One might wonder why they had made no effort to rent it out or obtain some payment from the person who was probably cultivating it illegally. Most likely, their age and the vulnerability of their household's survival deterred them from making any public effort to claim their land rights and some benefits from cultivation – unlike Mila, whose personality and energy made it possible for her to fight for her rights to resources. Zarifə and her sister seemed to be content with their trading business, and although their means were only enough to get by on, they were satisfied with their economic position.

Case 4: Leman's Case

Leman was my neighbour and friend, and she assisted me during some of my survey interviews. She lived close to my host family and was an intimate friend of my hostess, Könül. At the time of my fieldwork Leman was in her early forties, a widow since her husband died from illness caused by excessive drinking, leaving her alone with their three young children. When I was in Təzəkənd, she lived with her then young-adult sons and teenage daughter in a relatively large house that she had inherited from her husband, who had earned his living by running a small restaurant. Leman had married him immediately after finishing the compulsory eight years of school; she was proud to have fallen in love young and to have eloped with her good-looking husband, for the sake of whom she denied her parents the chance to decide whom she should marry. Apparently, her parents had wanted her to marry a man who was wealthier, but she decided her own fate at the age of 16. She remembered having a good, happy, but too brief life with her husband, despite the fact that he often beat her and the children when he was drunk, which she admits to herself and which her neighbours remember.

Leman never worked outside the home, having had her children soon after marriage. When her husband died, she had no income other than the orphans' payments the children were entitled to. Her mother-in-law was living with her own daughter in the nearby city, and her husband's only brother was ill and unable to support her. Although she did not have to pay anything for her house, she still needed income to cover daily expenses for herself and her growing children. She said she had support from her parental family and often accepted money from her mother and brother.

Leman's demands for loans from her kin were not always welcome. She developed a strategy of borrowing money from her relatives and friends in order to lend it for usury. When she made some profit, she repaid the loans. Nevertheless, she was constantly looking for ways to accumulate cash and turn it into income through usury. It was a risky business. When she lent money to others, she had no way to enforce repayment other than using gossip as a means of social control. I once accompanied her to the house of someone she had to reproach for not having returned a loan on time. All Leman could do was to talk to the woman, but she was not ready to pay the money back at the door. When it became clear that yet again the money would not be repaid, Leman started arguing, shouting reproachful words loudly enough for the neighbours to hear and understand what it was all about.

Yet there were limits to this kind of public slander. Leman did not want to risk earning a reputation as a troublemaker or a shameless (*hayasız*) woman, crying out in public for money, which was generally considered to be an immoral practice. Indeed, usury (*sələmçilik*) was a despised occupation. The whole village knew about the fate of a *sələmçi* woman who was killed by one of her business partners and how the hatred she incurred was so great that her tombstone was broken and desecrated.

Thus, Leman was taking a great risk. She had to access any cash resources available to her through her relatives, but at the same time she continually complained about her vulnerable situation as a young widow having to worry not only about her own honour but also that of her teenage sons and daughter. The sons had no training or education other than the compulsory eleven years. Leman was equally worried about her daughter, whom she had given in marriage to a distant relative immediately after the girl finished high school (despite my protests and those of many other neighbours that the daughter was still only a teenager), claiming she was worried about the girl's being kidnapped.

Leman also earned some money by doing discreet trading of her own produce. In winter she made many barrels of pickled vegetables, which sold well at the weekly market. Instead of having a stall at the market, for which there was a fee, she gave her pickles to a friend to sell and shared some of the earnings with her. She also sold her home-produced food within the neighbourhood, but that was only occasional, marginal income for her. She probably never considered cultivating the *pay* land her household had received, because she had no means to organise it on her own, given her activities and the fact that her sons were neither enterprising enough nor interested in working the land. Thus, together with neighbours who had received *pay* shares next to hers, she gave hers to a farmer. In return she received some wheat or flour, from which she made her bread. She received the same amount of payment as all the other *pay* owners and thought that was all right.

Leman's biography resembles Meliha's in that they both had relatively young families and sons with minimal education and no professional training. But Leman was a much more outgoing, extroverted, fighting type than Meliha. She definitely needed these qualities to engage in usury, and she used her social and rhetorical skills of gossiping and slandering as weapons for enforcing the repayment of loans. Her gendered kinship roles as mother and widow restricted her possibilities for engaging more fully in usury, but she could use those roles for mobilising support for herself from her neighbours, friends, and acquaintances. She managed to marry off her daughter and then her younger son with expensive, ostentatious wedding ceremonies. She gave her daughter a large dowry and bragged about it. The younger son married a young woman from a similar economic background; he was trying to earn money by doing day labour in construction in the *rayon*, earning the minimum daily wage of 10 manat (US$2) in 2002.

Leman's other great concern, the marriage of and a house for her elder son, was resolved through the exit option of migration: he left for Russia to find a job and then met a Russian woman, with whom he was still living and had a child in September 2005. Although Leman had not fulfilled the moral and social obligations of marrying him off properly and providing him with a house, she was pragmatic about the situation. According to her neighbours, she calculated the economic costs and benefits and said of her son, 'He saved his life/himself [*özünü qurtardı*]', because he found a woman to 'keep him [*onu saxlayır*]'. This was acceptable because Leman could not have provided with him everything she perceived him to have in Russia. Moreover, the elder son was not sending her any money, which she felt excused her for not having fulfilled her duties to him. After all, he was neither supporting her nor had returned to the village for a few years, and so in a way he was a lost (and saved) son for Leman. Even though she argued about her moral responsibilities and her son's expectations in these self-justifying terms, my hostess, Könül, was not entirely convinced about Leman's moral standards and jokingly teased her on many occasions for 'having sold her son to a Russian woman'.

Case 5: Terana's Household

Terana represents a different kind of woman head of household: she was a relatively wealthy and successful small businesswoman. Together with two of her four sons, she managed a small butcher shop just next to the marketplace, a convenient location for attracting customers. She and her sons all worked there, especially on Sundays, when the weekly food market took place and many people bought meat. In addition, the family sold meat from their home and had some storage space in the courtyard of their house.

Teranə lived with two of her sons, one of whom was newly married. She was in full charge of household affairs and strategies, despite having been widowed at a young age (usually, young widows return to their parental home). Her sons seemed to conduct no business without consulting her. Two of her unmarried sons were traders in Siberia, and the youngest worked as a butcher along with the only married son, Müşfik, who was a friend of the young men in my host family. Müşfik had been studying to become a customs officer, and Teranə organised a bribe to pay for a position for him at the nearby city customs office. Teranə's sons in Siberia sent home money that helped with household expenses such as higher education, Müşfik's marriage and the payment for his job, and costs associated with the meat trade. The family lived in a large, newly renovated house and had a new car.

When I asked where the family's starting capital had come from, I was told that Teranə's husband had been a butcher in the Soviet period and had earned a lot of money by illegally butchering meat in his own courtyard. Meat processing was officially under the control of the sovkhoz and kolkhoz administrations, but her husband, who was known as the 'informal' butcher, took advantage of private demands to buy fresh meat at unexpected times and in large quantities. After independence he made his business legal, but he died of illness not long afterwards. Teranə and her sons took over his customers and used his professional reputation to continue the business.

Teranə's success as a widowed head of household seemed to lie in her ability to manage the collective affairs of her sons. This might have been related to the sons' stage of life: they still needed to stick together and respect their mother, who was socially obligated to arrange their marriages and manage the acquisition of houses for them when they married. So far the only danger seemed to be the possibility that the sons in Russia might be tempted to find Russian wives or lovers for themselves. This was a serious concern for mothers of young men who worked and traded in the Russian Federation or in Kazakhstan; it reflected social expectations in the village that parents would secure suitable marriage partners for their children, ideally partners from Azerbaijan, but at least from a Muslim country such as Turkey or Iran. On the whole, Russians were considered undesirable as daughters-in-law, and as sons-in-law they were unthinkable. Unlike Meliha, Teranə could not accept her sons marrying Russian women, although it was more acceptable and, according to gossip, widespread – if publicly ignored – for young men to have Russian girlfriends. So Teranə spent a great deal of time looking for possible brides for her sons. She had the sons come back to the village at least once a year to present themselves as successful young men, loyal to their household while temporarily earning good money in Russia.

Despite her relative youth, Terənə had fully embraced the role of permanent widow, never thinking of remarrying but remaining fully dedicated to managing the household's financial and social matters. The large number of sons she had also helped guarantee her a good reputation, so long as the sons were socially respected and cooperated with each other. The privatised land share the household had received was rented to a larger cultivator, because all the sons were occupied in other trades and uninterested in cultivating it themselves.

Plate 5. 1980s house for sale (its owners have moved to Russia).

Case 6: Sakinə's Case

Sakinə was the only woman I knew in the village who, as a widowed female head of household, was a successful cultivator. Among the cases I describe here, she was the only woman who had an agricultural background, having been an agronomist in the kolkhoz. She lived in the former kolkhoz area and not in Leninabad like most of the other herb and tomato cultivators. She engaged successfully in cash crop cultivation and sold her produce to traders who came to households to buy it.

Sakinə lived in a large, well-furnished house, almost on her own, because her two daughters were married and her four sons were away in Russia and came to visit only occasionally. She had at least two young granddaughters who stayed with her to help with cultivation and household chores. For the harder work in the greenhouses, where she grew tomatoes and cucumbers, she employed short-term wage labourers. Besides her sons and daughters, Sakinə had several sisters and brothers, who made a web of influential kin for her. Her siblings were all well placed, with professions in the local bureaucracy. Although they were not among the local governing elites, they aspired to be so and were continually trying to establish links with such people.

There were, however, long-lasting conflicts among members of Sakinə's kin group. Two of her sons and several of her brothers' sons had been involved in the lucrative illegal trade of alcohol in Russia in the 1990s and owed debts to several members of the family as well as to other people in the community. This prevented them from coming back to the village, and Sakinə had to manage and help support their families along with managing her own household affairs. She also had to devote considerable energy to mediating and managing conflicts between quarrelling parties in her large kin group.

Sakinə had chosen a moderate scale of cultivation. She herself was hard-working and managed the cultivation of cash crops on her large *məhlə* with the help of paid labour and occasionally of her neighbours and kin. She could not have engaged in cultivation of her *pay* shares because of the shortage of labour and available men in her immediate kin group. Although having many sons and daughters could have increased her potential for economic success, in fact her kin group seemed to be more a burden than a resource for her. She had to work hard to support them socially and economically, rather than the other way around.

Summary

The preceding case studies of female-headed households show that although such households had a tendency to be economically vulnerable, the availability and successful management of close kin, especially of young men (sons), played a crucial role in economic success. The role played by social and economic capital accumulated during the Soviet period was also considerable, especially if the household head was able to employ it strategically, as in the cases of Mila and Teranə. Mila used her social capital in a negative but powerful way, employing knowledge about others to apply pressure in order to mobilise support. Teranə chose the more conservative, traditionally female strategy of playing the responsible mother, exploiting the social and

economic capital she inherited from her husband to achieve economic success through social control over her sons and by networking for support
among neighbours, members of her larger kin group, and customers.

None of these women could ignore their kin group and withdraw from
engaging in 'kin work' (see also Pine 1993, 2000). Even Mila had to be
concerned about the reputation of her daughters and ultimately could not
afford to ignore public opinion and the power of gossip. Such households
engaged in agricultural activities when they had tight control over their
household members and lacked other sources of income such as migration
and trade.

Finally, these female household heads laboured under harsher conditions than men in comparable situations. Men enjoyed greater socially accepted freedom to try out different strategies of survival and economic
accumulation, such as migrating and taking better-paying jobs in other
locations. There were no women migrants from Təzəkənd, although women
from the neighbouring city of Gəncə had migrated to Russia, and some
women had accompanied their men as labour migrants to Russia or Kazakhstan. It was also more common for men to remarry if they became widowers,
thus eliminating the pressure of raising children alone while having to secure
a livelihood – the inescapable dilemma facing female heads of household.

Households Coping with Shortages of Money and Unaffordable Prices

Many researchers have described transition economies as being cash shortage economies (see Ledeneva 1998; Seabright 2000; Gambold-Miller 2002).
Lack of cash is a chronic concern for rural households, even if they have
some agricultural produce for consumption or barter. The preceding case
studies illustrated how shortages of cash made households dependent on
cultivating cash crops on their *məhlə*s and selling the produce either in local
markets or to traders. Without this income, they would have been on the
verge of poverty. Households that cultivated their *məhlə*s had to see that the
produce got sold and not wasted, but they were aware of fluctuations in
prices according to the season, the quality of the produce, and the accessibil-
ity and demands of the markets.

Households that did not engage in active, extensive cultivation of
*məhlə*s met their needs for cash through a combination of strategies and uses
of material, labour, and human resources, trying to make the most of what
was available to them. My host family, for example, earned a little cash by
selling eggs from their few chickens, but the amount was so small that they
hardly recognised it as income. Indeed, Könül, my hostess, joked about

selling eggs as an example of how hard times were. In really desperate phases in the history of her household – such as when they needed cash to bribe the military not to send their son to the front when he was doing his military service during the years of the Karabakh conflict – she had to sell her deceased father's paintings. She remembered this with great sadness and embarrassment, because for her the paintings were the last symbolic remnants of her urban, educated family background, her ancestors having been wealthy landowners in the Crimea before becoming refugees.

Another household, in which the young adult daughters were teachers whose salaries were small and irregularly paid, exploited the daughters' baking skills. They were known for making fancy cakes, which were traditionally given as gifts at weddings and served to celebrate birthdays and other festive occasions. The teachers baked the cakes to order and were paid in cash and in kind. Other households, like Leman's, prepared foods such as pickled vegetables, marmalade, and conserves for sale, not at the marketplace but among neighbours, by word of mouth.

Cash shortages could also be partially remedied by performing wage labour for others. That labour, however, had to conform to certain rules of social hierarchy and status difference in the area. For example, owners of cars often drove others to hospital or on other business for a cash fee, but the price of the service could be higher, lower, or nothing at all depending on the relationship and status difference between the driver and the rider. If the two parties were close kin, the service might be free, and among young men who were friends and equals, the price might be simply the price of petrol. If the two parties were neighbours or acquaintances, then the driver might ask a minimum price for his services and petrol, which he would not exaggerate in order not to be seen as exploiting the acquaintance.

Other rules applied to offering one's services for agricultural work. Doing agricultural labour for friends and neighbours could be based on reciprocal or friendship relations, implying returns in the long term in varying spheres of exchange. On the whole, such labour exchange and reciprocity existed for the cultivation herbs, potatoes, onions, and other cash crop vegetables and fruits on household plots. Agricultural work on *pay* plots for unknown or unrelated people followed different rules. It required bargaining over the price of the labour, which caused resentment when the relationship was between people who lived in the same settlement. Agricultural labourers preferred to work in distant communities or at least not in their own.[126] Indeed, I met no agricultural labourer who worked in either the village or its

---

[126] In a way, this was like negative 'trust', such that knowing the person made the work relationship more ambivalent in terms of how to bargain for one's interests and rights. See also Gambetta (1988) and Torsello (2003).

close vicinity. All cases involved men or women working for landowners and cultivators in other communities or people organised for exchanges of labour such as rotational work and occasional help on a neighbour's plot.

Another widely practised strategy for coping with cash shortages was to buy goods on credit (in Azerbaijani, *nisiye*). This was practised at the discretion of the shop owner or trader, without a written contract, and required a relationship of trust between the buyer and the seller. Small shop owners in the village had such clientele, mostly neighbours. Könül, for instance, bought on credit at the shop owned by Naza across the street, because they had a relationship of mutual trust. Sometimes Könül's daughter-in-law, her son, or her grandchildren also purchased items at Naza's shop, not always with Könül's knowledge, and the cost was noted as a debt for Könül. Debts were usually paid when the debtors received their salaries, normally once a month. Naza was known as a fair and tolerant businesswoman and agreed to allow debts to be paid in instalments. Customers paid no interest, and Naza gave customers like Könül extra time to pay their balance when there were delays in the payment of salaries, such as those of teachers.

Many villagers expressed the hardship they experienced in terms of having access to cash with the words, 'If we could not buy food and goods with credit [*nisiye*], we would starve'. Nevertheless, *nisiye* relations did not prevent market competition between shop owners and petty traders. Opening a shop was a primary way of investing a modest amount of accumulated capital and creating a work space for women close to home, so despite the difficulty of working with *nisiye* relations, women in particular aspired to this kind of trading. They opened small shops on the same village streets and naturally fell into competition with one another for local customers, thus reducing their chance for significant gain, unless they offered a variety of goods and entrepreneurial innovation.

Buying on credit at the weekly market was not unheard of, although the common practice was to pay for goods upon purchase. For some foodstuffs such as flour, which one bought in 50-kilogram sacks, and feed for the chickens in the back yard, one could buy on credit if one had a trust relationship with the seller. Similar to examples from other ethnographies (Geertz 1963; Firth and Yamey 1964; Mintz 1964; Clark 1994; Mühlich 2001), such credit relationships were established between traders who had stable stands at the weekly market, to which they came regularly, and customers who had either a personal relationship with the seller or were known to have stable salaries, such as teachers and doctors. Such credit relationships were also sometimes extensions of trust relationships built up between sellers and customers in order to guarantee payment to the seller and good prices and product quality to the buyer.

Cash shortages could also be partially remedied by borrowing money from kin, friends, and neighbours. When those people could not lend money or when the sum needed was too large, borrowing money from a usurer (*saləmçi*) was the last resort. Interest rates for borrowing money on *saləm* (usury) were fairly stable and in 2002 reached 10 per cent per month of the amount borrowed. Rates might differ depending on the relationship between the lending and borrowing parties, but *saləm* always implied a substantial interest rate.

Lending money on *saləm* involved risks, as I mentioned earlier in the case of the woman head of household Leman. Her problem was not having enough cash to lend. She said that for the past three years she had been taking her mother-in-law's pension, eight şirvan per month (about US$16), which she was supposed to keep for her, but instead used it for her own household expenses and for lending money. She said she 'ate the money [*yeyib*]'. Then she got in trouble with her mother-in-law and that woman's daughter, Leman's sister-in-law. The mother-in-law, elderly and ill, lived in Gəncə, the nearest large city, and was cared for by her daughter. Leman rationalised – although she knew her argument was weak – that her aging mother-in-law would die anyway and would not need the money, and the daughter was taking care of her only because they lived in Gəncə, whereas Leman would have done the same if the mother-in-law had come to live with her in the village. In claiming that she was practicing her entitlement to her mother-in-law's pension, Leman referred to the patrilocal and patrilineal ideology that made provisions for women whose husbands had died and who had children to look after. They should ideally be taken care of by their in-laws, in this case by the mother-in-law.

Unfortunately, relations between Leman and her mother-in-law were not good, and the mother-in-law, like many others, preferred to live with her daughter, not least because there were better health care facilities in the city. And beyond her legitimate claim to support, Leman was transferring re-sources from her kin to earnings gained through usury, something that chal-lenged the moral economy and accepted spheres of exchange. Not only was usury a precarious way of earning money, but both money lenders and money borrowers were socially and morally deplored. Thus Leman had to endure the criticism of her neighbours and friends, even though they under-stood her need, as a widow with adult children, to engage in that business. Having to resort to usury was a tangible sign of despair, of being unable to meet emergency expenses, of needing large amounts of cash to pay bribes for jobs, funerals, and so forth, and of failing networks of supportive kin and friends.

Households and Conspicuous Consumption: A Self-Destructive Practice?

Life-cycle rituals such as wedding parties (*büyük toy*), circumcision feasts (*kiçik toy*), and funerals were occasions for substantial household expenditures in Təzəkənd. Households usually aimed to have savings and resources ready for at least the foreseeable life-cycle events. As I have detailed elsewhere (Yalçin-Heckmann 2001; see also Werner 1998), a marriage ceremony involved a lengthy process of negotiations, visits, prestations, and gift exchanges, in addition to the wedding party itself, all of which amounted to a considerable cash expenditure. Sometimes this practice reached a level at which it appeared self-destructive, involving showing off, conspicuous consumption, selfless giving, and extravagant gift exchanges. Although such practices were surrounded by ambivalence, they were ways of articulating social and emotional aspects of kinship relations and of claiming and displaying social and economic capital (Bourdieu 1977; Comaroff and Comaroff 1980; Tapper 1981; Werner 2002).

Life-cycle rituals put serious strains on household budgets, especially in an economy of shortage and in a consumerist culture in which goods were available but the means to pay for them were not. Excessive household expenses for weddings and funerals have been a concern in other former Soviet countries, too, and sometimes state authorities seem keen to discourage them through governmental policies and public propaganda.[127] In Azerbaijan, the issue is a fundamental part of local and national debates. One of my Baku acquaintances, an elderly, educated, professional woman, complained bitterly when news of lavish wedding parties and gifts for the son of a prominent politician was reported in the media. She criticised these expensive entertainments as decadences exemplifying low public and national morals. She interpreted the public's fascination with such extravagance as a way of blocking out consciousness of the consequences of the Karabakh war. She went on to express her sense of shame as an Azerbaijani when she travelled abroad and had to say that she came from Azerbaijan; she said she would rather claim she was from Turkey. She found it shameful that people enjoyed lavish parties and weddings: 'They celebrate their weddings and

---

[127] In Uzbekistan, a presidential decree banned ostentatious ceremonies, especially in weddings (Louw 2007: 77, citing Kandiyoti and Azimova 2004: 337). On the contested meanings and interpretations of old (Soviet) and modern weddings and marriage practices, see McBrien (2008: chapter 4) and also Werner (2002) and Light (2008).

enjoy themselves as if nothing has happened', referring to the national and political problems of post-war Azerbaijan, with its lost territories and hundreds of thousands of displaced persons and refugees. Yet despite such critiques, social pressure on brides' and grooms' families to outdo each other continues to dominate and even to drain households' scarce resources. One potential source of money for such consumption is labour migration, which I discuss next.

Plate 6. The arrival of the bride.

Migration: Taking Risks

Seasonal or longer-term migrations for work and education were relatively common in the Caucasian republics of the Soviet Union. Nona Shahnazaryan (2005: 236) wrote that such migrations were considered normal 'insofar as they were motivated mainly by the desire of rural men to live up to their traditionally prescribed gender role. This required considerable expenditure on things like gifts to family members, relatives, in-laws and other members of the community during various rituals of the life-cycle and, ultimately, the money earned during migrations was applied toward the major economic and symbolic investment of building the family home'. In the post-Soviet period, she observed, labour migration has been due to poverty and war, and 'migrants aim to secure basic survival'. The 'basic survival' syndrome should be viewed with caution, because many kinds of economic migrations and displacements have been portrayed in terms of such 'victimhood' (see Malkki 1997; Colson 2004). Yet the truth is that the new kinds of migrations involve risks, a great degree of uncertainty, lack of preparation for a long-term life strategy, and exposure to arbitrary state and non-state forces and actors.

As I described in chapter 4, 32 of the 77 households I surveyed (42 per cent) had migrants abroad. Nineteen of them had one or more sons abroad, and in five cases the household head or his or her partner was away. All but one of the migrants in the sample were in Russia, and that one was in Kazakhstan. The amount and regularity of remittances from these family members varied considerably, but only four households reported having received total remittances in excess of US$1,000 in 2001.

The case of Fərhad, a young man I knew as a friend of my host family and whom I interviewed for the survey, demonstrates the complexity of paths and strategies for seeking work abroad and the way family, kinship, and friendship ties can be strained and force the migrant to take risks. Fərhad and his extended family were people with whom I had relatively close contact, and I present his case on the basis of interviews and further talks with him, his family members, and his friends.

Besides being a good friend of the sons of my host family, Fərhad was the brother-in-law of one of their closest friends, Cəmşid. I met Fərhad many times at social gatherings, at wedding parties, during his visits with my host family, and when I went to visit his family. Fərhad's father was also an acquaintance of my host family's; he was considered an *aqsaqqal* (literally, 'one with a white beard', a respectable elderly person) in the settlement, having received higher education and worked in upper-level positions in the former socialist agricultural industries. Fərhad was a central figure for many young men, including friends of my host family's sons. He had gone to Russia several times to work and was considered an experienced young entrepreneurial migrant. He was thought to have knowledge of markets, sales, and job opportunities as well as links to other such people with jobs and opportunities. To what degree his image in the settlement reflected the reality of his situation becomes clear from the details of his story.

Fərhad was the youngest of five brothers: Firuz, Fərit, Fazıl, Fərman, and Fərhad (fig. 5.2). He also had two sisters, married and living in the same settlement, not far from their father's house. Of the five brothers, Fərit was registered as being, and said by their father to have been, in the same household with his parents. In fact he was away working in the Russian province of Irkutsk, together with his brothers Fazıl and Firuz. Fərhad, at the time of my interviews with him, had just come back from Irkutsk, having worked there with his brothers for some time, and was spending time with his young family – his wife, Cəmşid's sister, and their two young children.

Fərhad, his brothers and his business partners

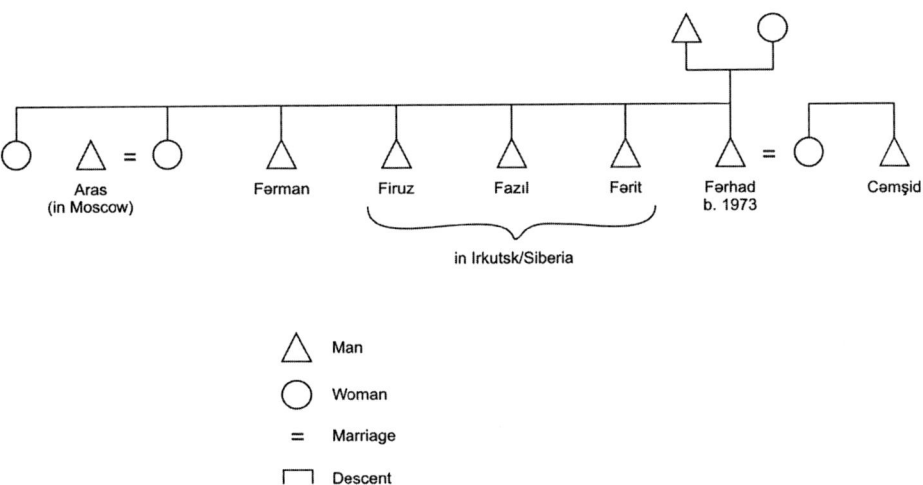

Figure 5.2. Fərhad, his brothers, and his business partners.

Born in 1973, Fərhad had studied wine production at the institute for wine-making in Ismayilli between 1990 and 1995. After that he was mostly unemployed for four years, finding nothing that suited him. The jobs he got paid at most US$10 a month, and even that not punctually. He decided to join his brothers, who had been involved in wine production and trade since the late 1980s, in Irkutsk. The brothers had worked in various wine factories in Azerbaijan during the late 1980s and early 1990s and had become involved in illegal wine sales. These took the form of stealing wine that was in transit from Azerbaijan to Russia by train, siphoning it off from railway containers with rubber pipes, and decanting it into bottles for sale in Russia. The remaining wine in the railway containers was then topped up with water. Since wine transport to Russia had stopped in the mid-1990s, the brothers no longer engaged in this activity.

In Irkutsk they had hired a wine-bottling factory and were producing bottled wine. To what degree they used illegal methods in this business, too, is difficult to say, but in areas where wine production was under state control and taxation, their business seems to have flourished for a while as they were able to organise access to large quantities of bottles and wine beyond state control. Fərhad said that filling one bottle of wine cost about 500–600 manat and would be sold for 1,000 manat (about US$0.25). Because of the bribes the brothers had to pay to the authorities, their profits were not very high. Fərhad thought he had not been well paid by his brothers, which was why he returned to Təzəkənd. He said he had received US$1,000 for the 13 months he spent in Irkutsk, which included his travel expenses.

After returning from Irkutsk, Fərhad stayed for only six months and then went to Moscow to work with his sister's husband, Aras, who was wholesaling vegetables and fruit. Aras had rented a container where the produce was stored, and Fərhad helped him with sales. Fərhad said that although he had been promised a salary of US$150 a month, he received no payment from his brother-in-law either, so after nearly a year in Moscow he again returned to the village.

Such return journeys were always full of expectations and tensions. Young men, especially when they had families whom they had left behind, either alone or with their parents, were expected to come back with enough money to last for some months, to cover household expenses, pay debts, and invest in postponed life-cycle rituals. The sum a returnee brought was publicly known; once the news of someone's return to the village was announced, the first question people asked among themselves was, 'How much money did he bring back'?[128] That Fərhad came back without any money was publicly known and was a loss of face for him.

To what degree could Fərhad have taken economic action by himself, and to what degree can his actions be seen as his individual strategies? His case illustrates a complicated mixture of individual and household strategies. Fərhad was pursuing a career very much under the influence of his elder brothers, studying the same subjects they had and seeking a career as a successful small businessman like them. But because he had no capital of his own, he was dependent on his brothers and his parental family to support him and his family throughout his migration career. If he had money, he said, he would have studied a different subject – tax accountancy – and sought a job in an accounting business, which would have situated him in the profitable state sector. With sufficient capital, too, he would have preferred to be an independent businessman, hiring a modest stand in a Moscow market and trading either on his own or with a hired labourer-salesperson. Without capital, he was bound by his family and affinal relations. Those

---

[128] On similar expectations and obligations of migrants in the mountainous parts of Poland, see Pine (1999, 2000).

people were committed to supporting him, but such inter-dependencies were not without tensions and resentments. Finally, Fərhad subscribed to the general discourse among young men in western Azerbaijani *rayon*s and rural settlements, which held that if jobs were available in Azerbaijan, then no one would leave his country for work abroad under such risky conditions.

From my interview with Fərhad's father, I knew that he had helped all his independent sons to build their houses. Moreover, the families of the three sons in Russia lived in the village, and the father said he looked after them. He said that the sons sent him money whenever they could, and in 2000 he received had approximately US$300–400 from them. He also took care of the empty house of one son, who had taken his family with him to Russia. Thus, the exchange of financial aid and solidarity between the parents and the sons seemed to be intensive.

Fərhad was typical of many young men of his age who grew up in the village with aspirations of getting white-collar jobs with salaries. Under the Soviet system of agricultural enterprise, young men like him might have found jobs as agronomists, agrarian experts, accountants, technologists in the wine industry, and the like. Fərhad had been pursuing this possibility in his education. Such a job would have made it possible for him to live in the rural settlement but have a fairly high standard of living and, most important, social recognition as a member of the local educated class.

During the transition from the socialist system to independence, Fərhad's education and qualifications, as well as the country's educational standards, were devalued and turned upside-down. The only option left open to him was to try to accumulate cash in order to 'pay for' an urban job. Although his family was still respected for belonging to the local educated class, it could not afford to pay for stable jobs for all its sons, nor could those jobs guarantee stable salaries. Hence, young men like Fərhad who did not aspire to agricultural work preferred to take the risk of out-migration. They would follow almost any acquaintance or relative who might help them escape the village economy. They preferred to sink or swim in the new, insecure economies of illegal petty trade and production, just about anywhere in the former Soviet realm that their networks might lead them.

Although such young men did not engage directly in agricultural production and so offered no competition to people who engaged in cultivation and or in accumulating land for sharecropping, they were still important economic figures in many households, which sought to build socially acceptable biographies for their sons and to secure social reproduction. If these young men were successful in accumulating enough to sustain living abroad over some years, they were also likely to turn their savings into conspicuous consumption and support for their kin group in rituals such as funerals and weddings. Without such successful migrants and their remittances, life-cycle ceremonies in the rural settlement would have been much more modest and socially looked down upon. In other words, even if migrants were out of the local production system, they were central to their households' production of symbolic capital – and in some cases, through their remittances, of real capital.

Vulnerability

A final case study is that of a three-generational household that had the structural preconditions for engaging in cultivation but nevertheless found itself in a vulnerable economic and social situation. The main character of this household, Ramin, was a man in his thirties who, because of his back-ground, was positively disposed towards agricultural activity, unlike Fərhad. Ramin engaged in intensive cash crop production on his household's plots, although he did not cultivate their *pay* share.

Ramin's name came up in the random sample for my survey, and my field assistant told me he was the son of another head of household who was also on my sample list. The two households were registered under different numbers because the adjacent household plots were originally given to two brothers, one of whom was Ramin's father, Əmin, when they came from Armenia in 1951. In 2001 the two plots were occupied by Əmin's wife, Gülzadə, their son Ramin and his family, and a deceased son's wife and son (fig. 5.3). Əmin's brother's son was not resident there, but apparently his claim to half of the land was still valid, for Ramin said that two village households (*təsərrüfat*) were registered in the village records on the same 25-*sotka* piece of land.

The story of Ramin's household in Leninabad began with his parents' displacement from Armenia in 1949. When Əmin and Gülzadə arrived in Leninabad in 1951, after having spent some time in other sites for the dis-placed, they had been married for a year. They had been paid compensation for their displacement by the Soviet state, an amount that covered the cost of their transportation from Armenia, and the two brothers were given free plots of land. Əmin and Gülzadə built a two-room, mud-brick house and over the years had eight children: four sons and four daughters. Əmin worked at the post office. In 1966, the year in which the house was regis-tered in the village registry books, the family began rebuilding it with stone, using their own labour and earnings (*öz əməyi ilə*). Gülzadə said they kept building and repairing the house until 1980, and this was the house in which she, Ramin, and other family members still lived.

Ramin's household

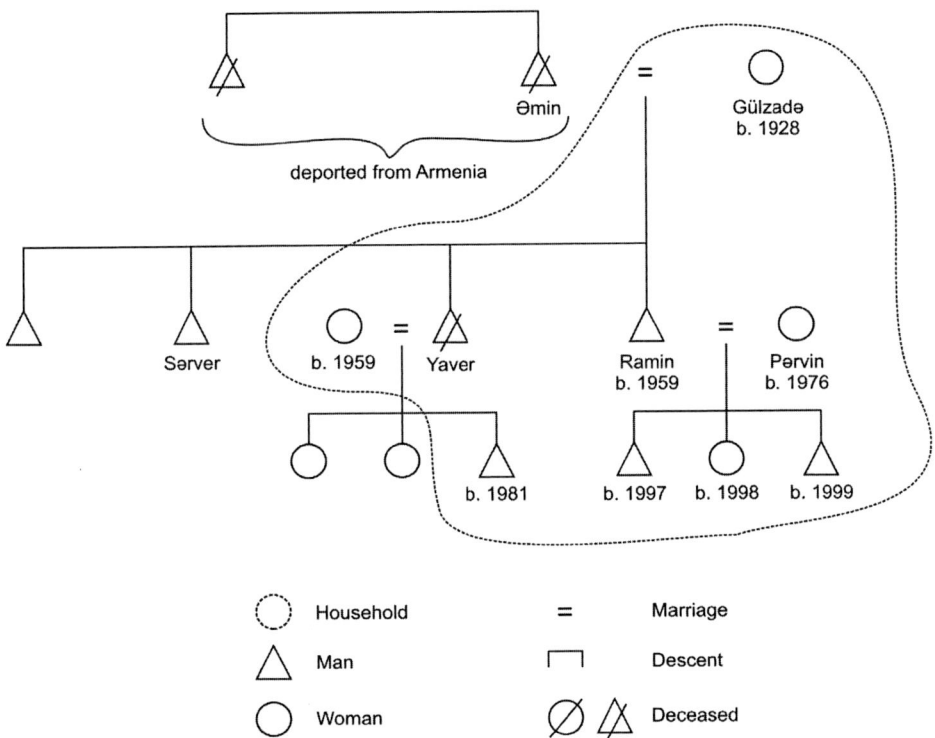

Figure 5.3. Ramin's household.

Soon after her arrival in Leninabad, Gülzadə started working in the local kolkhoz for cotton production. In the mid-1970s, when cotton ceased to be produced in the region, she went on to work as an agricultural labourer in the sovkhoz vineyards. She saw her worker status as related to her low level of education; because of World War II, she had gone to school for only five years. She was left an orphan when her father 'never returned from the war', having met the same fate as her brothers. Indeed, this was the first structural vulnerability in her biography: her having been deprived of a full education had limited the family's opportunities. However, she remembered that her family – presumably her mother and younger siblings – had been given 'blood money' (in Azerbaijani, *qan pulu*) by the state for the male family members who were missing in action. Her family's second vulnerability was its displacement from Armenia, for which she thought she had also received some compensation.

In 2001, eight people lived in the family house, which encompassed 60 square meters in four rooms. Əmin had died in the 1990s, and Ramin's brother Yaver, in 2000. Yaver's two daughters were already married and separated from the parental household.[129]

Ramin, Yaver, and a third brother, Sərver, had each applied for and received 8 *sotka* of land from the village administration in order to start their own households and build houses. The other two built houses on their plots, but Ramin said that although he had started building one in 1993, it was not yet finished. His prospects for finishing it were not good. Although he was the only one of the three brothers who had gone to vocational technical school (*texnikum*), becoming an electrician in 1988, he had worked for only two years after that. Since 1990 he had been officially unemployed (*bekar*), meaning that he did only odd jobs and received no stable salary. Until 1990 he was entitled to receive some products at a special state price, because of his status as a veteran of the war in Afghanistan. That privilege no longer existed, and he received a only symbolic payment as his veteran's salary. Ramin's wife, who had trained as an assistant nursery school teacher (*uşaq bağcası terbiyəcisi*), had never worked for wages because she stayed home to look after their young children. Thus, further vulnerabilities for Ramin's household were that despite his vocational training, he could not find a sustainable job; the state support he received as a war veteran was little to begin and dwindled further after independence; and his wife earned no wages.

The household of Ramin and his mother could be seen at the time of our interview as having a precarious existence. Yaver's death and the economic burden of his widow and teenage son must have further increased their vulnerability. Moreover, probably in order to cover the expense of mourning rituals for Yaver, Ramin had to sell Yaver's car, which the family had been using to transport vegetables and herbs for sale in Gəncə.

Since the mid-1980s the family had been selling produce grown on its household plot at local markets and in the city. Besides tomatoes, cucumbers, and other vegetables, they grew herbs and had some fruit trees. After 1991 they became more dependent on this income, and in 2001 Ramin was carrying out the trade on his own, taking the produce by automobile to the market in Gəncə. He also cultivated cucumbers on the second household

---

[129] The two daughters must already have been married before Yaver died, because after a father's death, daughters are not supposed to marry for at least a year, while the family is in mourning. They had been born in 1984 and 1985, respectively, so if they had married in 2000 at the latest, not long before their father died, they would have reached the ages of 15 and 16 at most. This is a very early age for marriage and might have been related to the household's difficulties in managing resources and strategies in the transition economy.

plot, where he was building his own house. Overall, the household could be said to have been using all its resources in terms of household plots. What is surprising is that despite the entitlements the family and household members had to privatised land shares, in 2001 they had not claimed the land or picked up their titles. A household of eight people should have received 112 *sotka* of land (14 *sotka* for each person). Ramin said he had gone to the village council and it had sent him away. It is unclear to me why he did not pursue his claim to receive this land, although it seems most likely that it was because of his limited capacity to work the land, since he and his nephew were the only men in the household.[130]

Overall, the vulnerability of this household was linked to the burden of life-course crises such as having to cover the brother's funeral expenses while experiencing diminishing input for successful agricultural production. In its earlier phase, selling produce in the markets, the household's large size and many dependents also contributed to its vulnerability. Although the household's size led it to receive substantial hectarage in *pay* shares, its actual composition was the primary reason it did not use this privatised land.

At first glance, Ramin's household seems to present an example of A. V. Chayanov's model of the economy of the peasant household, in which productivity is dependent on household size, and peasants 'are always balancing the drudgery of work against the return, and … have few desires beyond food and security' (Wilk and Cliggett 2007: 24). Upon closer examination, I believe Ramin's case does not fit Chayanov's thesis. The model maintains that when a household has enough land to feed its members, it will make no further effort to increase its land or productivity. But even if one could argue that Ramin's household had reached this self-satisfied stage, Ramin as head of household still had the culturally defined goal of building a house to secure the future of his children. He had just fulfilled another culturally defined obligation, that of taking on the great expense of funeral and mourning rituals for his father and brother, and he had plans to educate his children and support his deceased brother's young family. Hence, one cannot talk about the household's orientation being simply towards food and security. Even if Ramin and his household members were all engaged in cultivating the household plot, he saw himself not as a peasant but as an unemployed electrician, suggesting that if he were to find a job as an electrician, he would not be farming.

Finally, even if the household had benefited from enough labour to cultivate more land, it lacked capital for investing in cultivation – buying

---

[130] In addition, land the household might have received as *pay* would probably have needed to be irrigated, like most other *pay* shares, and irrigation was expensive, especially if a plot was not situated directly on an irrigation canal.

seeds, fertilizers, and pesticides, paying for a tractor, and so forth. Its members were also aware of market prices for wheat and barley, which failed to pay off many other cultivators' investments of cash and labour. Therefore, diverging from Chayanov's model, Ramin's case can be seen as typical of economically calculating cultivators, concerned with transaction costs rather than security and food for household members alone.[131]

Structural limitations on households like Ramin's had differential effects on household economic strategies and on the use of agricultural land in Təzəkənd. The quantitative data presented in chapter 4 showed that people in the village made limited use of their privatised land shares. The qualitative case studies described here help explain how and why some households raised cash crops, engaged in petty trade, pursued collective strategies for cultivating *pay* shares, resorted to migration as an exit option (albeit one still closely integrated with systems of ritual and symbolic exchange), and used moral discourses to resist vulnerability. They also reveal the ways in which household size, composition, and gender operated to promote or hinder the use of a variety of economic strategies.

---

[131] For other critiques of Chayanov's model, see Harris (1981), Donham (1981), and Torsello (2003: chapter 5).

Chapter 6
The Moral Economy of the Village: Norms and Practices of Exchange and Solidarity

> If kin were to eat the meat, [they] would not throw its bones away
> *[Qohum ətini yesə də, sümüyünü atmaz].*[132]
>
> Azerbaijani proverb, quoted in N. M. Q. Quliyeva,
> *Azərbaycanda Muasır Kənd Ailəsi və Ailə Məişəti*

Houses in Təzəkənd are typical of Azerbaijani villages in that they are built inside a courtyard (*həyət*) surrounded by a high wall with a metal gate opening onto the street. The house might be constructed with one wall towards the street, too, but this public face of the house is not used in everyday interactions, and its windows onto the street are normally kept tightly closed, with the curtains drawn. Household members perform many of their daily activities in the *həyət* – washing, cooking, cleaning, hosting guests, playing with children. The walls surrounding the courtyard, even if they are not particularly thick or strongly built, can shield the household from its surroundings, sealing family members off from their neighbours and the street. In other cases, depending on household members' relations with people around them, the walls might be high and solidly built but nevertheless permeable and easily ignored. Neighbouring women might chat across them and hand food or children over them. Neighbours might walk in after only a quick knock on the gate or after calling out the name of the household member they are looking for.

The sealed-off character of a household's or family's private life can be seen as an articulation of the family's social and economic relations within its rural community and beyond. The house and courtyard are where notions about society and the moral community are first learned and practised; they are the places from which social and economic relations with the

---

[132] That is, even if kin were to be mean and angry with a relative (and eat up his meat), they remain kin and would support the relative in need or difficulty.

outside ideally begin.[133] Within the household as a social unit, individuals cultivate notions of sharing, reciprocity, and hierarchy and also experience envy and competition.

In this chapter I examine normative and actual social and economic relations as they unfold from the perspectives of individuals as members of families and households, primarily in the rural community of Təzəkənd. I also look at other villages that I visited when following up the networks of my contacts in my two fieldwork sites. Such social and economic relations within a web of kin groups, friends, neighbours, and work colleagues are the social setting for 'concrete social property relations' (von Benda-Beckmann, von Benda-Beckmann, and Wiber 2006). Within this setting, the moral community is defined and activated, and relationships surrounding property such as household items, dowry objects, inherited goods, houses, courtyards, and gardens are learned, transmitted, transformed, or challenged.

Normatively, social relations in the village emphasised kinship solidarity as the ideal. Kin groups were seen as webs of persons and relationships within which social and moral obligations were fulfilled, reciprocal exchange took place, and individuals were socialised and expected to find recognition and support. Although a person's network of kin was given, in that he or she was born into a specific cluster of relationships, room and need still existed for each person to rearrange the network according to his or her personality, status, and abilities. Even if the ideal of solidarity among kin called for sociality and readiness to make concessions in the interest of the kin group, men and women were also expected to pursue their individual goals and interests and to become personalities beyond their immediate families. Using my fieldwork material, I examine the ways in which this tension was articulated, mediated, or developed into conflicts.

The relevance of kinship for individual status and for society in general is a well-explored theme in social theory and has been amply studied in anthropology.[134] Here I follow the work of other anthropologists who have specified the characteristics of Turkic language societies and of Azeris in particular, as well as those of other language and ethnic groups in the Middle East and Caucasus (see Stirling 1965; Meeker 1976; Schiffauer 1987; Holy 1989; Pfluger-Schindlbeck 1989; Delaney 1991; Yalçın-Heckmann 1991; White 1994). The kinship system I discuss conforms to the systems of these

---

[133] On the symbolic meaning of space and the spatial use of the house, see Bourdieu (1979: 133–153) and Carsten and Hugh-Jones (1995). For a recent discussion of the Muslim and Soviet character and symbolic meanings of Uzbek houses in Osh, see Liu (2007).

[134] For classic studies of kinship systems, see Fortes (1967 [1949]); Lévi-Strauss (1969); Goody (1975); Firth (1983 [1936]); Evans-Pritchard (2002 [1951]). For more recent studies, see Schweitzer (2000); Carsten (2004); Parkin (2004).

other societies in having certain cognatic kinship principles and weak notions of lineage membership (see Baharlı 1993 [1921]; Pfluger-Schindlbeck 2005). Its patriarchal bias is evident, despite substantial differences between rural and urban settings in the strength and effectiveness of patriarchy.

I neither trace the existence of lineage structures nor assess the significance of descent versus affinal ties. Primarily, I explore the significance of kinship ideology and familialism within the context of overall social, political, and economic relations in the countryside. More specifically, I ask to what degree the social and economic relationships surrounding hierarchy, reciprocity, debt, and exchange use and are embedded in terms, sentiments, and relations of kinship. I examine the direction and degree of change in kinship relations in interaction with changes in property relations and the system of agrarian production (cf. Ventsel 2005). My purpose is to assess the degree to which the rural community actually turns to principles of solidarity and moral support within the network of kin relations, as opposed to seeking solidarity and establishing relationships beyond that network. Thus my approach is similar to that of Peter Schweitzer (2000) and Janet Carsten (2004), who not only pursued post-Schneiderian efforts to understand kinship as a 'cultural system ... a system of symbols' (Schneider 1980: 1, cited in Schweitzer 2000: 2) but also looked at what kinship does and what people can do by using kinship notions, values, and norms.

The latter question is complex and difficult to tackle, because one's kin, especially in rural contexts, are usually also neighbours, work colleagues, potential spouses, and friends or foes. Kin are dominant in the social world of rural people, primarily through the economic and settlement structures within which they stay close to one another, but also through job opportunities, housing arrangements, and settlement and inheritance patterns. Given this obvious and natural dominance of kin ties within a rural community, it is nevertheless possible to trace trends of change in kinship relations as the state pursues policies for restructuring agrarian production and the rural economy (see also Kaneff and Yalçın-Heckmann 2003). Kinship has recently been discussed as having gained importance during the postsocialist crisis situation in many countries (see Pine 2002; Brandtstädter 2003; Dudwick et al. 2003; Gambold-Miller and Heady 2003). A return to household and kinship support in place of failing state support and resources has been predicted to be the general trend of social transformation in declining rural economies. I follow these discussions in this chapter by assessing the role of kinship in the construction and practice of a moral community and the way relations of solidarity, exchange, and rivalry interact with the ideology of kinship and property relations.

Relations of Exchange and Reciprocity: The Dominance of Kinship Solidarity and Family Ideology

Eldar and his family were my hosts during my stay in the town of Ismayilli. The family had kin living in a mountain village not far from the town; they were the mother's sister (MZ), mother's brother (MB), and cousins of Leyla, Eldar's wife. Leyla had grown up in this mountain village with her maternal grandmother (MM) and felt very close to her, as if she had been adopted by her. She had left the village when she married Eldar and moved into the town. Her parents and brothers all lived in Ismayilli, and a sister lived in another mountain village. Frequent visits and movements took place among these kinspeople; for instance, the children of various brothers, sisters, and in-laws would visit and stay sometimes for months in the households of cousins, uncles, and grandmothers. At any time a household might be hosting visiting cousins, nephews, and nieces, especially during school terms or for summer holidays.

The evening I expressed an interest in visiting Leyla's relatives in the mountain village, Eldar spontaneously decided that we would go immediately. That very night, at about ten o'clock, Leyla and her two sons, her mother, and I, with Eldar driving, crammed into his Lada Niva and left for the village. It lay in darkness when we arrived; everyone had gone to bed in order to make the usual early start taking care of the livestock and other animals.

We knocked loudly on the metal garden gate until it was finally opened by Leyla's uncle, the head of the family, a man in his fifties. It appeared that he had barely gotten dressed before welcoming us warmly. He assured us he did not mind being woken up, and in response, Eldar joked about village people going to bed early. Then he declared that we were all hungry, which was true, as we had missed supper. But we had arrived unannounced, late at night, so demanding food seemed to me impolite. The female family members did not immediately come out to greet us, but in the courtyard we could hear the hurried steps of women and girls getting food ready. This meant going to the chicken pen to find and catch a chicken of the right size and then slaughtering, cleaning, and cooking it as a stew and preparing rice pilaf and vegetables, all of which took no less than two hours.

Around midnight we were offered dinner. Until then the uncle kept us company, making small talk and discussing preparations for the upcoming wedding of his oldest daughter. We drank many cups of tea, served with a special jam typically used to sweeten tea. Eldar, Leyla, and their family displayed no embarrassment at causing so much commotion and work in the middle of the night. On the contrary, they complained that there should have been more tea, and when the table was set, Leyla demanded more salad and vegetables. The whole conversation involving demands for food and provision for kin and guests took place in a friendly, joking manner; no one seemed upset about the guests' turning up. There was no question whatsoever of our arrival's being untimely. It was understood that good kin would always prepare a full, delicious meal for relatives, no matter what the time of day.[135]

Such demonstrations of hospitality were common among kin and friends as well as for their invited guests. Probably my presence that night as an honoured guest of Eldar and Leyla's family contributed to the requirement of utmost hospitality and display in providing food, although by then I had been well incorporated into Eldar's family, had met nearly all of their kin network, and was no longer a novelty.

Had I been a complete stranger and gone to the village on my own, without the benefit of Eldar and Leyla's kinship network, I might have been refused hospitality altogether. That happened to me once in Təzəkənd, in late summer, when my host's household had run out of fruit. I thought I could go around the village with a young female companion and ask for grapes from other households that, I was told, might still have some (fruit was sold only at the weekly market in the village, on Sundays). My young friend Semayə and I did find a household that had grapes. Semayə introduced me to the female head of household as a visitor to the village and said that I would like to buy some grapes. But the woman did not know Semayə personally; she knew only her mother as a distant acquaintance. The compulsion of this distant relationship was weak, so she refused to sell us any. To smooth over her refusal, she said she had no grapes left.

Later during my stay in Təzəkənd, people repeatedly told this story about the woman, who subsequently became the mother-in-law of a niece of my host family, in order to tease her after I had met her on many other occasions. She was jokingly ridiculed for being ignorant and stingy, for not recognising the 'honourable guest' (əziz qonaq) of her future in-laws, and for refusing to help me have access to desirable food. The woman tried to make up for this lack of proper behaviour on all following occasions.

Showing generosity in the exchange of food and hospitality among kin and friends is a general rule in Azerbaijani society.[136] But on what principles

---

[135] The generosity and intimacy displayed on this occasion were typical of the overall closeness between Leyla and her MB's family and household. Later, in 2006, this closeness was transformed into marriage relations between the two families when Eldar and Leyla's oldest son got engaged to the younger daughter of Leyla's MB.

[136] The point here is not to highlight Azerbaijan's ethnic or national uniqueness but rather to underscore a shared norm of hospitality, which is in fact reported to be widespread and

are exchange relations based? When would a kinsman or kinswoman be refused generosity or exchange? Which principles of exchange are followed in order to expand or restrict access to resources among kin? Answering these questions requires further analysis of the concepts of reciprocity, exchange, and envy among kin and other villagers and how these help to promote or restrict individualism and collectivism in the rural community. Before turning to these questions, however, I outline the basic kinship structure and organisation in the rural settlement.

Basic Concepts and Structures of Family and Kin Groups

In Təzəkənd and nearby villages, households were primarily composed of families of various kinds – conjugal, extended, multi-generational, single parent, and incomplete. Most typical was the conjugal family, a married couple and their children, often living together with the parents of the husband or, less frequently, the wife. The household might also include the couple's married children and grandchildren. In my household survey, 43 per cent of households consisted of three or more generations living together. A household's size and composition depended primarily on its stage in the developmental cycle (Goody 1971 [1958]) and on wealth and occupation. The kinship ideology concerning household composition underscored the ideal of the extended, multi-generational family. Unmarried adult sons and daughters were never expected to separate from the parental household. Married sons usually resided with their parents so long as their children were small and not too many, and until they could afford either to build a house for themselves or to rent one.

Once the children were grown, if there were several of them, the older married sons and their families were expected to set up their own households. The parents were expected to support the construction of a separate house for each married, departing son. After marriage, residence followed the principle of patrilocality, so that women almost always moved to the house of their husband and his parents. When there was more than one son, the youngest was expected to stay with his parents after marriage and take care of them in their old age. This custom was open to negotiation and could be practised differently depending on the parental household's economic strategies and the sons' statuses and job arrangements, but it was seen as the

---

historical, as exemplified in travellers' accounts and in many ethnographic accounts of the Middle East, the Caucasus, and Central Asia. On competitive drinking and ostentatious hospitality in the Caucasus during the socialist period, see Mars and Altman (1987), and for a symbolic and social interpretation of the Georgian *supra*, or feast, during the post-Soviet period, see Mühlfried (2006).

traditional social security system for old age and was morally esteemed.[137] Later I describe occasional cases of elderly couples living alone, an arrangement that was considered improper and undesirable.

Genealogical kinship was traced cognatically (see also Pfluger-Schindlbeck 2005). Relations through both mother and father were important, although patrilateral kin were thought to carry more weight and influence, at least in principle. Affinal relations were close, especially those between a man and his parents-in-law and those between the parents of a husband and wife. The latter relationship was known as *quda*. In-law relations were considered to have been formal and prescribed in former times, and there was still some evidence of ritualised types of relationships, especially between daughters-in-law and fathers-in-law, as exemplified by avoidance behaviour and taboos in direct address and speech (see also Quliyeva 1997). In areas where people were thought to adhere more closely to tradition, daughters-in-law were said to avoid addressing their fathers-in-law directly. This custom has also been reported in other areas of the Caucasus and the Middle East (see Alekperov 1936; Yalçın-Heckmann 1991; Shahnazaryan 2005).

In-law relations were central to relations within the household as long as a daughter-in-law and her parents-in-law shared the same household. In such cases, cooperation and getting along, especially between the bride and her mother-in-law, were considered essential for the well-being and flourishing of the household and the multi-generational family.

Shifting from being a conjugal family to one encompassing two generations when sons married and brought their brides to live with their parents was considered a major, critical development in a household's life and composition. I was able to observe such a change in my host family, which, when I arrived in 2000, was a conjugal family with two adult sons. Towards summer that year, both sons announced that they had found girls whom they wished to marry, and two weddings took place (see Yalçın-Heckmann 2001). Such expansions of families into multi-generational ones were highly valued socially and culturally, as was evidenced by a frequently used expres-

---

[137] 'In Azerbaijani villages, according to popular custom, the youngest son is considered the legitimate heir, and thus the largest share of the property is transferred to him. This is called *minorat* [after the Russian term]. The youngest son is responsible for burying the father, paying off his debts, looking after the widowed mother, providing unmarried sisters with dowries, and paying for their weddings. If the father did not separate the households of his married sons, then after his death the eldest son becomes the household head, and arranging marriages for the unmarried brothers and sisters is considered his responsibility. Who will remain in the parental household is decided among the brothers collectively, and usually the decision favours the youngest son' (Quliyeva 1997: 89, my translation).

sion of good wishes to parents: 'May you see his [your son's] wedding [*toyunu görəsiniz*]'.

Parents were expected to organise and support their sons' weddings and settlement in the parental house, or else to provide for another house where the couple was expected to live. My host, Könül, and her husband, Həsən, were seriously concerned about providing their sons with equal means for starting new, married lives. In their case, the structural tension between male siblings in terms of receiving equal support, attention, and love from their parents – which might not be an issue when sons' marriages took place at intervals of some years – was felt socially and had to be carefully attended to by all parties involved. The brothers had to ensure that neither they themselves nor their future wives or wives' families placed unreasonable expectations on their parents. Könül and Həsən had to make sure that the sons received equal treatment and favours and that the whole family was treated with respect by the brides' families. Living arrangements immediately following the wedding parties had to ensure not only the equal treatment of both brides but also their partly normatively prescribed and ritualised incorporation into the new family.

The period immediately after a wedding was characterised by customary, ritualised visits between the affinal families and other relatives on certain days. During these visits, significant gift exchange, food sharing, and property exchange took place. The bride's dowry helped to establish her status and secure her recognition at the outset in her new husband's household and neighbourhood. In the case of my host family, only one bride could bring in her dowry, because of space limitations in the house. The other bride had to be treated specially, in order to compensate for the deficit concerning her status. Her dowry was still 'waiting' in her parental house, because the couple was to live for an indefinite time in Moscow, and her dowry – a bed set, several cupboards, sets of armchairs, a refrigerator, a washing machine, sets of porcelain, cutlery, crystal, vases, and so forth – could not be transported there. The bride who did bring her dowry to my hosts' house was expected to share her property with the other bride. This was an extra strain, because she also had to share it with her mother-in-law, who by tradition was expected to remain in charge of the household.

Although it was not expressed at the time, this tension was felt and apparently came up in later conflicts. Since 2000, the two brides had not lived together for any lengthy period. The couple in Moscow came nearly every summer for three or four weeks, but they did not have their own house or flat in Azerbaijan, and the parents could not provide them with one. This continued to strain the relationship between my hosts and their sons. The overlapping of the critical change from one type of household to another with the unequal distribution of household property affected the family's relationships and endangered the household's economic and survival strategies, as I discuss later.

Kin groups were sometimes neighbours in the rural community, but the settlement pattern did not allow for the consistent clustering of related people. As long as there was enough land on which to build houses, kin preferred to live close to one another. Otherwise, households within a neighbourhood were not necessarily kin.

Relations between neighbours, too, followed some moral and social norms. For instance, neighbours were expected at least to greet one another on the street and in other public spaces; this was the minimum expected sociality. When they did not, people interpreted their behaviour as evidence of hostility between them. Immediate neighbours might spend considerable time with one another, especially women and children, who shared much of their daytime. A child's first daily social contacts outside the household took place in the neighbourhood, and young girls and boys had their immediate friends there. Because kindergartens no longer provided preschool children with free food but demanded payment, parents did not send their children to kindergarten. Consequently, the street and the neighbourhood were the initial, primary social spaces for children until they began attending school.

For women who were not working in either the state sector (school) or an occupation such as trade, the neighbourhood and the street were the only morally and socially legitimate spaces available for spending time outside the household, and even that sociality was restricted according to age and marriage status. For instance, young brides were under stricter control concerning social relations such as visiting other women on the street than were young, unmarried daughters.

The household, then, was the social unit in which labour, food, and responsibilities were shared without specific, clear rules for immediate return and reciprocity (generalised reciprocity; see Sahlins 1972). The neighbourhood and friendship relations belonged to the category of sociality, in which reciprocity followed specific rules.[138]

Reciprocity and Exchange

When a strong expectation exists for the sharing of food, labour, and resources among kin and community, what sorts of rules apply to kin, non-kin,

---

[138] For further examples of community relations in postsocialist societies, see Ziker (1998), Ventsel (2005), and Heady and Gambold-Miller (2006).

neighbours, friends, and others concerning the obligations and expectations involved and the scale and timing of reciprocity?[139]

Expectations of reciprocity in my field sites were strong among kin, but their articulation depended on at least two elements. One was the kind of goods, resources (monetary or otherwise), or service being reciprocated. In general, this element was expressed in Azerbaijani as 'reciprocal help' (*qarşılıqlı kömək*).[140] The other was the element of time in reciprocity. I deal first with the kinds of goods or services being reciprocated.[141]

On the whole, goods being reciprocated were expected to be of equal value, especially in cases of reciprocity between kin, affines, neighbours, and friends, who were considered equals or structurally equivalent.[142] The less ceremonial and the more quotidian the reciprocal exchange was, the more the kinds of goods being exchanged were comparable. For example, when a neighbour sent food as a gift, for whatever reason, the family never returned the pot or the plate empty. The immediacy of the return and the equality of the things exchanged established and secured relationships and underscored the fact that the exchange had been completed. One received something and returned it immediately and unequivocally (following the principle of immediate return, à la Mauss and Sahlins).

Two basic ways of changing this equality and immediacy of reciprocation were to introduce the element of prestation into the exchange and to delay the return. The first way involved giving a gift to a relative or neighbour who could not immediately reciprocate in kind. A neighbour might send a sheep as a gift, for example, or someone might give his friend a mobile phone – both valuable items. The imbalance created in such an exchange must be interpreted within culturally extant categories of reciproc-

---

[139] Relations of reciprocity have been central themes in economic anthropology and have been elaborately discussed for both kin and non-kin by anthropologists such as Sahlins (1972), Malinowski (1978 [1922]), Godelier (1999), and Gudeman (2001). On gift exchange, the seminal work of Mauss 1990 [1924] revealed the work and meaning of gift-giving within the complexity of social relationships. My analysis here primarily follows Sahlins's model.

[140] *Kömək* means help or assistance. *Qarşılıqlı kömək* refers to mutual assistance and is not a neutral term such as *exchange*.

[141] Quliyeva (1997) noted that reciprocal help (*qarşılıqlı kömək*) existed more often between small households that did not have large networks of kin. Such families came together to help each other in agriculture and husbandry. Moreover, taking part in life-cycle rituals and helping others in times of misfortune were considered compulsory debts (*vacib borç*) of all rural families to all others. Although Quliyeva wrote that such reciprocal help existed earlier, at the beginning of the twentieth century, she also gave examples of reciprocal help in recent rural Azerbaijani society. My examples confirm the continued practice and norms of reciprocal help.

[142] On the significance of gift exchange and the meaning of gifts versus bribes in Central Asia, see Werner (2002).

ity, equality, and hierarchy. If a neighbour sends a sheep as a gift, it might be because he or she is appealing to an otherworldly authority or morality in a type of gift exchange called *ehsan*. The gift goes to the neighbour, but the addressee is God, to whom the giver is either appealing for a wish to be granted or paying for a fulfilled wish.

The other reason why a person might give an unreasonably large and expensive gift to a friend, neighbour, or relative is that he or she wishes to create a hierarchical relationship with the receiver. The excess of the gift as well as its embeddedness in a normative category of exchange creates pressure on the receiver to reciprocate. Because the gift cannot be reciprocated in kind, two possibilities emerge as responses. One is for the receiver to accept the superiority of the gift giver and accept the lower status in the hierarchical relationship (as between father and son, elder brother and younger brother, and *kirvǝ* father and *kirvǝ* son).[143] The other possibility is to introduce the element of time as a mediating factor to avoid or circumscribe hierarchy. The understanding is that one will find the time and the moment to reciprocate when one can. As long as this has not happened, however, one is in debt and dependency to the gift giver.[144]

One day I saw Semayǝ, the daughter of my host family's neighbour, busy sewing a blouse. I asked if she was making it for herself, and she replied that it was for the daughter-in-law of my host family. I was slightly surprised, because the daughter-in-law was neither of her age group nor her friend. At the time, Semayǝ was only a teenager and had been diligently trying to learn to sew by attending classes with a neighbour, which she had to pay for. Semayǝ's family had modest means; her mother, Meliha, whom I knew well, tried to make the best of her socially vulnerable position as a widow with three children by conducting petty trade and practising usury (see chapter 5). The fabric Semayǝ was using was certainly not the cheapest. The daughter-in-law of my host family was known for her taste for expensive clothes, which only her father could buy for her, even after her marriage. Semayǝ must have paid a substantial amount for the fabric. When I asked her why she was going to give it to the daughter-in-law as a present, she replied that this was her *pay* to her.

---

[143] A *kirvǝ* is the man who holds a boy during his circumcision ceremony, a role that entails a kind of ritual kinship. The families of the man and the boy refer to each other as *kirvǝ*, and the relationship is characterised by respect, ritualised exchange, gift exchange, protection, and emotional closeness. *Kirvǝlik* is commonly practiced in the Middle East and the Caucasus and has been described even across ethnic and religious boundaries, as in the case of *kirvǝ* relations between Muslim Kurds, Azeris, Orthodox Georgians, and Armenians in both historical and more contemporary contexts.

[144] For an analysis of the dependency created in such asymmetrical exchanges of money, gifts, and women, see Tapper (1981).

The word *pay* has a range of meanings in Azerbaijani. To begin with, it means 'a share of something', and in this sense it was used to denote the land shares (*pay torpağı*) that were distributed to rural settlers after the privatisation of former sovkhoz and kolkhoz land. But *pay* also means 'gift', as in both direct gift exchange and indirect and generalised exchange. That a gift always has this general meaning is expressed in the saying 'May you have lots of *pay*, gifts [*payın çox olsun*]', which is used when one receives a gift from someone. Semayə was referring to the generalised exchange notion of the word *pay* when she explained that she was sewing the blouse so that the daughter-in-law would have a share or gift from her ('*Onda payım ol-sun*'). The bride would have a share, a gift, from Semayə, which she would be expected to reciprocate sometime. In this way the relationship would have a long-term trajectory and an element of dependency, which Semayə hoped to use to further her own interests, to support her limited means and chances of accumulating social capital and relationships.

Marriage payments are an especially extravagant and complicated form of gift exchange (see also Comaroff and Comaroff 1980; Tapper 1981). During marriage rituals, kin, friends, and neighbours are expected to bring food, gifts for the trousseau (*cehiz*), and presents to include in *konça*s – trays given to the family of the bride at the time the bride is taken away from them in a ritual called *gəlin gətirmək*, 'to bring in a bride'. In such contexts, gift giving fulfils expectations between people with close relationships of kinship or friendship. The reciprocity is delayed, but maintaining balance in the exchange is important even if it takes place years later at another wedding, this time in the family of the person who originally gave the gift.[145]

The following passage is an excerpt from my field notes about gifts received during the marriage ceremonies for the two sons of my host family (for more on this example of marriage exchange and relationships, see Yalçın-Heckmann 2001). Besides the two marriage ceremonies themselves, three wedding parties were held: two at the respective brides' households, of a type called the girl's wedding party (*qız toyu*), and a final one at my host family's house, when the two brides were brought in, one after the other, in what is called the boy's party (*oğlan toyu*). On 19 October 2000 I wrote:

> The day after the first wedding [party]: yesterday morning I helped out a bit preparing *konça*s, the trays for the [second] bride's house

---

[145] Reciprocity in gift giving at weddings is a common practice in other parts of the Caucasus and among different ethnic and religious groups. See, for instance, Yalçın-Heckmann and Shahnazaryan (2005) on the trauma created when Armenian women who were neighbours regretted and mourned over unfulfilled reciprocal relationships when gifts such as carpets and bed sets could not be given to a beloved neighbour's daughter because their houses were destroyed and people were dispersed among different countries through war and forced displacement.

and her wedding party, the *toy*. The things given were two sets of clothes for Dilara [the first bride], two pairs of shoes, underwear, bath towels and soaps, cloth for her mother and sister, some night-gowns and morning-gowns, henna etc. Altogether, there were 11 trays [prepared by me and other women there] and three wedding cakes, one that was baked by Mila, Könül's younger friend and her neighbour Ulviyyə's bride, who is also Fahir's W, and the other by the daughters of another teacher, a friend of Könül's. The third one was brought in by Pəri, Könül's HZ [husband's sister], who paid to have the cake baked by someone who does such things quickly. At least three trays were brought in, one by Tamara, Könül's *kirvə*, an-other by Pəri, and another one by Hamiyyət, a teacher friend of Könül's. These were all women who also were attending the wed-ding in Dilara's place [her *qız toyu*].

Plate 7. Women dancing with the *konças*.

Exchanges of food, labour, and hospitality are most intensive among people who are related to each other in more than one way. The people just mentioned, who prepared the food and gifts to be elaborately packed as gift trays for the bride, were related to Könül in more than one way, and she expected them to show the closest, strongest support, materially, physically, and psychologically. Mila, for instance, was Könül's good friend, although she was much younger than Könül. Mila had studied to be a doctor but had never practiced, for she had married immediately after finishing her studies and moved to Russia with her husband, Fahir, who was then working as a trader. At the time of my fieldwork, Mila and her family had been living in Kazakhstan for some years, and she came to the village for vacations with her small children, staying with her mother-in-law, Ulviyyə, who was also a good friend and mentor of Könül's. Ulviyyə lived across the street from Könül and helped her in all matters, from daily chores to giving advice on Könül's economic affairs, such as how she should manage her land share or find a job for her unemployed son. Mila was doubly committed to helping Könül, as both her friend and the senior and much respected daughter-in-law of Ulviyyə.

There was another reason, too, for Mila's commitment to helping with the weddings. Her husband was considered to be earning well in Kazakhstan, and he certainly promoted that image by displaying his wealth during his home visits. Mila, therefore, could not simply give a modest gift but had to be one of the more generous gift givers, in order to maintain her status as the wife of a wealthy trader working abroad. Moreover, Mila was young and pretty and so was expected to take a leading role in all marriage prestations and visits, parties, and feasting ceremonies. By virtue of her relative youth and marital status, a woman like Mila was looked up to and admired by others as the epitome of success for a mature woman.

The other women who brought individual gifts or trays full of presents of various kinds (*konças*) were similarly women who had special, multi-layered relationships with Könül and her household. Tamara a good friend and elderly advisor of Könül's and also the widow of Könül's sons' *kirvə*, the man who had held them during their circumcision ceremony and was therefore a kind of godfather to them. The *kirvə* relationship exists not only between the boy and the man but also extends to relationships between the two families. The whole family of the *kirvə* is referred to as 'our *kirvə*', is treated with respect (*hörmət*), and is given special attention everywhere and all times. Throughout the boy's life, the family of the man chosen as *kirvə* has to give him and his family special, valued gifts, especially when he has grown up and is celebrating his second and major life-cycle ceremony (*büyük toy*, major feast). Thus, although Tamara's husband, who had been *kirvə* to both of Könül's sons, had died sometime earlier, she arrived for this part of the wedding festivities bringing the most suitable and generous gifts possible – a large cake as well as a tray full of presents for the future bride's

family. In this way she fulfilled people's expectations of her as the family's
kirvə and Könül's friend.

The biographies and motivations of other gift givers also reveal their
multiple ties to Könül and her family. Hamiyyət's and Pəri's relationships
with Könül can be seen as fulfilling formal and structural expectations, in
contrast to the personal relationship between Könül and the two women just
mentioned. Hamiyyət was a teaching colleague of Könül's and considered
herself a close friend. Könül was less committed to this collegial friendship
because she considered Hamiyyət to be rather calculating, someone who
cultivated friendships in order to strengthen her position in the teachers'
collective. She saw Hamiyyət's *konça* as an effort to impress and create
feelings of indebtedness rather than as a sincere gift.

Pəri was one of Könül's sisters-in-law, her husband's younger sister,
so it was her obligation to support and help in all phases of the life rituals of
her nephews. Pəri lived in another village in the *rayon* with her doctor husband and her own family. Although she could not come to help with the
wedding preparations and chores, she felt obliged to support the labour
involved in the preparations and was susceptible to criticism for failing to do
so. She brought a full *konça* to make up for what she could not do in person.
Könül's other sister-in-law, on the other hand, did not give a *konça* as a gift
but rather took on various prestigious chores of the wedding ceremony. She
was one of the women in charge of cooking and preparing the tables for the
major wedding party (*oğlan toyu*) in Könül's house, when the brides were
brought in. She also acted as *oğlan yengəsi*, the senior woman in charge of
helping the brides in the household of the grooms, Könül's sons. Thus she
contributed more in labour than in material gifts, although she and her family
also gave presents.

As a ritualised part of wedding celebrations, gift exchange shows that
even if gifts are prescribed and fairly standardised, the people who take part
in the exchange either display an existing relationship of kinship, friendship,
work colleagueship, or neighbourhood solidarity or are making a claim to
establish such a relationship. Gift giving is also related to labour exchange,
such that it may compensate for failing to provide labour for someone to
whom one is indebted. Finally, the gift may have the purpose of impressing
others and raising the status of the giver, who attempts to give it in such a
way (for example, in front of others) that it will be acknowledged and not
ignored.[146]

Exchange of labour and reciprocity in labour exchange is another important field of social relations. The case of Könül's sisters-in-law, just

---

[146] My analysis and findings here follow those of classic studies of gift exchange such as
those of Mauss (1990 [1924]), Weiner (1992), and Godelier (1999).

mentioned, shows that labour, too, is a resource that can be given as gift. Moreover, it is a resource that is used to fulfil social obligations in kinship, neighbourhood, and friendship relations. During Könül's preparations for her sons' wedding parties, she needed a great deal of help in the form of labour. Some of it had to be paid for, as in hiring a man to slaughter a calf and prepare the *kebab* for the guests, but not all the necessary labour could be obtained that way. Households must rely on their networks for labour support, and Könül's family had to plan carefully which kinds of labour support to ask of their friends, neighbours, and kin. I was told that some of the hired labour, such as the butcher and the musicians from the neighbouring city, who were friends of the younger son, had come at a special low price.[147]

Plate 8. Preparing a festive meal.

The careful planning of labour support follows the principle of asking help from people with whom one has steady, close relationships and with whom one wants to cultivate such relationships. If someone had been a

---

[147] Although the sons had a young male friend who could have done the job of butchering the calf, they did not ask him to do so, because he was to come as a guest of the wedding party and had already helped by putting up the tent for the party in the *həyət*.

friend but the relationship had cooled, an offer of labour help and its acceptance or rejection could determine the renewal or ending of the relationship.
One of Könül's friends, a teaching colleague, came to help with the food
preparation even though Könül had not asked her to do so. Könül found her
boastful and given to gossip, and there had been some dispute and cooling
off of their relationship. By coming to help without being asked, the colleague put Könül in a difficult position. She did not want to have her around
but could not tell her to go away. By accepting the unasked-for offer of
labour, Könül was forced to confirm that the relationship was still intact and
thus that she could be expected to offer reciprocal support in labour and
favours for the colleague.

Within a household, and later on between kin households, labour is
expected to be exchanged freely and upon need in a system of generalised
exchange. With the formation of households separate from the parental one,
the exchange of labour, gifts, and goods and the sharing and managing of
property become complicated, and the rules, increasingly disputable. The
case of Raqib, his parental household, and his brothers' households illustrates this complication. I met Raqib first through my household survey and
then a few times afterwards. I also knew neighbours and friends of his who
gave me further information about his situation.

Raqib had unclear and potentially strained relations with his father and
brothers, as was expressed in the course of our interview. I visited him at his
large *məhlə*, which he shared with his father's household, the two houses
being adjacent. The *məhlə* was being cultivated in herbs, the main cash crop
in that part of the village. Though Raqib's house was still under construction, he had moved into it with his wife and one child. The land on which to
build the house, as well for the garden, had been purchased by Raqib's father
for him and one of his brothers. The purchase was unregistered (I found no
entry for it in the village records), and Raqib seemed to feel uneasy about the
family's relationships regarding the property. During our conversation, he
said that he and his brothers exchanged labour reciprocally. But the father
was also present during my visit, and although Raqib was answering my
questions, the father seemed to have complete control over management,
earnings, consumption, and expenditures. He demonstrated this by loudly
explaining how much he had paid for the *məhlə*, how much the heating for
the greenhouse had cost, and what price the family was able to sell its tomatoes for. He said that those sales did not cover costs, and that was why the
construction of Raqib's house was unfinished.

Every time Raqib repeated that the *məhlə* and the house belonged to
him and his brother jointly, and that their father had bought the land for both
of them, another brother who was present during our conversation com-

mented that the property was only half Raqib's. Raqib got upset, saying that
he had put all his labour into the property, and if this was not enough, then
they should let him go away (*'Öyle isə qoyun gideyim'*). The tension inherent in this challenge and riposte was that a son was expected to give his
labour freely to his father and household, with no specific expectation of
return. In this case, Raqib had only labour to give and therefore continued to
be dependent on his father's household. In turn, the father kept Raqib under
his control by not clearly dividing the property and thus preventing his son
from making free decisions about the management of the property and the
labour involved in it. Raqib still had to obey his father as the manager of the
property. Since labour was his only resource, he could not give it as a gift,
but only as a dependent.

What Happens When Reciprocity Does Not Work?

Whereas reciprocity and equal exchange, whether in their generalised,
immediate, or delayed return forms, reproduce relations of equality and
solidarity (Sahlins 1972), other principles of social order such as gender,
generation, and age are related to hierarchical social relations. In this section
I deal with notions and relations of hierarchy as normative systems.

In Təzəkənd, gender and generational differences, the two basic crite-
ria for hierarchy, were partly articulated in rules of avoidance and deference.
Women and men were considered to be fundamentally different, and many
notions about this difference were similar to those found in many other
Middle Eastern and Caucasian societies.[148] The differences between the
genders were explained partly in biological terms (and could be due to either
divine creation or nature) and partly in psychological and social psychological terms. Women were expected to practice certain types of modest behaviour and to follow a modest dress code. Men were expected to socialise
primarily with other men and spend time mostly with them. Similarly, men
were socialised to be tough and 'manly' (*kişi kimi*), to be ready to challenge
other men and not give in to domination by their age mates, to dominate the
women and girls around them, to be spoiled during childhood, and to show
respect to elder men and women, especially kin. Although girls and boys
mixed with one another during their school years, they were nevertheless
expected to spend time with their own gender group, girls with their girl
friends and boys with other boys.

---

[148] The literature on gender roles and generational hierarchies in the Middle East is vast.
Some anthropological examples are Kandiyoti (1996), Abu-Lughod (1998), and Gilsenan
(2000). For an overview of contemporary discussions, see Moghissi (2005).

In addition to school, the neighbourhood offered a social space in which some contact between boys and girls was seen as proper or at least tolerable. In groups of age mates, girls and boys could see and talk to one another on the street. But the moment a private conversation took place between two young people who were not kin – even if it happened in a public space such as a plaza or the street – suspicion arose (often articulated in neighbourhood gossip) that an affair was going on between them. There-fore, passing time in groups was young people's most common behaviour, even for indicating interest in the other sex.

Such norms created ample means for adults to exercise control over young people's behaviour and social contacts, so girls and boys learned to choose friends among their neighbours, classmates, and kin in order to cultivate relationships of trust. In the company of such people, they had the freedom to meet members of the other sex, to socialise and have fun, to test their wit and cultivate humour, and to prove their prowess and beauty. Later, they could depend on this group for economic and political support. Socially, friendship (*dostluq*) between two people meant that they could visit each other in their homes, as long as they adhered to the rules of proper behav-iour, respecting their elders and following the rules for avoidance of people of similar age and the opposite sex.[149] Through friendships, one could culti-vate further social relationships and make partnerships of marriage or eco-nomic kinds. For instance, it was common to get to know one's future hus-band or wife in the household of a friend, where rules of cordiality and hospitality applied and where it was most acceptable for people of opposite sexes to be together.

The rules however, were also ambivalent and could cause misunder-standings and raise suspicions. For example, if a friend of a young man visited his household too often when an available young woman such as a sister or a cousin was there, it might raise suspicions that the friend was coming to see the girl more than the young man. This might lead to expecta-tions of courtship. Considerable social skills and mediation were needed to avoid rumours and misunderstandings.

Thus, I take gender and generation or age to be the two basic under-pinnings of hierarchy in rural society in western Azerbaijan. While basically following the pattern found in other Middle Eastern, Caucasian, and Muslim societies, gendered concepts in western Azerbaijan have been affected considerably by modernisation, education, and the introduction of salaried jobs in village economies, from as early as Soviet times. Girls are expected to go to school and perhaps learn a profession, depending on the family's

---

[149] For a recent study of a long-neglected social complex, that of friendship relations, see Schmidt et al. (2007).

socio-economic standing. They are allowed considerable freedom to pursue their educational and professional goals. Nevertheless, if a family has limited financial means, boys take priority for education and professional training. With Soviet modernisation and changes in rural economies, the most prestigious and broadly accepted professions for women in the countryside became teaching and working in the medical services as personnel and nurses. Women doctors, economists, and engineers, and those in administrative jobs, enjoy high esteem but are relatively rare among women from rural backgrounds. Such professional women do exist in rural settlements, but they may have urban backgrounds. Professional women in rural settlements enjoyed greater esteem and freedom of movement in Soviet times, especially when they were associated with high-prestige positions such as those in the kolkhoz and sovkhoz administrations. Such jobs no longer exist, and only teachers still enjoy esteem for having respectable, modestly paid female jobs. All women, with or without a profession, are obliged these days to conform to conventions of female modesty and chastity. How women were able manipulate such rules of gendered behaviour during socialist times is exemplified in the following story.

Looking through some old photographs in the home of Salimə, a doctor in Təzəkənd, I noticed that women's fashion in the 1970s had been the miniskirt. Salimə remembered those years with fondness and humour. She told how, as a young doctor at the local hospital at the time, she was put in charge of organising the female hospital workers for collective cotton picking, since all female medical personnel were expected to join other cotton picking brigades during the summers. The women were all wearing their everyday work clothes, mostly the fashionable miniskirts, when they had to interrupt what they were doing and go to the fields. They hated this work and felt humiliated toiling in the fields like 'unqualified people'. So Salimə went with her brigade of women but arranged with the party official in charge for her group not actually to have to pick cotton as long as they stayed in the vehicles or found a place to picnic near the fields. Other work groups noted their idleness, and someone complained to the head of the *rayon* party committee. Salimə defended herself by saying that all the hospital personnel were wearing short skirts, and it would have been immodest for them to bend over to pick cotton in front of men, who could have looked up the women's skirts. She claimed simply to have been worried about the chastity and good reputations of her colleagues. She would agree to do the work, she said, only if the head of the *rayon* party committee would bring his own female family members to pick cotton wearing skirts, too. Apparently her argument was persuasive, because those who were supposed to control collective female participation in cotton picking afterwards turned a blind eye to the hospital personnel.[150]

Gendered notions of chastity and the need to protect women and girls from shame and gossip could lead to difficult decisions concerning marriage. When young women had no parents, or when their parents belonged to lower social and economic status groups, they were especially vulnerable in marriage negotiations. The story of Hamza and Xulya, a young man and woman I knew from the neighbourhood, illustrates this vulnerability. Hamza, the son of Könül's best friend and neighbour, had been working in Kazakhstan for some years, together with his brothers. Könül's older son, my host in Təzəkənd, had joined him for a year to work in his business and earn some money. Hamza was under pressure from his mother, Ulviyyə, and sister to marry their neighbour's daughter, Xulya, so that, as they saw it, he would fulfil the ideal of establishing a family with an Azerbaijani girl (and leave his Russian lover). Xulya was under pressure to marry Hamza because she was an orphan and had no financial or other support from the rest of her family. I wrote the following entry in my field notes on 24 June 2001, after Hamza came back from Kazakhstan on a visit to his mother's household. Negotiations were going on for him to marry Xulya, and he was being talked about in the neighbourhood:

> The story of Hamza is going around. Dilara (Könül's daughter-in-law) and Könül were talking strongly against him. The fact that he never came here [to visit my host family] or had hardly any serious talk with Könül about [her son's] situation, and did not say when he was leaving, were all sources of concern for Könül. She said concerning him, '*Mənim ondan gözüm su içmir*', which means 'I do not trust him', after observing his behaviour. Then she was warned by Mila [Könül's friend and Hamza's brother's wife], who privately told her that Hamza was an untrustworthy person and that Könül's son should not spend a lot of time with him. Since then, Könül is determined to ask him [her son] to return in September. ...
>
> Mila reported to Könül that apparently Hamza had a fight with his mother and sister and has been throwing things around; probably this is all related to the story of the Russian woman. He [was supposed to have] said openly that he will keep the woman and that he has bought and renovated a house for her. His sister, when I confronted her with this problem and asked her what she would do to convince him to leave the woman, said that the woman wants only

---

[150] Forced cotton picking was common throughout the Soviet period. During Stalin's purges, deported people were the major labour force (see Pohl 2007). Forced labour by women and children continues to be practised in post-Soviet Uzbekistan (see Cannell 2007).

his money and she will prevail over her brother. When I asked her why he should not marry the Russian woman, she said two of her mother's brothers had married Russian women, and they no longer had any sense of family (*ailələri hamı dağıldı*). On the other hand, Könül and her husband, Həsən, say they feel sorry for the girl [Xulya], but no one has the courage to say they disapprove of the match as this will then be held against them by Ulviyyə and Hamza's sister. They also say the relatives of the girl were stupid (*ahmak*). This match is, in fact (*günah*), a sin as Xulya is a neighbour, Həsən and Könül say. Dilara thinks Xulya is bewitched, because a short time ago she said she would not marry Hamza because he is keeping a Russian woman. Now, however, Dilara says that whatever they say to convince her, it is as if she has been bewitched by a *cadı* (a witch): Xulya believes now that he will take her [in marriage] and that he will come back and marry her. The news we had from the children [of Hamza's sister], however, is different. [Accordingly] Hamza left for Kazakhstan on Friday and the family say he will come back soon for his wedding. The child says he will not come back.

In this extract from an even longer and more complicated story involving a few households on the street close by, with people who were kin, friends, work mates, and neighbours, the following social and moral values are highlighted and strategies and limitations displayed.

Xulya was considered a pretty and modest young woman with an unfortunate fate, since she had lost her father and later her mother before getting married. This is one of the worst misfortunes that can happen to a young person in Azerbaijan, and it always evokes pity and feelings of moral responsibility in people close to the orphan, whether they are kin or immediate neighbours. Xulya was under enormous pressure from the whole neighbourhood, with constant rumours and gossip going around about whom she should marry and why. At the time, Hamza's mother played a crucial role. She was considered a wise older woman, and her sons had all made their way to become traders in Kazakhstan. They were earning fairly well, although people also gossiped about whether or not the money was earned illegally. Hamza's mother had been a good friend of Xulya's mother and said that the two had long before promised each other to become *quda* (in-laws) by having their children marry. When Xulya's mother died after a short illness, Hamza's mother, Ulviyyə, said she felt an extra responsibility for Xulya, because she had promised this marriage to her mother.

Xulya, according to Azerbaijani marriage ideals, would have been a good match for a number of candidates, but there was no adult who would take seriously the responsibility for arranging a marriage for her. Her sisters wanted her to be married off as quickly as possible to a well-to-do household, and Hamza, according to this criterion, was not a bad prospect. But he also had serious drawbacks: he was ugly (as he was in Xulya's eyes, too), and he had a Russian lover whom he refused to give up. It was said that the girlfriend knew about his illegal alcohol trade and threatened to report him to the authorities, and that he was a drug addict and the Russian woman knew how to cope with it. Hamza, it was said, had invested all his earnings in buying property and luxury items for the woman in Kazakhstan, as well as taking her on holidays in Turkey.

In a way, marrying Hamza to Xulya was a last effort to restore his credibility and reputation. It might cleanse him of the rumours and accusations about dealing in illegal trade and cheating other young men from the settlement who came to work with him in Kazakhstan. It might help him heal from his addiction – which everyone knew about but no one spoke of openly – and separate him from his Russian woman friend, who had become, in the eyes of his mother and sister, the symbolic witch who had virtually possessed Hamza with her sex appeal and her cunning management of his illegal earnings. Not only Hamza's reputation but also his money needed to be rescued.

Hamza's mother could be said to have had a good, morally supportable motive for promoting the marriage in order to keep her promise to Xulya's mother. In the neighbourhood, though, general opinion underscored the mismatch between Xulya and Hamza: she was young and pretty; he was ugly and not at all interested in her. Yet although the adults in the neighbourhood felt strongly that the match was morally wrong, no one was responsible or courageous enough to challenge the appropriateness of the marriage, especially when it came to influencing Hamza's mother. No one wanted to risk having bad relations with her household, because she was considered an influential woman who controlled the economic and social strategies of all her children and even her son-in-law. The status she held through her combination of gender, generation, wealth, and strong personality made her immune to direct challenge.

Even her son could not resist her decision, and the story of Hamza and Xulya ended on a sad note. They did get married, though the wedding was another source of scandalous gossip, because Hamza did not come to the wedding party. Xulya travelled to Kazakhstan with her husband, and according to stories reported by other young men from the settlement who worked with Hamza, she was extremely depressed there because Hamza kept his Russian lover and spent his time primarily with her. Moreover, Hamza did not recover from his addiction but died from it only three years after his marriage. The last time I saw Xulya was in September 2005, when she came back from Kazakhstan to accompany Hamza, who was undergoing drug therapy at the time.

After his death, it was unclear with whom Xulya should live. She stayed temporarily in her parental house with her unmarried young brother. Her financial situation was also unclear, since her mother-in-law, Ulviyyə, had died more than a year earlier. The wives of her brothers-in-law as well as her sister-in-law wanted her now to take on the responsibility of looking after Ulviyyə's alcoholic husband. None of the sons wanted to do so – and being away working in Kazakhstan, they had a partially acceptable reason – and the daughter simply could not cope with him. So Xulya, although she had benefited by marrying into a family of some economic means (and displayed this with gold jewellery and fancy clothes) found herself reduced to dependency, commanded to take care of the young and the sick in the larger family group.

As Hamza's mother's role in this case demonstrates, age and generational differences are factors in maintaining hierarchical relations in the rural community. Young people are expected to obey those who are older than themselves, especially among kin and family members. This expectation is demonstrated in terms and forms of address and behaviour, such as lowering the voice when speaking, using certain terms of address, being properly shaved and dressed, and avoiding certain practices in the presence of the elderly. The head of the household is traditionally the oldest male – the father or, in a three-generational household, the father's father. Respect is shown in everyday behaviour such as not speaking loudly in the presence of older kin (something especially incumbent upon young women in the presence of older men), attending to the needs and wishes of the older generation, not speaking before an older person does, sitting in a composed way, and not smoking in the presence of elders. Again, these rules of respect for elders are common among many other traditional Middle Eastern, Caucasian, and Muslim societies.

Respect for older people is reciprocated in the form of protection and affection for the younger generation.[151] On the whole, children are always at the centre of adults' attention and are shown much love and affection. They are often spoiled, especially if they happen to be the first and only boy. Children's birthday parties are celebrated almost as lavishly as circumcision ceremonies and parties, especially the first birthday. Affection and attention to children are accompanied by the obligation to care for their needs, education, and life-cycle rituals throughout their lives. It is not uncommon, for

---

[151] For an elaborate study of intergenerational respect and affection among Turkish migrants and villagers, see Pfluger-Schindlbeck (1989).

instance, for older brothers to take full responsibility for providing for the education of younger brothers.

Earlier I mentioned Eldar, one of my hosts in Ismayilli. An agrarian economist and a founding member of an agrarian credit company, he had a hard-working wife, Leyla, and two teenage sons going to school. Eldar's father had died when Eldar was still a young man and his own children were small. Before his death, the father summoned Eldar, his six brothers, who were both younger and older than he, and his two sisters and made Eldar promise that he would always take care of his mother and siblings. This had serious consequences for Eldar's plans for life with his own family. It meant he had to find money to support the marriages of all his unmarried brothers and sisters, and he had to organise financial support for his mother, who had just started living on her own after Eldar's family separated from the parental household. He also had to finance the education of all his younger brothers and cover their living expenses during their military service.

Eldar had started building a house for himself, but in ten years he had managed to build only a single room and a foyer, a stall for the cow, and a toilet. Leyla told me how plans for a second room, a kitchen, and a bathroom had to be regularly postponed, especially because of the financial demands they faced when one brother needed money to study in Baku, another was studying in Gənca, a third had to be helped to buy a tractor, and a sister needed funds for her marriage. During my visit to Eldar in September 2005, he proudly listed all the financial support he had been able to give his extended family: he had bought a tractor, a combine, and an old van and distributed them among his brothers; he had helped one brother get married in Baku and found him a job (with the financial support of that brother's father-in-law); he had helped another brother find employment in the city of Ismayilli; and he had sent his own sons to a private boarding school to prepare them for university.

Surprisingly, in spite of all this, Eldar's prosperity was flourishing. He had expanded his herd of cattle, which Leyla took care of at home. The only thing remaining to be resolved was the construction of his house. He still could not find the means to build another room, which was badly needed now that his sons had grown up and had to share one room with their parents. Leyla added, good-humouredly, that the house probably would not be finished for years to come, since now they had to finance their own sons' education. Happily, at the time of my visit in September 2007, their financial situation had improved and stabilised. The couple proudly showed me their new land and the house they had begun building on it for their two sons, the elder of whom was attending university and expected to get married when the house was finished. But Eldar and Leyla still had not finished their own house.

Not all families and kin groups follow these norms of filial solidarity, but they are considered morally desirable and are valued by everyone. The most desirable behaviour is for kin to support one another at all costs. Even when someone is known to be cheating or being corrupt and making 'unjust' money, if the money goes to support family members, the behaviour is considered acceptable.

The brother of a young friend of Aydın, the son of my host family, had gone to Russia to earn a living. He later became an affine to my host family by marrying one of Aydın's cousins. Aydın and the brother of his friend Muhammed saw each other occasionally in Moscow, especially after the young wife, Aydın's cousin, arrived there. Shortly after the wedding, Muhammed's mother became seriously ill with kidney disease and needed expensive dialysis treatment. Muhammed, by then also in Russia, was supporting his family back in the village, even though the family had some income from the father's keeping cattle. The mother's treatment demanded about US$100 for each round of medication, an amount hardly anyone in the village could afford for long. When I asked Aydın how Muhammed managed to earn money in Moscow, Aydın said that in spite of the danger, Muhammed was working with a mafia group, stealing car parts from a car factory in another Russian town and transporting them to customers in order to make huge sums. Aydın resented the fact that Azerbaijani men working in Russia got involved in illegal trade and mafia business, but his friend's activities were acceptable to him because the money he earned was used to pay for treatments for his desperately ill mother back home.

Favour and Corruption

As Muhammed's case shows, obligations to care and provide for one's family can be used as excuses for corrupt and criminal behaviour.[152] Everyone in Təzəkənd had heard of cases in which a teacher received money for giving good grades, a policeman took money not to charge someone for driving without the required documents, or a customs officer valued a parcel at less or more than its real price in return for money. As long as the behaviour was practised by an outsider who was not a relative or friend, it was condemned as corrupt. The moment such behaviour was observed on the part of a relative or friend, it became understandable and even admissible.

---

[152] For a fine critical examination of the concept of corruption, see Gupta (1995). For further anthropological and international discussions, see Pardo (2004), Haller and Shore (2005), and Nuijten and Anders (2007).

The most common excuse for tolerating corruption was, 'After all, he or she is doing this for the children, the family, the brothers, sisters, or parents'. Another strategy for tolerating corrupt or immoral behaviour was turning a blind eye to it and not acknowledging it in public.

Aydın, who had been working as a vegetable trader in Moscow for some time, had incurred considerable expenses and large debts, which he did not tell his parents about. Some of this was due to his own and his brother's upcoming wedding expenses, and some was due to his business, which was risky and in which he was still an apprentice. Surely his parents suspected that he owed large debts, for they were astonished that Aydın could provide such large sums for the wedding expenses. Only his mother, Könül, shared her discomfort and suspicion with me, saying she was unsure how Aydın was earning such amounts and how he came to have such generous friends, lending him large sums for the wedding costs. Könül was worried that Aydın might fall into corrupt business activities and often sermonised to him on how important it was for him – the son of a village elder (aqsaqqal), a descendant of the prophet Muhammad's family (seyyid) in the village, and the son of parents who had always earned their living through honest means, as state employees – to stick to legal and morally acceptable ways of earning his living and not be tempted, like so many other young men, to make large sums quickly.

Aydın never challenged his mother when she preached to him, although he often told his parents stories about other people's dangerous mafia dealings and about how he himself had lost money that was intended for the agricultural producers in the village when his couriers were beaten up and robbed in the street. In a private conversation with me, however, he confessed that he could not earn his living in Moscow by being honest, and like other traders in the marketplace, he cheated with his scales. Once was caught, he said, and had to pay a fine. He did not have the courage to confess this to his mother.

Envy, Competition, and Conflict

For people in Təzəkənd, the biblical story of the brothers Cain and Abel is the historical and religious example of the roots of envy. Sharing resources and labour with kin is considered to be morally proper behaviour. Yet envy and competition between peers and siblings are common (see also Heady 1999). Brothers are thought to envy (paxıllıq, həsəd) or at least have the potential to envy each other, even when they are expected to support each other for life. Similarly, neighbours are thought to envy each other. Fear of being envied forces people to restrain themselves from consumption and ostentatious displays of wealth and fortune. Envy inclines people to be disparaging of others, and people who are incompetent or unsuccessful in their economic endeavours are thought to be easily envious. Indeed, many people told me that envy of others' success and wealth was an endemic problem of Azerbaijani society and was partly behind the strength of the Azerbaijani mafia in the Russian Federation.

Most important among kin is that the balance between who wins and who loses in sharing, reciprocity, and distribution of family and household resources is always open. Accounts are never settled, and expectations of support and sharing continue for lifetimes. Feelings of envy among peers, friends, siblings, and kin are routine as long as they remain within limits and are not articulated as bad talk, slander, or gossip (*qeybət*). Indeed, at times when family property is redistributed, as upon the marriage of a family's daughter, the daughter's siblings and friends are expected to admire and envy her trousseau when it is displayed for neighbours and guests. Young girls use this chance to compare the gifts and property being given as the trousseau and to inform themselves about the latest trends in consumer goods.

My neighbour's daughter, Leyla, who was about 16 years old, followed such trousseau displays with intense interest. She lived with her widowed mother and two brothers, one younger and one older, and she expected not have a large trousseau because her family was poor. She expressed her worries to me as we looked over the new furniture and other items in the trousseau of my host family's future daughter-in-law. Leyla admired the fashionable new china sets and crystal vases, as well as the many huge stuffed toys that came with the trousseau. Like other girls of marriageable age, she followed the fashions and knew the prices of all the common trousseau items. She compared the other young woman's trousseau with what her own mother had been buying and saving for her as a trousseau over the previous five years or more. She identified the items she already had and told me what her mother had paid for them. None of this conversation was a secret; other young girls, neighbours and kin, made the same comparisons and price estimates. The common attitude was that the more one got, the better. Young women always compared themselves with other women in terms of trousseaus, and never with their brothers, who might stand to receive land or a house upon marriage or through inheritance, even though women could inherit under civil law. Envying another girl's luck was acceptable as long as one did not exaggerate either praise or criticism of the other girl's trousseau.

Although the redistribution of property and wealth among families on occasions such as marriages is expected, sharing and the devolution of property are not always free of conflict, as the following story illustrates.

The head of my host family, Həsən, had inherited his parents' house and family plot because he had lived with the parents the longest and married last, even though he was the oldest of the three brothers. Traditionally it is the youngest brother who receives the parental house and garden. But Həsən said that before his parents died, he had helped build his next younger brother's house, and after their deaths, he financed the youngest brother's wedding and house and his remaining sisters' marriages. Normally, the brothers would have been expected to contribute money and labour when Həsən's sons got married, but to my surprise, neither of the brothers appeared for the wedding, no immediate member of their families came, and they contributed none of the labour or to any of the financial costs.

Həsən was not on speaking terms with one brother, who had a teahouse in the centre of town, because of an old conflict between them over the third brother, who had gone to work in Russia. His wife became the subject of rumours while he was away, and the source of the rumours was the wife of the teahouse-owning brother. Həsən claimed he warned that brother to control his wife and stop her from spreading such rumours, and this was the cause of the conflict between them. After some time, the brother in Russia came to collect his family, but the relationship between him and the rest of the family had died since then. That the brother in Russia took no part in any wedding finances or preparations was especially remarkable because family members working abroad are normally drawn into all wedding arrangements and in many cases cover most of the financial expenditures.[153]

Although people mostly followed social norms and traditions about how property should be distributed and inherited among brothers and sisters, exceptions to and disagreements over the norms were not rare. The possibility for reinterpreting the norms usually arose from the long-term character of reciprocal relationships. As in Həsən's case, if one son is closer to the parents, gets married later than the others, and stays with the parents in their house the longest, he may be designated to inherit the parental property. For a daughter to inherit the parental property is rare and happens primarily when there are no sons to inherit. Therefore, the case of Könül, my host in Təzəkənd, seems to have been an exception, although it is difficult to say how rare such a case might be. Her story illustrates the way conflict over property can lead to the break-up of even the closest and most obligatory kinship relations.

---

[153] Years later, after Həsən died, his brother in Russia died shortly after him. Despite all the social distance between Həsən's family and that of the brother, it was Həsən's sons who had to finance the mortuary rituals and funeral expenses for the dead brother.

Könül married into the village of Təzəkənd, where she had just started her professional life as a young teacher. She had an older brother, Behruz, whom she described as having made a successful career as an engineer in the Soviet system. He had moved to Moscow to study, stayed there to work, married a Russian woman, and lived there ever since. He was now pensioned. When Könül's parents got old and ill, she had to care for them, because according to her, Behruz never came back to Azerbaijan, least of all when they were ill and about to die. According to Könül, Behruz did not get along with his father and came only briefly for the funeral. He helped little with its expenses and left immediately afterwards for Moscow. Their mother was left to Könül's care, and Könül travelled back and forth between Təzəkənd and Gəncə on the *elektrichka* every day at that time to help and cook for her ailing parent. She did this in addition to her job, her party offices, and family and household obligations.

Könül remembered this extremely strenuous period with bitterness, because her brother scarcely helped her with anything, either financially or organisationally. Ultimately, when her mother became bedridden and had to be cared for in Könül's home in the village, she did so with the help of her neighbours and friends in the village. The mother died in Könül's house, but the funeral had to be held in Gəncə, where their father was buried. Könül said that Behruz came only at the end and contributed hardly anything to the funeral expenses. All this time, she had shouldered the responsibility of caring for their elderly parents when, according to tradition and moral expectations, this should have been the son's responsibility. Könül said that the parents, especially her father, had nearly rejected his only son, and it was only through Könül's reassuring intervention that he agreed not to change the ownership of the city flat where they have been living. Könül discussed this conflict with her brother and told him that she did not want to own the flat, but she begged her brother to allow her son to live there as long as Behruz remained in Moscow. Whenever he returned to Azerbaijan, he could have the flat.

When the parents died, according to Azerbaijan's civil inheritance laws, which date from Soviet times, she and her brother should have shared the inherited property. Behruz went on living in Moscow, and Könül kept the flat, partly renovating it for her younger son to live in when he got married. But the conflict between the brother and sister continued. Behruz accused Könül of greed (*açgözlülük*) for taking over the flat and not recognising his right to sole inheritance and ownership. Könül argued back that he had left for Moscow for his own career and life and never supported his parents in their old age, and she was only practising use rights and not ownership. In the end, the property was transferred to her, and after some years she sold it, when her now married son needed money in order to survive with his own trade in Moscow. The relationship between Könül and her brother seems to have completely broken down, and Könül had no other kin to rely upon, much like her brother who lived as a lonely widower in Moscow.

That civil laws and traditions do not always match has been well researched anthropologically (Mundy 2002; Moore 2005; von Benda-Beckmann and von Benda-Beckmann 2006). Civil laws may have been better applied in the urban context during the Soviet period; the rural context was apparently more resistant to the application of civil laws alone. Könül's case illustrates a rural context with urban extensions where she and her brother got caught up in the discrepant legal system and she was able to exploit the civil system despite her brother's traditional moral right. The traditional moral right, however, prescribes not only that the son should be the sole inheritor of the property but also that he should be the main person to take care of the aging parents. Thus Könül could argue, within the same system of moral imperatives, that her brother had not fulfilled his obligations as a son, and that she had had to assume his duties towards their parents. Such ambivalences arising out of long-term reciprocity in generational and family relationships allows for the breaking of the traditional rule of patrilineal transfer of property.

Concluding Remarks

Why people in some households in Təzəkənd were inclined towards or discouraged from engaging in the agricultural use of privatised property cannot be understood on the basis solely of statistical evidence about household strategies. One must also understand the values and norms that raise certain expectations and sometimes fulfil them. Solidarity among kin was a dominant ideology, prescribing certain generational and gender hierarchies and offering models of support and property exchange alternative to those of civil law and socialist practices. If the rule of civil law seems to have been firmer during socialist times, nevertheless gender, kinship, and generational values and practices were accommodated. In the postsocialist period, despite the opening up of some possibilities such as free travel, contacts abroad, free trade, and privatised land shares, the withdrawal of state support and, more important, the waning of the security that people believe they had under the former system forced people to rearrange their kin and social relations. Formerly, the parental generation could be fairly sure of having the means to provide their offspring with education, houses, and jobs – that is, they had security of reproduction.

What happens behind household walls – how family members cultivate emotional, intimate relationships but also follow economic and hierar-

chically prescribed relations of exchange and solidarity with one another –
influences decisions concerning property and the household economy. That
households in Təzəkənd have expanded spatially, such that migrants in
faraway Siberian and Russian places interact with their home locality, is
taken into account when expenses and resources are calculated and redistributed. Or family members are symbolically and socially cast out of the moral
community when intimate and economic relations between those who are
gone and those remaining behind become difficult to maintain. Families try
desperately to tie long absent sons to the community through arranged
marriages. Daughters-in-law who cannot be amply provided with trousseaus
are especially consoled so that envy does not ruin intra-familial relations.
Sons who cannot acquire houses and garden plots when they want to can be
kept under paternal control by restricting their access to the limited cash
capital of the kin group.

Chapter 7
Economic Strategies of Landless IDPs

Pir is a settlement of internally displaced persons (IDPs), most of whom were first displaced from the Azerbaijani district (*rayon*) of Laçın. I visited the settlement on a cold, sunny day in March 2000 and spent the day talking to Azmi and his family in their two-room dwelling. Azmi's wife, Gülüş, and their youngest son, Məhman, received my assistant and me in their sparsely furnished rooms: they had a table, some chairs, and a glass-fronted cupboard. Their bedding was neatly piled to one side. Azmi was not home when we arrived and had to be called back from herding sheep. While waiting, we conversed with Məhman, an unemployed university graduate from Baku. Gülüş stoked the wood-fired oven for us, and in the background we could hear the daughters of the family preparing tea. Before long, Azmi arrived. He was an elderly looking man in his mid-sixties, with a strong limp. He greeted us with a stern look as he entered the room.

By way of introduction, I explained to Azmi that I was a researcher with an interest in Kurds, that I had lived with and written about Kurds in Turkey, and that I wanted to learn about the Kurds in Azerbaijan. I said I had been referred to him by his brother-in-law, an important man in Baku with a university job and political ambitions, president of a centre for Kurdish people in the capitol. Listening to all this, Azmi replied in Azerbaijani to my few words of Kurdish, stating that his family were Kurds and did not try to hide it, but although they understood Kurdish, they no longer spoke it. From this modest beginning, we talked throughout the afternoon about a wide range of topics: the family's place of origin in Laçın *rayon*; the number of Kurdish villages that had existed there; the policy of naming the villages and registering people as Kurds during Soviet times; and finally, at length, about the family's flight from the Laçın district in 1992, during the war over the autonomous region of Karabakh, and their settlement in Pir, in the district of Ismayilli in northern Azerbaijan.

When I asked whether or not the family owned the fields around the settlement where they cultivated wheat and barley, Azmi could barely control his anger and frustration as he recounted his quarrel with the authorities. I could feel the intensity of his anger as he told me how he had had to fight for the IDPs' right of access to fields in and around Pir. He had lobbied the representative responsible for the settlement of IDPs, additionally contacting acquaintances among some officials and bureaucrats of the *rayon*. When he tried to plead the case for IDPs' access to farmland, the assistant governor retorted that the fields had been privatised and distributed to other villagers, and if the IDPs wanted land, they should 'go and get the land where their ancestors are buried' (in Azerbaijani, *atalarının basıldığı torpaqlardan alsınlar*).

Azmi was so infuriated by the assistant governor's reply that he had to be physically restrained from getting into a fight with the indifferent bureaucrat. Undaunted, he pursued the IDPs' claim with the support of local and national representatives of the IDPs, taking his protest to the governor's office and eventually writing petitions to the office of President Heydər Əliyev.

My conversation with Azmi and his indignation at being so callously dismissed – on top of being denied access to land – made me reflect on the meaning of land in a comparative sense, especially as I was already investigating reasons for under-cultivation and under-use of agrarian land in my first research site in Azerbaijan, Təzəkənd. Up to that point, my primary focus in Təzəkənd was on the economic value and use or non-use of agricultural land and on trying to clarify the economic and social limitations on agricultural activity by individuals and households. Azmi now offered a different discourse on land: he was alluding to it as territory and homeland, and its economic use as a resource was being contested. I was already interested in the effects of war, state and international politics, and displacement on notions of land and practices of land use (see Yalçın-Heckmann, Behrends, and Leutloff-Grandits 2003). Azmi's story and the field site of Pir offered an opportunity to look into those effects again and to compare the situation in Pir with that in Təzəkənd.

I believe it is important to discuss the situation of IDPs in relation to property in Azerbaijan because a large proportion of IDPs (*məcburi köçkün*) and refugees (*qaçqın*) still exists there. Estimates for the two categories together total nearly 1 million people, out of a total Azerbaijani population of somewhat over 8 million. State and political discourses on territory, especially in relation to values and practices pertaining to agricultural land and rural property in Azerbaijan, are also important. Not only is the number of displaced persons in the country large, but the land under Armenian occupation is estimated at nearly 20 percent.[154] Between 1988 and 1994, Azerbaijan lost territory, received refugees, and had to accommodate the displaced in other parts of the country. The Armenian population, too, left or fled between 1988 and 1992, and emigration by Russians and Jews increased after the end of the Soviet Union.[155] In short, some land was lost as Azerbaijani territory while other land became available through the eviction of the Armenian population. How this affected agricultural land tenure, property regimes, and production systems is the core issue to be explored here.

Also implicated in the function of land as territory or economic resource are citizenship practices in Azerbaijan.[156] IDPs are all Azerbaijani citizens, but they have been structurally and legally hindered from receiving privatised land shares. Their obtaining of rights to own privatised shares has been 'postponed' until the lost territories are recovered. This closely allies the economic survival of IDPs with political debates in Azerbaijan on Karabakh, on occupied territories, and on the difficulties of re-settling IDPs. With their fate linked to the outcome of the Karabakh war, IDPs constitute visible and articulate lobbying groups in governmental politics. In this they are similar to groups such as veterans' associations and families and mothers of martyrs. Unlike many non-displaced villagers, IDPs do have special, if limited, access to state resources.

The case study I present here should not be read as representative of the situation of all IDPs in Azerbaijan. Rather, I use it to explore the relationship between land as resource and as territory. Without further comparative studies of IDPs and refugees settled in other climatic and agricultural zones, it is difficult to make a general statement about IDPs' 'hunger for land'.

In the rest of this chapter, I discuss first the status of IDPs from administrative, legal, and organisational points of view. I then deal with the ethnic category 'Kurd', to which more than half the IDPs in Pir belong,

---

[154] Veliyev and Asadov (2003: 207) provide the figures of 700,000 internally displaced persons and 20 percent of Azerbaijani land under occupation, not including the disputed territory of Karabakh. According to UNHCR representative Vugar Abdusalimov, there were approximately 620,000 IDPs, 200,000 Azerbaijani refugees from Armenia, and 50,000 Meskhetian Turks in Azerbaijan in 2000 (interview, 3 April 2000).

[155] Perevedentsev (1993: 26) noted that Russians had been leaving Transcaucasia since the 1960s, and Azerbaijan specifically since the 1970s. In 1989, Russians made up 5.6 per cent of the population of Azerbaijan, the second smallest proportion among the former Soviet republics, after 1.6 per cent in Armenia.

[156] The case of IDPs in Azerbaijan is strongly indicative of the significance of legal and political norms and practices concerning property (von Benda-Beckmann, von Benda-Beckmann, and Wiber 2006: 16–19). For similar analyses of citizenship practices and property regimes, see James (2006) and Leutloff-Grandits (2006).

because ethnic discourses and politics have an effect on local and broader strategies adopted by IDPs. I recount the history of the settlement in Pir as provided by the narratives of IDPs and other settlers and then present data on land use and other economic activities by settlers in Pir. Finally, I offer a comparative discussion of why IDPs are 'hungry for land', what they do to satisfy that hunger, and how successful they are in juxtaposing land as territory and as an asset.

The Category of Internally Displaced Persons (IDPs)

By general definition, internally displaced persons are people who have become displaced within the boundaries of a state because of war or threat of war and violent conflict.[157] Owing to the nature of displacements, to the similarities between refugees and IDPs in terms of their flight and living conditions, and to the sheer number and scale of displacements, IDPs have been a matter of concern to the United Nations High Commission for Refugees (UNHCR) since the 1970s. Beginning in the 1990s, the UNHCR and the United Nations (UN) took several decisions that would allow the UNHCR to take responsibility for IDPs, as it does for refugees, with the consent of the state concerned.[158] The rationale for the UNHCR's getting involved in helping and protecting IDPs has been explained in reference to the similarities between 'the causes and consequences of their displacement and humanitarian needs' and those of refugees and the fact that 'had they crossed an international frontier, [they] would have had a claim to international protection'.[159]

The Republic of Azerbaijan, following international standards, legally defines an internally displaced person as follows:

A forcibly displaced person (someone displaced within a country) is a person who has moved to another place within the territory of the Republic of Azerbaijan (RA), being forced to leave his or her permanent residence due to military attacks or natural or technological disasters. A citizen of the RA who arrives in the RA after being

---

[157] Forced displacement is a broader category encompassing people who are re-settled because of development projects, natural catastrophes, and the like. Anthropological studies of displacement have indicated the need to see it 'as an outcome of a combination of causes involving a multiple set of factors' (Shami 1994: 3). See also Malkki (1997) and Pilkington (1998).

[158] For a discussion of the history of the UNHCR's involvement with IDPs, see Mattar and White (2005).

[159] 'Internally Displaced Persons: The Role of the United Nations High Commissioner for Refugees', UNHCR position paper, Executive Committee of the High Commissioner's Program, 20 June 2000, p. 3.

forced out of his or her permanent residence in another country under conditions similar to those that apply to refugees can be granted
IDP status by the relevant executive authority [my translation].[160]

A 2001 amendment to this law stipulated that IDPs and refugees arriving from Armenia who had not so far been permanently re-settled were to be
treated comparably to IDPs from within Azerbaijan:

Article 2: Forcibly displaced persons and persons comparable to
them.

Those persons who have had to leave their permanent residence
within the territory of the RA due to military attacks from outside,
occupation of territories, or having to live under constant gunfire are
considered forcibly displaced persons for the purposes of this law.
Those persons who have arrived in the RA because they had to leave
their permanent residence as a result of ethnic cleansing in the Republic of Armenia or in other countries and have not (as yet) been
permanently settled will be treated as having a status comparable to
that of forcibly displaced persons [my translation].[161]

Some international legal observers have commented that treating IDPs
and refugees as forcibly displaced persons is problematic[162], and I believe it
hinders the effectiveness of certain aid policies. The UNHCR has been
reducing international relief aid to Azerbaijan since the late 1990s and has
been encouraging the Azerbaijani government to implement settlement
policies for refugees and IDPs.[163] According to the UNHCR, the category
'refugees' in general includes, apart from refugees of other nationalities,
such as Afghans and Chechens, Azerbaijanis who were displaced from

---

[160] 'Law of the Azerbaijani Republic on the Status of Refugees and Persons Forcibly Displaced within the Country, 21 May 1999, part 1, article 1 [Qaçqınların və məcburi
köçkünlərin (ölkə daxilində köçürülmüş şəxslərin) statusu haqqında, Azərbaycan Respublikasının Qanunu, 21 may 1999–cu il, № 668–IQ, I fəsil, maddə 1]'. It is important to note
that according to this article, in order to receive the status of IDP, an Azeri person who has
been displaced from another country must possess Azerbaijani citizenship.

[161] 'Law of the Azerbaijani Republic on social protection of forcibly displaced persons and
persons comparable to them, May 21, 1999; additions and amendments, 15 November 2001
and 23 November 2001 [Məcburi köçkünlərin və onlara bərabər tutulan şəxslərin sosial
müdafiəsi haqqında, Azərbaycan Respublikasının Qanunu, 21 may, 1999–cu il, № 669–IQ,
Əlavə və dəyişikliklər: 1, 15 noyabr 2001, N 214–II QD, q.m.t. 1.01.2002; 2, 23 noyabr
2001]'.

[162] Veliyev and Asadov (2003: 276, 329–330) note that the concept of forcibly displaced
person in the national legislation 'goes beyond the notion of IDP insofar as it is also applica-
ble to refugees'. They consider this a weakness in the law, causing confusion, and believe it
would be better to have separate laws for IDPs and refugees.

[163] Interview with Vugar Abdusalimov, the local officer of the UNHCR in Baku, 3 April
2000.

Armenia between 1988 and 1991. The Azerbaijani refugees from Armenia are generally considered to be economically and structurally well integrated into the Azerbaijani state, because they have had support not only from the state (in part from the former Soviet state) but also from their kin. With the aforementioned amendment, their status was made comparable to that of IDPs.

People who were displaced during the Nagorno-Karabakh war, between 1992 and 1994, make up a much larger group than refugees per se. Many were from rural backgrounds and regions. Needing urgently to be settled, many received inadequate public housing in Baku and several other cities. Since 2000, all the refugees and IDPs have been provided for and supported by the Azerbaijani State Oil Fund. Among other things, this fund pays for new housing construction and provides food rations for refugees and IDPs (*Azerbaijan International* 2002). A careful reading of the quarterly online journal *Azerbaijan International* shows that the majority of housing that has so far been built for forcibly displaced persons has gone to people who fled Armenia before the Karabakh war, and thus it has been available only to some IDPs. The latter are returnees to two provinces that had been under Karabakh-Armenian occupation but have been partly reclaimed by Azerbaijani forces (as has happened in Fuzuli *rayon* and some parts of Ağdam) (*Azerbaijan International* 2002). Hence, through legislation and by placing the Azerbaijanis from Armenia and IDPs together and labelling them forcibly displaced persons (*məcburi köçkün*), the government is able to manipulate and disguise who genuinely gets help and who is settled permanently. It could be argued that in this way the government is fulfilling UNHCR recommendations by settling the forcibly displaced persons while underscoring the rights of IDPs in the arena of internal politics by claiming to pursue the recovery of lost territories for them.

Legislation in Azerbaijan also links the legal status of forcibly displaced persons and internally displaced persons to their permanent settlement status, whether they are settled in their original place of residence or another location. An internally displaced person loses his or her IDP status when 'he or she returns to the place of his or her former residence or is provided with other and equivalent accommodation in the same region; [or when] the abovementioned does not occur and he or she is provided with a proper accommodation and residence by a special decree of the state' (my translation).[164]

Conditions for Azerbaijani IDPs returning to their former places of residence depend on state and international politics – that is, whether and

---

[164] 'Law of the Azerbaijani Republic on the Status of Refugees and Persons Forcibly Displaced within the Country', 21 May 1999, part 3, article 14.

how peace is achieved in the Nagorno-Karabakh conflict and whether the state can, through intervention, provide IDPs with equivalent residence and property in the same region, as has been the case in parts of Fuzuli *rayon*, where some returnees have been re-settled. State bodies could decide to settle IDPs by special decree, which would mean politically that the Azerbaijani state accepted the loss of its territory. State officials clearly make the connection between the settlement of IDPs and international political interests. In 2002 I interviewed Əli Həsənov, then the vice prime minister and head of the State Committee for Refugees and IDPs, who expressed this relationship as follows: 'If we were to settle and integrate all the IDPs within Azerbaijan, how could we legitimately struggle any further for regaining the lost territories?'[165]

State involvement in the welfare of IDPs can be seen further in the state's support for their employment. According to existing legislation:

> State bodies responsible for employment issues shall assist refugees and IDPs in job seeking. The restoration of the work record shall be implemented in the order established by the legislation. If away from the job, because of improving his/her professional training or mastering a new profession, a refugee or IDP shall be paid an average salary at the new place of employment for the new specialisation. The difference in salary for the full period of the job because of changing the specialisation without being apart from the job shall be paid to the refugee or IDP by the firm or organisation, which has signed a labour agreement with him/her.[166]

In one respect, Azerbaijani laws reflect the Soviet system of guaranteeing equal treatment for IDPs, because they have had to flee their homeland and lose their employment. Yet even if the law stipulates that state authorities should assist IDPs in job seeking, IDPs have no employment priority, in the sense of affirmative action, for jobs that are also sought by other unemployed people. And if IDPs have no personal networks of patronage and protection (*arxa*, literally, 'back', meaning 'backing someone') in the areas where they are settled, then they have little chance of finding employment in either the state or the private sector.

In Pir, some IDPs had indeed been provided with training programmes in the mid-1990s. Azmi's eldest daughter, Sevim, for instance, received some training as an assistant nurse (*medsestra*), learning how to take care of the ill, administer first aid, measure blood pressure, and give injections. She

---

[165] Excerpt from notes taken during an interview in Baku on 10 October 2002.

[166] 'Law of the Azerbaijani Republic on the Status of Refugees and Persons Forcibly Displaced within the Country', 21 May 1999, part 3, article 16. English translation provided by the IOM Office in Baku, courtesy of Alovsat Əliyev, September 2005.

had hoped to find a job at a health centre, but because the family had only one car and daily transport to any health centre was difficult and costly, she remained without a proper job and only gave occasional injections in the settlement for a modest fee. Məhman, Azmi's youngest son, was attending university while his family was settled in Pir and re-joined them after he finished his degree. Despite his father's many efforts, involving pleas to local administrators and substantial bribes to some of them, Məhman never found a job in the city or the locality and was frustrated by the fate of being a university graduate reduced to working as a shepherd. The only state employment available in Pir was at the school for IDPs. There, the teachers all had salaries according to the category in which they would have fallen in their original place of settlement, the *rayon* of Laçın. In the end, Məhman found income supplementary to that from herding as a teacher in the settlement.

Azerbaijani laws concerning refugees and IDPs also declare the state's responsibility for providing dwellings for them: 'The provision of refugees and IDPs with dwellings shall be implemented by the relevant authorities. ... In accordance with the desire of the refugee or IDP, she or he may be given a loan bearing no interest for ten years and, depending also on her or his place of residence, a land plot within a determined area' (my translation).[167] The second sentence of this article is important, for it guarantees that the state will take responsibility for providing not only lodging but also a plot of land, of which the size and location will be decided by the local executive authority. This was the central argument of the IDPs in Pir for occupying the agricultural land around them, a point I discuss later.

It is clear that on the legislative level, the state assumes the role of protector and guarantor of the economic and political well-being of IDPs and forcibly displaced persons and seeks to assist them in accessing jobs, lodging, and economic survival. In addition, the status of IDPs and forcibly displaced persons is linked to their own strategies of access to permanent settlement and property ownership. Later in this chapter I look at the ways IDPs in Pir make use of legislative acts and develop their own strategies of political and economic survival. In the next section I deal with another important aspect of IDPs' political life in Pir: the significance of ethnic affiliations and local politics.

---

[167] 'Law of the Azerbaijani Republic on the Status of Refugees and Persons Forcibly Displaced within the Country', 21 May 1999, part 3, article 17.

Ethnicity in Pir: Kurds and Others

More than half the households in Pir identified themselves as Kurds. Kurdish identity was based on stories of origins and settlement and on the emic and etic perspectives of identifying oneself as such. In our conversations about why people identified themselves as Kurds, Azmi frequently said, 'Those who deny their origins are scoundrels [*aslını inkar eləyən, haramzadədir*]'.[168] For him and others in his kin group who had the same village background, being Kurdish was simply acknowledging their common origins. Use of the Kurdish language was not expected for this self-identification, although quite a few of the adults claimed that they at least understand it. Broadly speaking, they considered themselves to share a common identity with Kurds in Turkey and in other parts of Azerbaijan, but they were also keen to emphasise their differences. For instance, they criticised the Kurdish radio broadcast from Baku (which incidentally they could not receive in the settlement) and the Kurdish alphabet books they had received from the Kurdish cultural organisation in Baku so that teachers could teach children Kurdish after school, because they were in a different dialect and accent that they did not understand. However, I never heard the Kurds speak Kurdish among themselves, and they admitted that they spoke it rarely, and only in situations when they did not want a third party to understand what they were saying.[169]

The constitution of the Republic of Azerbaijan recognises the existence of ethnic groups in Azerbaijan and guarantees them equal rights and non-discriminatory treatment. Gidaiat Orudzhev (Hidayət Orucev), policy advisor for nationalities affairs for the Azerbaijani state, has quoted the 1995 constitution as recognising the rights of every citizen, 'regardless of race, nationality, religion, language, gender, origin, property status, social position, convictions, and affiliation to political parties, trade unions and other public organizations' (Orudzhev 2003: 139). He cites 20 national minorities, including Kurds but not Armenians (Orudzhev 2003: 140). These 20 minorities are said to have received financial assistance from the state on several occasions 'and do not have to pay rent on facilities where their associations are located'. Some groups, including the Kurds, have radio programmes and newspapers and other publications in their own languages. In Parliament, the nationalities are represented at the level of minister and deputy minister. A

---

[168] *Haramzadə* is a word from the Muslim context suggesting the violation of the Islamic prohibition of engaging in acts involving things, persons, and objects that are *haram*, religiously forbidden. In everyday usage it means 'scoundrel' or 'crook'.

[169] This may be why they never spoke Kurdish when I was present, because many knew or thought I could understand their Kurdish. The only exception to this was an elderly man in the settlement, a retired bus driver and self-taught poet who wrote poetry in Kurdish and Azerbaijani and who had been teaching his granddaughter some Kurdish.

Consultative Council of National Minority Representatives functions under the Azerbaijani state nationalities policy adviser, Orudzhev himself. He expresses the opinion that the preservation of ethnic identity enriches Azeri culture and that ethnic minorities should have cultural autonomy. At various conferences, 'all the republic's minorities were represented. ... In this way, Azerbaijan, which is a multiethnic society, is showing the whole world its attitude toward its national minorities, and they can demonstrate to the world community their true status in a democratic state, which keeps a constant and careful watch over them' (Orudzhev 2003: 140).

Orudzhev's is the formal political position, but in fact ethnic relations have recently been problematic, and ethnic minorities have had to reassert their place in the new Republic of Azerbaijan. Besides the ethnic cleansing of Armenians from Azerbaijan in 1988–1992 because of the tensions and military conflict over Nagorno-Karabakh, other ethnic tensions have involved Talish speakers in the south of the country and Lezgis in the north. Moreover, Orudzhev provides no explanation of how representation by minority delegates at conferences is achieved or guaranteed. He articulates the official interpretation of the limits of political representation as follows:

> With respect to the activity of the national minorities, it should be kept in mind that one of the ways to encourage separatism is to form political parties and movements based on national characteristics. But there are basically no such trends in Azerbaijan. The activity of the Armenians in Azerbaijan is the only exception[170], which is supported from the outside, primarily and largely from Armenia and from the Armenian lobby abroad. ... The leaders of the national minorities in Azerbaijan are against any such incautious and hasty decision [such as wanting to form their own political parties] and operate within the framework of the national-cultural societies, hand-in-hand with the country's government and social structures (Orudzhev 2003: 141-142).

Orudzhev further emphasises that the government cares for and supports the well-being of minorities, giving examples of famous non-Azeri artists, scientists, and other prominent people from Azerbaijan to demonstrate what tolerant people the Azerbaijanis are. These statements from a state bureaucrat in charge of minority affairs suggest how ethnicity is implicated in many other political, economic, and historical issues in contemporary Azerbaijani society.

Elsewhere, Daniel Müller and I have argued that the existence of Kurds as an ethnic minority in Azerbaijan today relates to six factors: their

---

[170] Up to this point, there is no mention of Armenians in Orudzhev's article under any topic – available schools, publications, broadcasting, and representation.

early and long-lasting linguistic and cultural assimilation; socialist policies concerning ethnic and national minorities; developments in postsocialist Azerbaijan; the Nagorno-Karabakh war; the existence of Kurds as a marginalised minority among other ethnic groups; and the economic decline in postsocialist Azerbaijan, which rendered ethnic concerns less important than they once were (Müller and Yalçın-Heckmann 2004: 153). The ethnic identity of the Kurds in Pir can be seen in connection to all of these factors.

First, the area they came from has been affected by the long, gradual assimilation of Kurds into Azeri identity (see Müller 2000, 2002; Müller and Yalçın-Heckmann 2004). Intermarriage and religious affiliation between Shia Kurds and Azeris seem to have been both cause and effect of this process. Second, the Kurds in this region were subjected to different policies of recognition and denial throughout the Soviet period (Müller 2000). Even if memories of those policies linger among some elder Kurdish IDPs in Pir – such as recollections of having a Kurdish newspaper published in Laçın or having been registered as Kurds after political lobbying of Moscow by Azerbaijani Kurdish leaders – such factors have not led to any active political ethnic movement.[171] Many are keen to emphasise other aspects of their economic and social lives in their place of origin. For instance, they all took part in domesticating the Soviet economy of animal husbandry by 'privatising' sheep and cows and keeping them in kolkhoz herds in the mountains and in winter pastures of Ağcabədi (see map 1).[172]

The Kurds seem neither to assign any specific identity concerns to their Soviet history nor to claim any special status because of their ethnic identity in post-Soviet Azerbaijan. Rather, their situation highlights the common fate of post-Soviet economic decline and displacement, because of the war over Nagorno-Karabakh and the struggle of the Kurds, along with all the other ethnic and Azeri groups, to return to that region. As Müller (2000, 2002) has shown, ethnic politics and self-assertion naturally link to overall political concerns and even to the international politics of Azerbaijan, yet the small number of people who identify themselves as Kurds in Azerbaijan present Kurdishness not as a dominant, assertive ethnic identity but rather as

---

[171] People also remember local involvement in international Kurdish politics. Azmi recalled that 'Barzani's Kurds' were exiled from Iran and subsequently were accomodated by the Soviet government in various kolkhoz and sovkhoz buildings in their area. See also Müller and Yalçın-Heckmann (2004: 170 note 41).

[172] One of the most valuable pieces of ethnographic writing on the Kurds of this region is the work of Alesker Alekperov (1936). He said that although animal production was collectivised in 1928–1933, some nomadic Kurds were still moving over the mountains between summer and winter pastures (pp. 37–39), similar to the movement in the late socialist years. Alekperov also noted that almost all the Kurds spoke Azerbaijani and not Kurdish. I thank the late Atiga Izmailova and Gesine Koch for translating this text for me.

one among other minority identities, having close links and shared values with the majority population (see also Cavadov 2000: 135–166).

The Rural Settlement of Pir

Visitors to Pir are struck by how sparse its vegetation is. The absence of trees and vineyards resulted from the grape vines having been cut up and destroyed after the dissolution of the local sovkhoz, particularly when the vineyards were privatised in the midst of the cash and energy shortages and cold winters in the second half of the 1990s.

Plate 9. Fields around Pir.

The history of Pir's population reflects the changing composition of the settler communities. Administratively, the settlement of Pir resulted from two Soviet agricultural farm structures: the hillside and large animal sheds were part of a livestock kolkhoz that was turned into a livestock farm (*firma*) in the late 1980s. The arable land belonged to a sovkhoz that specialised in growing seeds and also had vineyards in this location.

Since 1988 the population of the settlement and the locality has changed dramatically. As ethnic tensions arose from the dispute over Nagorno-Karabakh and ethnic cleansing began in both Azerbaijan and Armenia, the Armenians, who lived close to the vineyards in which they worked, left the area. Other stories of flight and deportation are inscribed in Pir's history, too. Ethnic Lezgis, the main national group of Dagestan, had been living there since the 1930s, when they fled Stalin's collectivisation in Dagestan.[173] Around 1988–1990, when the Armenians left the area, some Azerbaijani refugees from Armenia were settled there. After 1990 the locality received other groups of deported peoples. Meskhetian Turks arrived from Uzbekistan.[174] Azeris arrived from Georgia in the early 1990s and rented some of the houses of the Meskhetian settlers, who are still said to be the owners of these few houses.[175]

One reason for settling the refugees in Pir must have been the exodus of Armenians from the area, as a result of which land and houses became available. There was also the state farm, where some grapes were still being grown and the settlers could be employed.

The IDPs of the Karabakh war were settled in Pir in stages. My host, Azmi, and his kin group came first, and later some of their neighbours and members of their larger kin group arrived from their village in Laçın district. Azmi recalled that in 1992, after having spent time in the traditional winter pastures of Laçın, he started looking for a more climatically suitable place for the animals in summer and ultimately found it in Pir, with the advice of a police director of the *rayon* who was a good friend of Azmi's brother-in-law in Baku. Sheep, goats, and some horses arrived from the Laçın *rayon* along with the people. Mostly the property of the livestock kolkhoz in Laçın, they were divided among the IDPs partly through the privatisation and agrarian

---

[173] Only the former, early residents of the locality around Pir, Lezgis and Armenians, are represented in the local graveyard. Although the Armenian gravestones seem to have been removed, local people know that there are Armenian graves there. Now the graveyard is used only by Lezgis. The IDPs carry their dead more than 400 kilometres away, to be buried in their ancestral land in the *rayon* of Ağcabədi.

[174] The assistant representative of the central administration of the sub-district said that in 2001 there were 492 refugees (*qaçqın*) registered in the sub-district, and 555 IDPs (*məcburi köçkün*). Meskhetian Turks were deported mainly to Uzbekistan in 1944; those in Pir had been allowed to come to Azerbaijan when pogroms broke out against them in Uzbekistan's Fergana Valley in 1989. See Tomlinson (2004) for the memories of the refugees, and Yunusov (2000), among others, for the fate of Meskhetian Turks who were deported more than once. UNHCR sources give the total number of Meskhetian refugees from Uzbekistan to Azerbaijan as 46,000 (*UNHCR Refugees Magazine* 1996).

[175] Apparently the Georgian Azeris arrived in Azerbaijan after being subjected to pressure and violence in Georgia in the early 1990s. However, they were not formally recognised as displaced, so they have the status neither of refugee (*qaçqın*) nor of IDP (*məcburi köçkün*). Many consider themselves to have been displaced and forced to migrate, even if some still have contact with and travel to Georgia.

reforms of the mid-1990s. Azmi said he and others also took the many animals among the kolkhoz herds that they already owned privately.

At first the IDPs kept their animals in the run-down livestock sheds of the former kolkhoz, close to where the families were to build their shelters. At that time there were few animals, because the IDP population consisted of only about ten households. In the summer months the animals were taken to a faraway mountain pasture, and later they were taken to valleys beyond the nearby hills. During the first years after the IDPs settled in Pir, the sovkhoz vineyards still existed, and some people worked in them as well.

The first dwellings were built in 1995 with the support of the UNHCR and the World Peace Organisation (WPO), an American non-governmental organization. Azmi's family members still remembered how an American officer from the WPO came to Pir many times to assist with the construction. However, the financial aid had to be administered through the local authorities, and many IDPs believed the money was embezzled by the bureaucrats. Instead of the aid money's being spent to construct substantial housing for the IDPs, the shelters they got were of poor quality. For the IDPs, the embezzlement was confirmed by the anger and disappointment of the WPO officer, 'Tom', who shouted angrily and hit the thin walls with his fist when he saw the end result. Azmi's son claimed to have heard him complain of 'robbers' and 'impostors'.

The IDPs had stayed in these poor-quality shelters over the years, trying to make them more comfortable by renovating the interiors, constructing extensions, and building animal sheds using the cement posts that remained from the vineyards. Despite their efforts, survey data that I collected from 48 households in Pir showed that the mean living space available to households was 56 square metres, and standard housing still consisted of the one- and two-room dwellings originally provided by the aid organisations.[176]

All the houses had electricity, although in early 2000 there were long power cuts. This situation seems to have improved subsequently. Heat was provided by stoves fuelled by animal dung produced in the settlement and wood purchased by residents. There were no paved roads and no sewage system in the settlement. Water had to be carried from a single well down the road, something done mostly by women and children. When I re-visited

---

[176] More than 80 percent of surveyed households had living space measuring between 6 and 60 square metres. Only 7 of the 48 households had living space of more than 100 square metres; these were people living in the half-finished houses that had been built for the Meskhetian Turks. Some IDPs moved into houses left vacant by the Meskhetians, as did all the Georgian Azeris.

the settlement in summer 2008, the water situation remained unaltered.[177] The only infrastructural change was the building of a new school in 2005, and it had neither heating nor sewerage.

In 2001 there were 60 households in Pir, and I was able to carry out a survey of 48 of them, for a total of 252 people.[178] The majority of these households ($n = 28$) consisted of IDPs from the *rayon* of Laçın, almost all of them from one village ($n = 24$) and the rest from other *rayon*s under occupation. Nine households in the settlement consisted of migrants or refugees from Georgia.

In general, the households were relatively large. Mean size was 5.25 persons, and 27 per cent of households (13 of 48) comprised 7 or more persons. In comparison, nearly one-third of the surveyed households in Təzəkənd had 7 or more persons, suggesting that larger households were more feasible in Təzəkənd than in Pir.

Ethnically, 28 household heads (HHHs) were Kurds, 16 were Azerbaijani Azeris, and 4 were Georgian Azeris. Because Kurdish households – defined here as those with a Kurdish HHH – formed such a large proportion of the small survey group, Kurds were represented heavily in all household size categories. Nevertheless, nearly half the Kurdish households (13 of 28, or 46 per cent) had 6 or more people, whereas fewer than one-third of Azeri households (5 of 16, or 31 per cent) had that size.

Household size was linked closely to length of stay in Pir (the mean number of years spent in Pir was 6.94), and number of years of residence in Pir correlated significantly (Pearson's correlation = .300) with the ethnic identity of the HHH. Of the 48 surveyed households, 28 had lived in Pir for 8 years or more, and nearly half those households (13 of 28) were headed by ethnic Kurds, confirming the settlement story told by Azmi. This can be explained by the extensive kinship networks of Kurdish households and their links to the winter pasture IDP settlement in Ağcabədi, which I discuss later. Suffice it to say that 90 per cent of all households had kin in the Pir settlement. The tendency to have kin in Pir was very strong among Kurdish households (96 per cent), and 75 per cent of Azeri households (4 out of 16)

---

[177] Azmi tried many times to organise financial support from international aid organisations through the mediation of the IDPs' representatives. Once the community was provided with a turbo engine for pumping water from the well, but the machine soon broke down and could not be replaced because of lack of funds. In any case, getting a new pump would not have sufficed; the settlement needed to be fitted throughout with water pipes, for which there was no prospect of the IDPs acquiring funding.

[178] The members of the other 12 households were either temporarily or permanently away from Pir at the time of my stay in 2001.

also had kin in the settlement. The population of Pir was predominantly young, with 41 per cent of persons aged 18 or younger.[179]

Table 7.1. Occupations of Heads of Household (HHHs) in Pir.

Occupation	Number of HHHs	Percentage
Farming	4	8.3
Herding	3	6.3
Farming and herding	11	22.9
Driver	5	10.4
Teacher	12	25.0
Pensioner	10	20.8
Construction worker	1	2.1
Administrator	1	2.1
Trader	1	2.1
Total	48	100.0

Table 7.1 shows the distribution of occupations of household heads in the Pir survey sample. Altogether, 18 of 48 HHHs (38 per cent) were involved in farming, herding, or farming and herding together, meaning that they were dependent on the availability of land around the settlement for agricultural production, pasture, and hay cutting.[180] The answers given by pensioners, teachers, and administrators indicated that they received salaries, but as the interviewees categorised themselves, being pensioners, teachers, drivers, and so forth did not necessarily exclude agricultural or herding activities. Even if such HHHs were not personally involved in herding animals or cultivating land, other family members might be so engaged. Therefore, it is plausible to conclude that agricultural and herding were the dominant economic activities in Pir.

Agriculture and Animal Production in Pir

Almost all the households I surveyed in Pir (46 of 48) said they cultivated land. Table 7.2 shows that plots of between one and two hectares were the most commonly cultivated. As recorded by Azmi during the land distribution

---

[179] Six households out of 48 had no children in the age group of 18 or younger, and another 6 had 4 or more children in that age group. The largest number of households (17) had 2 children in that age group. Mean age of household heads was 46. There were 41 male-headed households and 7 female-headed households.

[180] In Təzəkənd, only 18 per cent of HHHs were clearly occupied in the agrarian sector, and 39 per cent of HHHs were pensioners, relative to 21 per cent in Pir.

that took place semi-formally within the settlement, the total area used by the 60 households in Pir amounted to about 224 hectares.[181] In 1999 the IDPs distributed the land among themselves; according to Azmi, until then they had been renting land for cultivation (*icarə*, in Azerbaijani) and for pasture, primarily from the sovkhoz mentioned earlier. Up to that time, implementation of the agrarian reforms in this region was slow, but once the sovkhoz land the IDPs had been renting became the property of residents of neighbouring villages, a decision had to be made. Azmi and other representatives of the IDP households in Pir (mostly his kin and other villagers from Laçın district) sought the right to use the cultivable area around their settlement. This led to the dispute and confrontation mentioned at the beginning of the chapter, when the local authorities were not initially inclined to grant use rights. By lobbying various patrons and committees that had to do with the IDPs, Azmi and others threatened the villagers who were in fact entitled to the land and managed to get use rights for an indefinite time (*muvəqqəti istifadə*).

Table 7.2. Sizes of Plots Cultivated by Households in Pir, in Hectares.

Plot Size	Number of Households	Percentage
0 (no land)	2	4.2
0.01–1.00	9	18.8
1.01–2.00	26	54.2
2.01–3.00	5	10.4
3.01–4.00	3	6.3
5.01 or more	3	6.3
Total	48	100.0

The inconsistency between Azmi's figure of 224 hectares (of which each household received 4 hectares) and the figures given by the interviewed

---

[181] When asked how the household had obtained the land it cultivated, some people said they had been given the land by a central administrative body such as the Land Office (*Torpaq Şö'bəsi*) or by the governor (*icra hakimi*) himself, on the basis of a presidential decree concerning land use rights for IDPs. Others said the land had come from the municipality (*bələdiyyə*) of Pir (of which Azmi, significantly, was the representative), and yet others said it was the municipality of the neighbouring settlement. Some said Azmi had taken the land by force and given it to the people. Everyone knew, however, that the use rights were temporary (*muvəqqəti*). Those who said the municipality had given them the land claimed to pay taxes of about US$2 per hectare a year for use rights.

HHHs, which added up to 110 hectares[182], can be interpreted in various ways. First, it is possible that Azmi simply lied about the figure, but I see no reason why he would have done so, because he knew I was carrying out the survey and asking everyone how much land he or she cultivated. A correlated possibility of untruth is that all the respondents gave smaller plot sizes than they actually cultivated. Again, there is no reason to suspect this was the case, since the respondents were all aware that I was talking to Azmi and other leading figures in the settlement about land and property issues.

Further possible explanations might be related to variations in household size, such that households lacking a sufficient labour force were unable to cultivate four hectares. Table 7.3 shows the relationship between size of land holding and household size. Nearly half of households of 4 to 5 persons were cultivating plots of 1 to 2 hectares, as were more than half of households of 6 to 7 persons. There was no increase in plot size as household size increased, suggesting that Chayanov's model might apply here. But contrary to Chayanov's assumption, almost all Pir cultivators were keen to cultivate more land if they had the possibility and land was available. Hence, the fact that they were not cultivating more land was not because of a disinclination for the drudgery but because no additional land was available to them.

Table 7.3. Sizes of Cultivated Plots in Pir, in Hectares, by Size of Household.

| Plot Size | Number of Persons in Household | | | | |
	2–3	4–5	6–7	8+	Total
0 (no land)	0	2	0	0	2
0.01–1.00	2	5	2	0	9
1.01–2.00	5	10	9	2	26
2.01–3.00	0	2	1	2	5
3.01–4.00	0	1	1	1	3
5.01 or more	0	1	2	0	3
Total	7	21	15	5	48

It is possible, too, that the ethnic identity of the HHH somehow made a difference in the amount of land a household had under cultivation. Half the Azeri settlers were cultivating plots of less than one hectare, whereas

---

[182] A small number of respondents said they had received land as registered resident Georgian Azeris, out of the land being distributed under the agrarian reforms. One such HHH was cultivating 12 hectares, part of which was the land share (*pay torpağı*) he had received inside the boundaries of the neighbouring municipality.

among the Kurdish settlers, only one HHH had a plot that small under cultivation.[183]

Another possible explanation for people's not using four hectares of land could be the fluctuations of residence and occupation that resulted when some people left the settlement temporarily or permanently for trade or to seek other employment, such that occupational restrictions hindered the use of all the available land. However, the relationship between occupation of HHH and land size per household showed no such tendency. Indeed, among the 12 teachers, 6 had land sizes of 1 to 2 hectares, and the rest had more than 2 hectares under cultivation.

It might have been that for a combination of the foregoing or other reasons, household members had given land to others for cultivation. Yet no respondents said they had given land to which they were entitled under the semi-formal distribution to someone else.

The reason people most often gave was meagre economic resources and the nature of the rural economy: they simply could not afford to cultivate any more land, and as I discuss shortly, they needed land to graze their animals. Nevertheless, the settlers of Pir demonstrated a strong interest in cultivating more land if ownership and use rights could be clarified and settled in a more permanent way than they were at the time of the survey.

Besides agriculture, keeping and herding animals was common in Pir, with 45 of 48 households saying they had animals. Thirty-eight households owned sheep, and of those, 15 (nearly 40 per cent) owned flocks of 11 to 20 sheep. Only 3 of the 38 households owned flocks of more than 50 sheep.

Sheep herds had grown smaller since the IDPs had been displaced (table 7.4). The interviewed household heads acknowledged that they had privately owned substantial numbers of sheep even during the socialist years. Before displacement, 24 households had 51 sheep or more, and in 4 extreme cases, more than 200. In 2001 only 3 households owned 51 sheep or more. Only 1 of the 24 households that formerly had 51 sheep or more still had the same size herd in 2001. Previously, 19 households had herds of only 1 to 50 sheep, where in 2001, 35 did so. The popularity of keeping small herds seems to have corresponded to the subsistence economy, the limited area available for pasture and hay cutting, and the strategies households had developed to manage insecure ownership and limited access to investment possibilities for herding and agriculture.

---

[183] More than half of the Kurdish households and more than one-third of the Azeri households were in the average land size category, 1 to 2 hectares. Eight Kurdish households had land in the categories of 2.01 hectares and more.

Table 7.4. Numbers of Households Owning Certain Numbers of Sheep in 2001 and before Displacement.

Number of Sheep Owned in 2001	Number of Households Owning the Following Number of Sheep before Displacement			Total Households Owning Sheep in 2001
	0	1–50	51 or More	
No information	0	1	0	1
0	1	5	3	9
1–50	3	12	20	35
51 or more	1	1	1	3
Total	5	19	24	48

Land use and ownership of livestock in Pir present interesting implications. If owning a herd of 51 sheep or more reflects people's having possessed the means, experience, skills, and desire to keep relatively large herds, then after war and displacement nearly the half the surveyed households had had to give up those means, skills, and intentions. It is ironic that under the former socialist system of Soviet Azerbaijan, the residents of Laçın *rayon* had better chances of keeping large private herds than they did in 2001, under the privatised economy.

Most surveyed households in Pir engaged in a combination of animal husbandry and agriculture. Only three households said they kept no animals, and only two said they engaged in no cultivation. Agriculture was primarily a subsistence activity, and agricultural products were often used as animal fodder. When agricultural produce was used as fodder, the animals were often seen as a form of savings, having the function of a bank in ensuring the livelihood of the household. People referred to the number of animals they had to sell for certain life-cycle rituals or for financing major expenditures such as repairing the old car, bribing an authority for a favour, or making some repairs to their dwelling.

Animals were also the means to financial accumulation. If households became somewhat better off, it was because of their diligent planning and effective use of animals, their meat, and their other products such as cheese, butter, hides, and wool. Yet even if households sought to accumulate money or at least economic security through successful herding and agriculture, their desires were all related to having settled lives, if not back in their homelands, then in big cities such as Gəncə and Baku. This desire arose from their lack of security in their property and residences and from their ambivalence about settling permanently in Pir, where IDPs saw little future in the slow pace of infrastructural and general life improvement. They did not see themselves becoming large landowners or large herders in the long run, but rather traders, shopkeepers, and state employees, mostly living in urban areas. I heard of no former resident of the settlement moving to another rural settlement; any moves that did occur were either to Baku or to a small town in the area, mostly for jobs in petty or middle-scale trade. Thus, even among this group of farmers and herders, who had considerable agricultural experience from earlier times and were keen to occupy land for subsistence, when people managed to accumulate some resources, they planned to expand not in the rural economy but in the urban sector. A side effect was the conversion of accumulated capital from rural land into urban houses by those who set their minds on moving to urban centres.

Chapter 8
Conclusion

> While property should up to a point be held in common, the general
> principle should be that of private ownership. If the responsibility for
> looking after property is distributed over many individuals, this will
> not lead to mutual recriminations; on the contrary, with every man
> busy with his own, there will be increased production all around.
>   – Aristotle, *The Politics*, Book 2

These ideas of Aristotle, written around 336 BCE while he was living in
Athens as a foreigner and thus was neither a citizen nor a property owner,
have influenced many social and political philosophers and inspired much of
liberal economic thought. Yet Aristotle recognised that even if property
flourished in private hands, it should be combined with a fair distribution of
profits, and citizens should be guaranteed the right to use property communally
(Aristotle 1962). Property rights, then, have for centuries been seen to be
intrinsically involved with rights and systems of distribution as well as with
rights of political belonging and citizenship. These ideas and their repercussions
can be seen in the ideologies, policies, values, and attitudes of people
in contemporary Azerbaijan.

My starting point in this book was the question, why do rural dwellers
in postsocialist Azerbaijan not cultivate the land they received for free
through the agrarian reforms? Were Aristotle and dozens of others after him
wrong when they recommended private ownership of land as the primary
and even sufficient motivation for use of the land? Or did Azerbaijan's long
socialist experience as a Soviet republic thoroughly erase memories of the
experience of private ownership and convince rural communities of the
superiority of communal property and state agricultural organisation? Do we
have here a case of postsocialist adjustment problems?

I began seeking answers to these questions with reference to three
theoretical frameworks for human economic behaviour: political economy,
an actor-oriented approach, and a moral economy model. The political

economic framework offered a broad approach in which the social nature of human behaviour, which shapes much of decision-making, is seen in relation to individuals' belonging to and taking action within certain social groups.[184] Such groups might be households, clans, or social classes (see also Ortiz 2005; Wilk and Cligett 2007: 42–43), and they interact with political interests in the larger society. Such a political economic approach necessitates a discussion of the historical formation of social groups and political interests – in this case, instances of historically determined, path-dependent effects of local Azerbaijani history on property relations and concepts of private, communal, and state property.

My look at regional history in chapters 2 and 3 leads to the following conclusions. First, the region under scrutiny lay on the border between competing Persian, Russian, and Ottoman empires into the early nineteenth century. It saw repeated conquests by and then withdrawals of military forces and therefore repeated settlement and flight of resident populations. In this period the smaller princedoms seem to have played the major role in political rule, and the region was under the immediate influence of competing Georgian and Muslim Azeri and Kurdish princes, khans and bəgs, and feudal lords.

Second, in the nineteenth century the region was already integrated far more than other parts of the Caucasus into larger economic structures. This was especially true for the *rayon* of Şəmkir, as it came to be known during this century, which flourished in wine production carried out mainly by German colonists and entrepreneurs from western Azerbaijan.

Third, because of western Azerbaijan's relative wealth and industrial and economic development, the Soviet regime early on introduced collective agricultural structures such as sovkhozes into the region. Despite the regime's use of rhetoric claiming that it was taking land from big landlords and nationalising it for collective use, the region had in fact experienced state ownership of land for many centuries. The big landlords were either German colonists, who were liquidated after World War I, or Muslim bəgs, who were linked to the local population through ties of kinship, lineage, and clanship and thus did not hold the kind of legal and economic power over rural settlers that feudal lords held in Europe.

Fourth, the Soviet period introduced greater infrastructural development to the area. Under the Soviets, central agrarian policies dictated cultivation and production patterns and controls while integrating the area into the centralised command economy of production and redistribution. The notion

---

[184] For a discussion of the narrower and more historical use of the political economic approach and its relationship to economic anthropology, see Robotham (2005).

of the state as provider, controller, and property owner seems to have become especially well developed during the Soviet era.

Fifth, in the memories of local people in Şəmkir district, the late socialist era is associated with relative wealth and the freedom to market agricultural produce. On one hand, this allowed them to make good gains; on the other, entrenched corruption necessitated coping with nepotism and favouritism.

The framework of political economy, then, underscores the role played by the state as a strong determinant in property relations. For centuries, rural people in Azerbaijan have had to cope with states and other political entities that have conquered, controlled, and withdrawn. Rural dwellers reacted to each state action and developed their own relations to property: land could be gained and lost; it could be given freely and taken away; it could be an asset or, lacking other economic support systems, a liability. All these local experiences advance the interpretation that agrarian property acquires or loses significance within a larger economic system, as part of market relations and political rule.

My second framework for understanding people's economic behaviour and property relations was the actor-orientated approach. In chapters 4 and 5 I looked at individual and household behaviour in appropriating land, choosing to cultivate one or both of the two major kinds of land in western Azerbaijan – household plots, or *məhlə*s, and privatised shares, or *pay* – and making decisions for acquiring, accumulating, and spending household capital. The actors were assumed to be self-interested and also embedded in more or less restrictive social and economic relationships, a social context in which they have possibilities for making 'good' or 'bad' decisions. I found that social and economic relations concerning agrarian land were directed primarily by the profitability of markets. People and households cultivated the strips of land they had long held or had recently acquired through privatisation if they thought they had access to profitable markets.

Household size, gender and generational composition, and internal relations were all found to affect whether or not household members acted collectively and how they did so. Households that could mobilise their own members as well as larger kin networks for cultivating and marketing produce seem to have had better chances of economic survival and even economic accumulation than those that could not. Migration and remittances from migrants were also crucial factors in household economic strategies. When local migrants successfully marketed fresh vegetables to consumers in Moscow and St. Petersburg, production in household plots of herbs and vegetables increased, and rising prices became strong incentives for cultivating formerly unused plots, provided that irrigation and fertilisers were available.

In short, the actor-orientated framework, while supporting the argument that rural property was tightly linked to larger economic structures and markets, enabled a deeper exploration of the way households understood and developed strategies for using or not using land. Applying this approach helped me highlight the reasons for Azerbaijanis' different attitudes towards different kinds of land and to explain why land remained unused when a household's gender, age, and generational composition hindered its adopting a collective strategy. Under certain household circumstances, land and private property could become a liability instead of an asset.

My third framework placed human economic behaviour within a moral economic ideology (Wilk and Cligett 2007: 43–46, 117–151) that was locally manifested in notions of kinship solidarity and support, reciprocity and exchange, and competition and envy. The community of Təzəkənd, like the community and 'mutuality within the base' discussed by Stephen Gudeman (2001, 2005), followed the ideology of solidarity and support according to Islamic notions and socialist ones equally. Socialist policies of state support for the needy and disadvantaged were seen as positive qualities of the former system that people wished to see from the present state as well. But the former system had not created a moral community based on the notion of the superiority of collective property (cf. Hann 2007). People saw collective property as having been the property of a central state that had forced people to come up with fictitious production numbers, which they could then use, through creative local and national subversions, to steal and cheat, as in the *pripiska* scandals in cotton and wine production.

Through the moral economy framework, then, we can understand how local notions and networks of kinship and solidarity can further restrain or allow property to be valued and used. Like property, kinship relations in Təzəkənd could be an asset or a liability, so their balanced use and cultivation were essential for converting property into economic wealth.

The legacy of socialism and postsocialist structures render this case study in Azerbaijan comparable to other cases in formerly socialist countries (see, for example, Hann 2003, 2005b, 2007). Comparison with other socialist cases and postsocialist paths of transformation necessitates historical grounding (Hann 2007: 301) as well as taking into account contemporary geo-political and economic conjunctures. In particular, any comparison must consider the following points:

- In many countries of central and eastern Europe, pre-socialist property was restored to its former owners or their descendants (see

Cartwright 2001; Verdery 2003; also Hann 2007: 302), but this did not happen in Azerbaijan, Russia, or Ukraine.

- Azerbaijan, unlike the central and eastern European countries, has so far had no access to European markets for its agricultural produce. The only markets with any attraction for Azerbaijani producers are those in Russia.

- Trade in Russian markets requires a mixture of labour migration (for gaining experience and establishing contacts), transnational links (for which knowing Russian is important), and risk-taking (as exemplified in the narratives and biographies provided in earlier chapters).

- The distance and spatial aspects of trade contacts, as well as the uneven economic development created in Azerbaijan by a booming oil industry and a flourishing construction industry in the capital, have had a deep effect on the country's postsocialist agrarian changes.

A further difference that affects comparisons between Azerbaijan and other postsocialist countries is the former's unresolved conflict over the status of Nagorno-Karabakh and the situation of internally displaced persons (IDPs), who continue to strain economic and political resources and can be used and abused in political discourse. In relation to IDPs, land can be neither private nor communally owned but transformed into *territory*. Land for IDPs is negotiated by keeping them in the legal limbo of internal displacement and granting them use rights to land – but not ownership of it – through presidential decrees and patronage.[185]

Moreover, Azerbaijan is subject to a particular mixture of continuing socialist and authoritarian structures that, together with nationalist discourses and market-orientated ideals and changes, have influenced the transformation of agrarian property in specific ways. Local understandings of the Azerbaijani state associate it clearly and firmly with power holders in the centre, and less so with local power holders. Rules and regulations exist, but access to their implementation seems to be biased and works to the benefit of those in power. The role of the state as the provider and protector of property has declined; people acknowledge that nepotism and favouritism existed in the former system, but the present, supposedly free-market system has made these practices even more rampant. People perceive the markets not to be free but rather controlled by monopolies. The oil industry, people often said, belonged to the ruling clan, and other, less profitable markets were distrib-

---

[185] Andrew Gilbert (2006: 14–18) made the similar point that in post-war situations such as that in Bosnia-Herzegovina, much of the postsocialist transition is mediated through the prism of war and post-war experiences, rendering discussions of the socialist past obsolete and undesirable in the public arena. I thank Chris Hann for drawing my attention to this article.

uted among lesser power-holding networks, all clients of 'those at the top'. Substantial economic gains could not be had, people believed, without the support of the power holders or without one's being able to pay extortion money to those who guarded the niche of economic profit-making in question.

Turning to the outlook for the rural economy in western Azerbaijan, I want to underscore the surprising role played there by emigration. The remittances of migrants contribute to a certain economic livelihood in the region. In September 2007 a regional wholesale marketplace was opened near Təzəkənd, built by a local migrant then working in Russia. The goods sold there were all global products, not local ones, but residents were pleased at least to have job opportunities for some of the young unemployed people of the *rayon*. Migrants' capital continued to play a substantial role in 2008 in maintaining links for trading herbs and vegetables from Təzəkənd, and their investments were visible in an emerging market for livestock for national consumption. The booming city of Baku was seeing increased consumption of meat, and animal husbandry was becoming the second strongest economic sector in the western Azerbaijani *rayon*s. In Təzəkənd some households had begun cultivating clover on their *pay* shares, in response to demand for animal fodder. Some migrants were making economic alliances with local power holders in order to keep certain land as pasture and were raising cattle and sheep there. The IDPs in Pir, too, had discovered the gains that could be made by selling livestock in Baku and were getting involved in such trade relations.

As migrants support the regime with their economic investments, they take pressure off the politicians and free the centre from having to provide for substantial and thorough change in the countryside. Ironically, once migrants are successful enough to return to the country, they do not come back to their rural homelands but settle in Baku. Hence, despite the relative economic development in the rural sector, the goal expressed by İrşad Əliyev, the former minister of agriculture (chapter 3) – that of a countryside where rural residents stay and flourish – seems no more attainable now than it was in when I interviewed him in 2000. Even if private property has returned to rural Azerbaijan, rural people are more inclined to leave that property for out-migration or for jobs and more desirable lives in the urban metropolis of Baku.

Appendix

Table 1
Numbers of Households by *Məhlə* Size and Settlement Group

	Məhlə Size (in *Sotka*)					
Settlement Group	0–5	6–12	14–19	20–29	30+	Total
Leninabad-Düzqışlaq	0	12	6	19	2	39
Demiryolu altı and üstü	12	16	2	6	0	36
Total	12	28	8	25	2	75

Table 2
Numbers of Households (HHs) Producing Cash Crop Vegetables in the Previous Year, by *Məhlə* Size

		Did Household Produce Cash Crop Vegetables?		
Məhlə Size in *Sotka*	Did HH Produce during Previous Year?	No	Yes	Total
No information	Yes	1	0	1
0–5	No	1	0	1
	Yes	4	2	6
6–12	No	2	0	2
	Yes	9	15	24
14–19	Yes	3	5	8
20–29	No	1	0	1
	Yes	4	20	24
30+	Yes	0	2	2

Table 3

Numbers of Households (HH) Producing Cash Crop Vegetables in the Previous Year, by Məhlə Size and Household Size

Məhlə Size (in *Sotka*)	Number of Persons in Household	Did Household Produce Cash Crop Vegetables?		
		No	Yes	Total
0–5	1–3	1	0	1
	4–6	4	1	5
	7–9	2	1	3
	Total	7	2	9
6–12	1–3	3	6	9
	4–6	6	6	12
	7–9	2	3	5
	Total	11	15	26
14–19	1–3	2	0	2
	4–6	1	1	2
	7–9	0	3	3
	10–12	0	1	1
	Total	3	5	8
20–29	1–3	2	3	5
	4–6	2	6	8
	7–9	1	8	9
	10–12	0	1	1
	13+	0	2	2
	Total	5	20	25
30+	1–3	0	1	1
	4–6	0	1	1
	Total	0	2	2

Table 4

Household Cultivation of *Məhlə* Plots and *Pay* Land in Leninabad-Düzqışlaq, by Occupation of Head of Household (HHH)

Occupation	Number of Households	*Məhlə* Use in Previous Year		Cash Crop Grown on *Məhlə*		Received *Pay* Share		Cultivated *Pay* Share	
Pensioner	14	Yes	14	Yes	13	Yes	13	Yes	3
				No	1	No	1	No	11
Agricultural labourer	7	Yes	7	Yes	7	Yes	7	Yes	0
								No	7
Farmer	8	Yes	8	Yes	8	Yes	7	Yes	4
								No	3
						NI*	1	NI*	1
Unemployed	4	Yes	4	Yes	4	Yes	4	Yes	0
								No	4
Tractor driver	2	Yes	2	Yes	2	Yes	2	Yes	0
								No	2
Private sector	2	Yes	1	Yes	1	Yes	2	Yes	0
		No	1	No	1			No	2
Trader	2	Yes	2	Yes	2	Yes	2	Yes	0
								No	2
Total	39		39		39		39		39

* NI = No information

Table 5

Household Cultivation of *Məhlə* Plots and *Pay* Land in Demiryolu altı and üstü, by Occupation of Head of Household (HHH)

Occupation of HHH	Number of Households	*Məhlə* Use in Previous Year		Cash Crop Grown on *Məhlə*		Received *Pay* Share		Cultivated *Pay* Share	
Pensioner	16	Yes	13	Yes	2	Yes	15	Yes	3
		No	3	No	13	No	1	No	13
				NI*	1				
State employee	6	Yes	4	Yes	0	Yes	6	Yes	0
		No	1	No	5			No	6
		NI*	1	NI*	1				
Self-employed	5	Yes	5	Yes	1	Yes	5	Yes	0
				No	4			No	4
								NI*	1
Trader	3	Yes	2	Yes	0	Yes	3	Yes	1
		No	1	No	3			No	2
Housewife	4	Yes	1	Yes	1	Yes	4	Yes	0
		No	3	No	3			No	4
Unemployed	1	Yes	1	Yes	1	Yes	1	Yes	0
								No	1
Tractor driver	1	Yes	1	Yes	1	Yes	1	Yes	0
								No	1
Administrator	1	Yes	0	Yes	0	Yes	1	Yes	0
		No	1	No	1			No	1
Farmer	1	Yes	1	Yes	1	Yes	1	Yes	1
Total	38		38		38		38		38

* NI = No information

Table 6
Agricultural Production Strategy by Size of Household

Number of Persons in Household	Strategy	Leninabad-Düzqışlaq	Demiryolu Altı and Üstü	Total
1–3	No cash crop on *məhlə*	1	8	9
	Cash crop by no *pay* cultivation	8	2	10
	Total	9	10	19
4–6	No cash crop on *məhlə*	0	13	13
	Cash crop by no *pay* cultivation	7	1	8
	Cash crop and *pay* cultivation	5	2	7
	Total	12	16	28
7–9	No cash crop on *məhlə*	1	4	5
	Cash crop by no *pay* cultivation	11	2	13
	Cash crop and *pay* cultivation	1	0	1
	Total	13	6	19
10–12	Cash crop by no *pay* cultivation	1	0	1
	Cash crop and *pay* cultivation	1	0	1
	Total	2	0	2
13+	Cash crop by no *pay* cultivation	2	0	2

Bibliography

Abrahamian, L. 1997. Typology of Aggressiveness and National Violence in the Former USSR. *International Journal on Minority and Group Rights* 4: 263–278.

Abrahams, R. (ed.). 1996. *After Socialism: Land Reform and Social Change in Eastern Europe.* Providence, RI: Berghahn.

Abu-Lughod, L. (ed.). 1998. *Remaking Women: Feminism and Modernity in the Middle East.* Princeton, NJ: Princeton University Press.

Acheson, J. M. (ed.). 1994. *Anthropology and Institutional Economics.* Lanham, MD: University Press of America.

——. 1996. Household Organization and Budget Structures in a Purépecha Pueblo. *American Ethnologist* 23 (2): 331–351.

Adam, V. 2001. Why Do They Cry? Criticisms of Muharram Celebrations in Tsarist and Socialist Azerbaijan. In R. Brunner and W. Ende (eds.), *The Twelver Shia in Modern Times: Religious Culture and Political History,* pp. 114–134. Leiden: Brill.

——. 2005. Umdeutung der Geschichte im Zeichen des Nationalismus seit dem Ende der Sowjetunion: Das Beispiel Aserbaidschan. Deutschland, Armenien und der Kaukasus. In F. Adanır and B. Bonwetsch (eds.), *Osmanismus, Nationalismus und der Kaukasus: Muslime und Christen, Türken und Armenier im 19. und 20. Jahrhundert,* pp. 21–42. Wiesbaden: Reichert Verlag.

Alekperov, A. 1936. K voprosy ob izučenii kul'tury Kurdov. In *Akademija Nauk SSSR Trudy Azerbajdžanskogo Filiala XXV. Serija Istoričeskaja,* pp. 33–62. Baku.

Alexander, C. 2004. Value, Relation, and Changing Bodies: Privatization and Property Rights in Kazakhstan. In K. Verdery and C. Humphrey (eds.), *Property in Question: Value Transformation in the Global Economy,* pp. 251–273. Oxford: Berg.

Allahverdiyev, H. 1980. *Azərbaycan Kəndinin Sosial İnkişafı.* Bakı: Azərbaycan Dövlət Nəşriyyatı.

——. 1986. *Sosial İnkişafın Planlaşdırılması Problemləri.* Bakı: Azərbaycan SSR Ali ve Orta İxtisas Təhsili Nazırlığı.

Allina-Pisano, J. 2003. *Soviet Men into Peasants: Property Rights and Economy in the Black Earth, 1991–2000.* PhD dissertation, University of Michigan.

Altstadt, A. L. 1992. *The Azerbaijani Turks: Power and Identity under Russian Rule.* Stanford, CA: Hoover Institution Press.

Aristotle 1962. *The Politics.* Translated by T. A. Sinclair. Middlesex, UK: Penguin.

Atabaki, T. 2002 [1993]. *Azerbaijan: Ethnicity and the Struggle for Power in Iran*. London: I. B. Tauris.

Auch, E.-M. 2001. *Öl und Wein am Kaukasus: Deutsche Forschungsreisende, Kolonisten und Unternehmer im vorrevolutionären Aserbaidschan*. Wiesbaden: Reichert Verlag.

Azərbaycan Respublikasında milli iqtisadiyyatın inkişaf etdirilməsi istiqamətləri. 2004. Bakı: Elm.

Azərbaycan Respublikasında 1–i Sentyabr 2000–ci İl Vəziyyətinə Aqrar İslahatın Gedişi Haqqında. 2000. Bakı.

Azərbaycan Tarixi, Yeddi cilddə. 1998–2003. Seven volumes edited by F. Magsudov; vol. 5 (2001), edited by M. İsmayılov et al. Bakı: Elm.

Azərbaycanın Regionları. 2001. Bakı: Səda.

Azərbaycanın Statistik Göstəriciləri. 2001. Bakı: Səda.

Azerbaijan International. 2002. Update on Refugees (by Vugar Abdusalimov). Vol. 10, no. 4. www.azer.com/aiweb/categories/magazine/ai104_folder/104_articles/104_refugee_update.html.

Azerbaijan Soviet Encyclopaedia [Azərbaycan Sovet Ensiklopediyası]. 1987. Vol. 10. Baku.

Baberowski, J. 2003. *Der Feind ist überall: Stalinismus im Kaukasus*. München: Deutsche Verlags-Anstalt.

———. 2004. Verschleierte Feinde: Stalinismus im sowjetischen Orient. *Geschichte und Gesellschaft* 30 (1): 10–36.

Baddeley, J. F. 1999 [1908]. *The Russian Conquest of the Caucasus*. Richmond, UK: Curzon.

Baharlı, M. V. 1993 [1921]. *Azərbaycan: Coğrafi-Təbii etnoqrafik və iqtisadi mülahizat*. Baku: Azərbaycan Dövlət Nəşriyyatı.

Bailey, F. G. 1969. *Stratagems and Spoils: A Social Anthropology of Politics*. Oxford: Blackwell.

Barth, F. (ed.). 1963. *The Role of the Entrepreneur in Social Change in Norway*. Oslo: Norwegian University Press.

———. 1992. Towards Greater Naturalism in Conceptualizing Societies. In A. Kuper (ed.), *Conceptualizing Society,* pp. 17–33. London: Routledge.

Bellér-Hann, I. 1998. Crafts, Entrepreneurship and Gendered Economic Relations in Southern Xinjiang in the Era of 'Socialist Commodity Economy'. *Central Asian Survey* 17 (4): 701–718.

Berry, S. 2002. Debating the Land Question in Africa. *Comparative Studies in Society and History* 44 (4): 638–668.

Bertelsmann Stiftung. 2007. *BTI 2008: Azerbaijan Country Report*. Gütersloh: Bertelsmann Stiftung.

Bezemer, D. J., and J. R. Davis. 2003. The Rural Nonfarm Economy in Transition Countries: Findings from Armenia. In M. Spoor (ed.), *Transition, Institutions, and the Rural Sector,* pp. 163–184. New York: Lexington Books.

Bourdieu, P. 1977. *Outline of a Theory of Practice.* Cambridge: Cambridge University Press.

———. 1979. *Algeria 1960.* Cambridge: Cambridge University Press.

Bournoutian, G. A. 1996. The Ethnic Composition and the Socio-economic Condition of Eastern Armenia in the First Half of the Nineteenth Century. In R. G. Suny (ed.), *Transcaucasia, Nationalism, and Social Change: Essays in the History of Armenia, Azerbaijan, and Georgia,* revised edition, pp. 69–86. Ann Arbor: University of Michigan Press.

Brandtstädter, S. 2003. The Moral Economy of Kinship and Property in Southern China. In C. Hann and the Property Relations Group, *The Postsocialist Agrarian Question,* pp. 441–459. Münster: LIT Verlag.

Bridger, S., and F. Pine (eds.). 1998. *Surviving Post-socialism: Local Strategies and Regional Resources in Eastern Europe and the Former Soviet Union.* London: Routledge.

Brunner, R., and W. Ende (eds.). 2001. *The Twelver Shia in Modern Times: Religious Culture and Political History.* Leiden: Brill.

Bünyadov, Z. 2004. *Azərbaycan Atabəyləri Dövləti (1136–1225–ci illər).* Bakı: Pedagogika.

Burawoy, M. 2000. Grounding Globalization. In M. Burawoy et al. (eds.), *Global Ethnography,* pp. 337–351. Berkeley: University of California Press.

———, and K. Verdery (eds.). 1999a. *Uncertain Transitions: Ethnographies of Change in the Postsocialist World.* Lanham, MD: Rowman and Littlefield.

———, and K. Verdery. 1999b. Introduction. In M. Burawoy and K. Verdery (eds.), *Uncertain Transition: Ethnographies of Change in the Post-socialist World,* pp. 1–18. Lanham, MD: Rowman and Littlefield.

Cahen, C. 1986a. Atabak (Atabeg). In *The Encyclopedia of Islam, New Edition,* vol. 1, pp. 731–732. Leiden: E. J. Brill.

———. 1986b. Iqta. In *The Encyclopedia of Islam, New Edition,* vol. 3, pp. 1088–1091. Leiden: Brill.

Cannell, E. 2007. The Role of Children in Uzbekistan's Cotton Harvest. In D. Kandiyoti (ed.), *The Cotton Sector in Central Asia: Economic Policy and Development Challenges,* pp. 216–222. London: School of Oriental and African Studies, University of London.

Carsten, J. 2004. *After Kinship.* Cambridge: Cambridge University Press.

------, and S. Hugh-Jones (eds.). 1995. *About the House: Lévi-Strauss and Beyond.* Cambridge: Cambridge University Press.

Cartwright, A. L. 2001. *The Return of the Peasant: Land Reform in Post-communist Romania.* Aldershot, UK: Ashgate.

------. 2003. Private Farming in Romania: What Are the Old People Going to Do with Their Land? In C. Hann and the Property Relations Group, *The Postsocialist Agrarian Question,* pp. 171–188. Münster: LIT Verlag.

Cashdan, E. (ed.). 1990. *Risk and Uncertainty in Tribal and Peasant Economies.* Boulder, CO: Westview Press.

Cavadov, Q. 2000. *Azərbaycanın Azsaylı Xalqları və Milli Azlıqları (Tarix və Muasırlık).* Bakı: Elm.

Cellarius, B. 2003. Property Restitution and Natural Resource Use in the Rhodope Mountains, Bulgaria. In C. Hann and the Property Relations Group, *The Postsocialist Agrarian Question,* pp. 189–218. Münster: LIT Verlag.

Clark, G. 1994. *Onions Are My Husband: Survival and Accumulation by West African Market Women.* Chicago: University of Chicago Press.

Colson, E. 2004. Displacement. In D. Nugent (ed.), *A Companion to the Anthropology of Politics,* pp. 107–120. Malden, MA: Blackwell.

Comaroff, Jean, and John L. Comaroff (eds.). 1980. *The Meaning of Marriage Payments.* London: Academic Press.

Comaroff, John L. 1982. Dialectical Systems, History, and Anthropology: Units of Study and Questions of Theory. *Journal of Southern African Studies* 8: 143–172.

Connerton, P. 2009. *How Modernity Forgets.* Cambridge: Cambridge University Press.

Cornell, S. E. 2001. Democratization Falters in Azerbaijan. *Journal of Democracy* 12 (2): 118–131.

Delaney, C. 1991. *The Seed and the Soil: Gender and Cosmology in Turkish Village Society.* Berkeley, CA: University of California Press.

Derlugian, G. M. 2002. Azeri Orientalists as Mirror of the Post-Soviet Revolution. In C. Leys and L. Panitch (eds.), *Fighting Identities: Race, Religion, and Ethno-Nationalism,* pp. 93–113. London: Pluto Press.

------. 2005. *Bourdieu's Secret Admirer: A Word-System Biography.* Chicago: University of Chicago Press.

de Waal, T. 2003. *Black Garden: Armenia and Azerbaijan through Peace and War.* New York: New York University Press.

Donham, D. L. 1981. Beyond the Domestic Mode of Production. *Man* 16 (4): 515–541.

Dudwick, N. 2000. Postsocialism and the Fieldwork of War. In H. G. De-Soto and N. Dudwick (eds.), *Fieldwork Dilemmas: Anthropologists in Postsocialist States,* pp. 13–30. Madison: University of Wisconsin Press.

———, K. Fock, and D. Sedik. 2005. A Stocktaking of Land Reform and Farm Restructuring in Bulgaria, Moldova, Azerbaijan, and Kazakhstan. In *Environmentally and Socially Sustainable Development: Europe and Central Asia Region.* Washington, DC: World Bank.

———, E. Gomart, A. Marc, and K. Kuehnast (eds.). 2003. *When Things Fall Apart: Qualitative Studies of Poverty in the Former Soviet Union.* Washington, DC: World Bank.

Dunn, S. P., and E. Dunn. 1967. *The Peasants of Central Russia.* New York: Holt, Rinehart and Winston.

Durrenberger, E. P. (ed.). 1984. *Chayanov, Peasants, and Economic Anthropology.* Orlando, FL: Academic Press.

———, and N. Tannenbaum. 2002. Chayanov and Theory in Economic Anthropology. In J. Ensminger (ed.), *Theory in Economic Anthropology,* pp. 137–154. Walnut Creek, CA: Altamira Press.

Dwyer, D., and J. Bruce (eds.). 1988. *A Home Divided: Women and Income in the Third World.* Stanford. CA: University of California Press.

Eidson, J. R. 2006. Cooperative Property at the Limit. In F. von Benda-Beckmann, K. von Benda-Beckmann, and M. G. Wiber (eds.), *Changing Properties of Property,* pp. 147–169. Oxford: Berghahn.

Ələkbərli, Ə. 2000. *Garbi Azərbaycan: Cild 1, Vedibasar Mahallı.* Bakı: Ağrıdağ.

———. 2002. *Zəngibasar, Gərnibasar və Qırxbulaq Mahalları.* Bakı: Ağrıdağ.

———. 2006. *Monuments of Western Azerbaijan.* Bakı: Ağrıdağ.

Ələsgərov, A. K., and H. A. Qasımov. 1972. *Azərbaycan SSR Kənd Təsərrüfatının İnkişafının Mühüm Problemleri.* Bakı: Elm Nəşriyyatı.

Əliyev, İ. 1997. *Heydər Əliyev və Azərbaycanın Kənd Təsərrüfatı.* Bakı: Azərbaycan Dövlət Nəşriyyatı.

Ellis, F. 1998. *Peasant Economics: Farm Households and Agrarian Development.* Cambridge: Cambridge University Press.

Ensminger, J. 1998. Anthropology and the New Institutionalism. *Journal of Institutional and Theoretical Economics* 154: 774–789.

———, and J. Knight. 1997. Changing Social Norms: Common Property, Bridewealth, and Clan Exogamy. *Current Anthropology* 38 (1): 1–24.

Evans-Pritchard, E. E. 2002 [1951]. *Kinship and Marriage among the Nuer.* Oxford: Clarendon Press.

Finke, P. 2004. *Nomaden im Transformationsprozess: Kasachen in der post-sozialistischen Mongolei.* Münster: LIT Verlag.

Firth, R. 1983 [1936]. *We, the Tikopia: A Sociological Study of Kinship in Primitive Polynesia.* Stanford, CA: Stanford University Press.

——, and B. S. Yamey (eds.). 1964. *Capital, Savings and Credit in Peasant Societies.* London: George Allen and Unwin.

Fortes, M. 1967 [1949]. *The Web of Kinship among the Tallensi.* Oxford: Oxford University Press.

Gambetta, D. (ed.). 1988. *Trust: Making and Breaking Cooperative Relations.* New York: Blackwell.

Gambold-Miller, L. L. 2002. Communal Coherence and Barriers to Reform. In D. J. O'Brien and S. K. Wegren (eds.), *Rural Reform in Post-Soviet Russia,* pp. 221–242. Baltimore, MD: Woodrow Wilson Center Press.

——, and P. Heady. 2003. Cooperation, Power, and Community: Economy and Ideology in the Russian Countryside. In C. Hann and the Property Relations Group, *The Postsocialist Agrarian Question,* pp. 257–292. Münster: LIT Verlag.

Geertz, C. 1963. *Peddlers and Princes: Social Change and Economic Modernization in Two Indonesian Towns.* Chicago: University of Chicago Press.

Gəncə Şəhərinin Tarixi. 2004. Elmi-praktik konfransın materialları. Gəncə Şəhərinin İcra Hakimiyyəti. Bakı: Nurlan.

Gəncə Tarixi Oçerk. 1994. Azərbaycan Elmlər Akademiyası, A. Bakıxanov adına Tarix İnstitutu. Bakı: Elm.

Gilbert, A. 2006. The Past in Parenthesis: (Non)post-socialism in Post-war Bosnia-Herzegovina. *Anthropology Today* 22 (4): 14–18.

Gilsenan, M. 1976. Lying, Honour, and Contradiction. In B. Kapferer (ed.), *Transaction and Meaning,* pp. 191–222. Philadelphia: Institute for the Study of Human Issues.

——. 2000. *Recognizing Islam: Religion and Society in the Modern Middle East.* Revised edition. London: I. B. Tauris.

Gleason, G. 1992. The 'National Factor' and the Logic of Sovietology. In A. J. Motyl (ed.), *The Post-Soviet Nations: Perspectives on the Demise of the USSR,* pp. 1–29. New York: Columbia University Press.

Godelier, M. 1999. *The Enigma of the Gift.* Cambridge: Polity Press.

Golden, P. 1992. *An Introduction to the History of the Turkic Peoples: Ethnogenesis and State-Formation in Medieval and Early Modern Eurasia and the Middle East.* Wiesbaden: Otto Harrassowitz.

——. 1996. The Turkic Peoples and Caucasia. In R. G. Suny (ed.), *Transcaucasia, Nationalism, and Social Change: Essays in the History of*

Armenia, Azerbaijan, and Georgia, revised edition, pp. 45–67. Ann Arbor: University of Michigan Press.

Goltz, T. 1998. *Azerbaijan Diary: A Rogue Reporter's Adventures in an Oil-Rich, War-Torn, Post-Soviet Republic.* London: M. E. Sharpe.

Gomart, E. 2003. Between Civil War and Land Reform: Among the Poorest of the Poor in Tajikistan. In N. Dudwick, E. Gomart, M. Alexandre, and K. Kuehnast (eds.), *When Things Fall Apart: Qualitative Studies of Poverty in the Former Soviet Union,* pp. 57–93. Washington, DC: World Bank.

Goody, J. (ed.). 1971 [1958]. *The Developmental Cycle in Domestic Groups.* Cambridge: Cambridge University Press.

———. 1975. *The Character of Kinship.* Cambridge: Cambridge University Press.

Grant, B. 2004. An Average Azeri Village (1930): Remembering Rebellion in the Caucasus Mountains. *Slavic Review* 63 (4): 705–731.

———. 2009. *The Captive and the Gift: Cultural Histories of Sovereignty in Russia and the Caucasus.* New York: Cornell University Press.

Gray, P. 2003. Volga Farmers and Arctic Herders: Common (Post)socialist Experiences in Rural Russia. In C. Hann and the Property Relations Group, *The Postsocialist Agrarian Question,* pp. 293–320. Münster: LIT Verlag.

Gudeman, S. 1978. *The Demise of a Rural Economy: From Subsistence to Capitalism in a Latin American Village.* London: Routledge and Kegan Paul.

———. 2001. *The Anthropology of Economy: Community, Market, and Culture.* Oxford: Blackwell.

———. 2005. Community and Economy: Economy's Base. In J. G. Carrier (ed.), *A Handbook of Economic Anthropology,* pp. 94–106. Cheltenham, UK: Edward Elgar.

Gupta, A. 1995. Blurred Boundaries: The Discourse of Corruption, the Culture of Politics, and the Imagined State. *American Ethnologist* 22 (2): 375–402.

Haller, D., and C. Shore (eds.). 2005. *Corruption: Anthropological Perspectives.* London: Pluto Press.

Hanke, S. 1998. *Aserbaidschans Weg zur Marktwirtschaft: Fünf Jahre Wirtschaftstransformation seit der Unabhängigkeit.* Frankfurt: Peter Lang.

Hann, C. 1998. Introduction: The Embeddedness of Property. In C. M. Hann (ed.), *Property Relations: Renewing the Anthropological Tradition,* pp. 1–47. Cambridge: Cambridge University Press.

------ (ed.). 2002. *Postsocialism: Ideal, Ideologies and Practices in Eurasia.* London: Routledge.

------. 2003. Introduction: Decollectivisation and the Moral Economy. In C. Hann and the Property Relations Group, *The Postsocialist Agrarian Question,* pp. 1–46. Münster: LIT Verlag.

------. 2005a. *Property Relations: The Halle Focus Group 2000–2005.* Halle/Saale: Max Planck Institute for Social Anthropology.

------. 2005b. Postsocialist Societies. In J. G. Carrier (ed.), *A Handbook of Economic Anthropology,* pp. 547–557. Cheltenham, UK: Edward Elgar.

------. 2007. A New Double Movement? Anthropological Perspectives on Property in the Age of Neoliberalism. *Socio-Economic Review* 5: 287–318.

------, and the Property Relations Group. 2003. *The Postsocialist Agrarian Question: Property Relations and the Rural Condition.* Münster: LIT Verlag.

------, and M. Sárkány. 2003. The Great Transformation in Rural Hungary: Property, Life Strategies, and Living Standards. In C. Hann and the Property Relations Group, *The Postsocialist Agrarian Question,* pp. 117–141. Münster: LIT Verlag.

Harris, O. 1981. Households as Natural Units. In K. Young, C. Wolkowitz, and R. McCullagh (eds.), *Of Marriage and the Market: Women's Subordination Internationally and Its Lessons,* pp. 136–155. London: Routledge and Kegan Paul.

Heady, P. 1999. *The Hard People: Rivalry, Sympathy and Social Structure in an Alpine Valley.* Amsterdam: Harwood Academic.

------, and L. L. Gambold-Miller. 2006. Nostalgia and the Emotional Economy: A Comparative Look at Rural Russia. In M. Svasek (ed.), *Postsocialism: Politics and Emotions in Central and Eastern Europe,* pp. 34–52. Oxford: Berghahn.

Hegaard, S. E. 1977. Nationalism in Azerbaidzhan in the Era of Brezhnev. In G. W. Simmonds (ed.), *Nationalism in the USSR and Eastern Europe in the Era of Brezhnev and Kosygin,* pp. 188–199. Detroit, MI: University of Detroit Press.

Heyat, F. 2002. Women and the Culture of Entrepreneurship in Soviet and Post-Soviet Azerbaijan. In R. Mandel and C. Humphrey (eds.), *Markets and Moralities: Ethnographies of Postsocialism,* pp. 19–31. Oxford: Berg.

Hivon, M. 1998. The Bullied Farmer: Social Pressure as a Survival Strategy? In S. Bridger and F. Pine (eds.), *Surviving Post-Socialism: Local*

    Strategies and Regional Responses in Eastern Europe and the For-mer Soviet Union, pp. 33–51. London: Routledge.

Holy, L. 1989. *Kinship, Honour and Solidarity: Cousin Marriage in the Middle East.* Manchester: Manchester University Press.

Humphrey, C. 1983. *Karl Marx Collective: Economy, Society and Religion in a Siberian Collective Farm.* Cambridge: Cambridge University Press.

———. 1998. *Marx Went Away but Karl Stayed Behind.* Ann Arbor: University of Michigan Press.

———, and K. Verdery. 2004. Introduction: Raising Questions about Property. In K. Verdery and C. Humphrey (eds.), *Property in Question: Value Transformation in the Global Economy,* pp. 1–26. Oxford: Berg.

Ibrahimov, I. 1998. *Aqrar İslahatın Təşkilati-İqtisadi Mexanizmi.* Bakı: Azərbaycan Dövlət Nəşriyyatı.

James, D. 2006. The Tragedy of the Private: Owners, Communities and the State in South Africa's Land Reform Programme. In F. von Benda-Beckmann, K. von Benda-Beckmann, and M. G. Wiber (eds.), *Changing Properties of Property,* pp. 243–268. Oxford: Berghahn.

Joyce, A. A, and M. Winter. 1996. Ideology, Power, and Urban Society in Pre-Hispanic Oaxaca. *Current Anthropology* 37 (1): 33–46, 70–73.

Kaiser, M. 2007. *Eurasia in the Making: Revival of the Silk Road. A Study on Cross-Border Trade and Markets in Contemporary Uzbekistan.* Bielefeld: Transcript.

Kalb, D. 2002. Afterword: Globalism and Postsocialist Prospects. In C. Hann (ed.), *Postsocialism: Ideals, Ideologies and Practices in Eurasia,* pp. 317–334. London: Routledge.

Kandiyoti, D. (ed.). 1996. *Gendering the Middle East: Emerging Perspectives.* New York: Syracuse University Press.

———. 1998. Rural Livelihoods and Social Networks in Uzbekistan: Perspectives from Andijan. *Central Asian Survey* 17 (4): 561–578.

———. 1999. Poverty in Transition: An Ethnographic Critique of Household Surveys in Post-Soviet Central Asia. *Development and Change* 30: 499–524.

———. 2002. *Agrarian Reform, Gender and Land Rights in Uzbekistan.* Geneva: United Nations Research Institute for Social Development.

———, and N. Azimova. 2004. The Communal and the Sacred: Women's Worlds of Ritual in Uzbekistan. *Journal of the Royal Anthropological Institute* 10: 327–349.

Kaneff, D. 2002. The Shame and Pride of Market Activity: Morality, Identity and Trading in Postsocialist Rural Bulgaria. In R. Mandel and C.

Humphrey (eds.), *Markets and Moralities: Ethnographies of Postso-
cialism,* pp. 33–51. Oxford: Berg.
——, and L. Yalçın-Heckmann. 2003. Retreat to Cooperative or the House-
hold? Agricultural Privatisation in Ukraine and Azerbaijan. In C.
Hann and the Property Relations Group, *The Postsocialist Agrarian
Question,* pp. 219–255. Münster: LIT Verlag.
Karagiannis, E. 2002. *Energy and Security in the Caucasus.* London:
RoutledgeCurzon.
*Kolxoz, Sovxoz və Təsərrüfətlararası Kənd Təsərrüfəti Müəssisələrinin Əsas
Iqtisadi Göstəriciləri 1985–1990 cu İllər.* 1991. Bakı: Azərbaycan
respublikası dövlət statistika komitəsi.
Lambton, A. 1991. Land Tenure and Revenue Administration in the Nine-
teenth Century. In P. Avery, G. Hambly, and C. Melville (eds.), *The
Cambridge History of Iran,* vol. 7, pp. 459–505. Cambridge: Cam-
bridge University Press.
——. 2000. Tiyul. In *Encyclopedia of Islam, New Edition,* vol. 10, pp. 550–
551. Leiden: Brill.
Ledeneva, A. V. 1998. *Russia's Economy of Favours: Blatt, Networking,
and Informal Exchange.* Cambridge: Cambridge University Press.
Leonard, P., and D. Kaneff (eds.). 2002. *Post-Socialist Peasant? Rural and
Urban Constructions of Identity in Eastern Europe, East Asia and
the Former Soviet Union.* Basingstoke, UK: Palgrave.
Lerman, Z. 2004. Successful Land Individualization in Trans-Caucasia:
Armenia, Azerbaijan, Georgia. In D. A. Macey, W. Pyle, and S. K.
Wegren (eds.), *Building Market Institutions in Post-Communist Ag-
riculture: Land, Credit, and Assistance,* pp. 53–75. Lanham, MD:
Lexington.
——. 2006. The Impact of Land Reform on Rural Household Incomes in
Transcaucasia. *Eurasian Geography and Economics* 47 (1): 112–
123.
——, C. Csaki, and G. Feder. 2004. *Agriculture in Transition: Land Policies
and Evolving Farm Structures in Post-Soviet Countries.* Lanham,
MD: Lexington.
——, and A. Mirzakhanian. 2001. *Private Agriculture in Armenia.* Lanham,
MD: Lexington.
Leutloff-Grandits, C. 2006. *Claiming Ownership in Postwar Croatia: The
Dynamics of Property Relations and Ethnic Conflict in the Knin Re-
gion.* Münster: LIT Verlag.
Lévi-Strauss, C. 1969. *The Elementary Structures of Kinship.* Boston: Bea-
con Press.

Light, N. 2008. Alliance and Prestation in Kyrgyz Marriage Rituals. Paper
    delivered at the Max Planck Institute for Social Anthropology,
    Halle/Saale, Germany.
Liu, M. Y. 2007. A Central Asian Tale of Two Cities: Locating Lives and
    Aspirations in a Shifting Post-Soviet Cityscape. In J. Sahadeo and R.
    Zanca (eds.), *Everyday Life in Central Asia: Past and Present,* pp.
    66–83. Bloomington: Indiana University Press.
Louw, M. E. 2007. *Everyday Islam in Post-Soviet Central Asia.* London:
    Routledge.
Malinowski, B. 1935. *Coral Gardens and Their Magic.* London: Allen and
    Unwin.
─────. 1978 [1922]. *Argonauts of the Western Pacific.* London: Routledge
    and Kegan Paul.
Malkki, L. 1997. *Purity and Exile: Violence, Memory, and National Cos-
    mology among Hutu Refugees in Tanzania.* Chicago: University of
    Chicago Press.
Mamedov, A. I. 1985. *Ekonomicheskie vzaimootnosheniya v regional'nych
    APK.* Moscow: Agropromizdat.
Mandel, R., and C. Humphrey (eds.). 2002. *Markets and Moralities: Ethno-
    graphies of Postsocialism.* Oxford: Berg.
Mars, G., and Y. Altman. 1987. Alternative Mechanisms of Distribution in a
    Soviet Economy. In M. Douglas (ed.), *Constructive Drinking: Per-
    spectives on Drink from Anthropology,* pp. 270–279. Cambridge:
    Cambridge University Press.
Mattar, V., and P. White. 2005. Consistent and Predictable Responses to
    IDPs: A Review of UNHCR's Decision-making Processes. Paper of
    the UNHCR Evaluation and Policy Analysis Unit. Geneva, Switzer-
    land.
Mauss, M. 1990 [1924]. *The Gift: The Form and Reason for Exchange in
    Archaic Societies.* New York: W. W. Norton.
McBrien, J. 2008. The Fruit of Devotion: Islam and Modernity in Kyr-
    gyzstan. PhD Thesis, Martin-Luther University, Halle-Wittenberg,
    Germany.
Meeker, M. 1976. Meaning and Society in the Near East: Examples from the
    Black Sea Turks and the Levantine Arabs. Parts 1 and 2. *Interna-
    tional Journal of Middle Eastern Studies* 7: 243–270, 383–422.
Meillasoux, C. 1981. *Maidens, Meal and Money.* Cambridge: Cambridge
    University Press.
Məmmədov, Q. 1998. *Azərbaycan Torpaqlarının Ekoloji Qiymətləndirilmə-
    si.* Bakı: Elm.

Məmmədova, F. 2004. Gəncə Şəhərinin Alban Tarixinde Rolu (VII–XII əsrlər). In *Gəncə Şəhərinin Tarixi 2004* (Elmi-praktik konfransın materialları), pp. 15–19. Gəncə Şəhərinin İcra Hakimiyyəti Gəncə Dövlət Universiteti. Bakı: Nurlan.

Ménard, C., and M. M. Shirley (eds.). 2005. *Handbook of New Institutional Economics.* Dordrecht, Netherlands: Springer.

Mintz, S. W. 1964. The Employment of Capital by Market Women in Haiti. In R. Firth and B. S. Yamey (eds.), *Capital, Saving and Credit in Peasant Societies,* pp. 256–286. London: George Allen and Unwin.

Moghissi, H. (ed.). 2005. *Women and Islam: Critical Concepts in Sociology.* 3 vols. London: Routledge.

Moore, S. F. (ed.). 2005. *Law and Anthropology: A Reader.* Malden, MA: Blackwell.

Mostashari, F. 2006. *On the Religious Frontier: Tsarist Russia and Islam in the Caucasus.* London: I. B. Tauris.

Motyl, A. J. (ed.). 1992. *Thinking Theoretically about Soviet Nationalities: History and Comparison in the Study of the USSR.* New York: Columbia University Press.

Mühlfried, F. 2006. *Postsowjetische Feiern: Das georgische Bankett im Wandel.* Stuttgart: Ibidem Verlag.

Mühlich, M. 2001. *Credit and Culture: A Substantivist Perspective on Credit Relations in Nepal.* Berlin: Reimer.

Müller, D. 2000. The Kurds of Soviet Azerbaijan, 1920–1991 (with Special Reference to 'Red Kurdistan'). *Central Asian Survey* 19 (1): 41–77.

——. 2002. Fata Morgana mit Folgen: Das 'Rote Kurdistan' in Sowjetaserbaidschan. *Kurdische Studien* 2 (1): 5–61.

——, and L. Yalçın-Heckmann. 2004. Zwischen Assimilation und Akkomodation: Zur Geschichte und Gegenwart der Kurden in Aserbaidschan. In S. Conermann and G. Haig (eds.), *Die Kurden: Studien zu ihrer Sprache, Geschichte und Kultur,* pp. 151–206. Hamburg: EB-Verlag.

Mundy, M. (ed.). 2002. *Law and Anthropology.* Aldershot, UK: Ashgate.

——. 2004. Ownership or Office? A Debate in Islamic Hanafite Jurisprudence over the Nature of the Military 'Fief', from the Mamluks to the Ottomans. In A. M. M. Pottage and M. Mundy (eds.), *Law, Anthropology, and the Constitution of the Social,* pp. 102–104. Cambridge: Cambridge University Press.

Mustafayev, S. 1999. Orta Əsrlərdə Azərbaycanda Türk Etnik Şüurunun İnqişaf Mərhələləri. *Milli Özünüdərkətmə Beynəlxalq Elmi Kollokiumun Tezisləri,* pp. 102–104. Bakı: Qərb Üniversiteti.

———. 2007. The History of Sovereignty in Azerbaijan: A Preliminary Survey of Basic Approaches. In B. Grant and L. Yalçın-Heckmann (eds.), *Caucasus Paradigms: Anthropologies, Histories and the Making of a World Area*, pp. 95–117. Berlin: LIT Verlag.

Netting, R. 1993. *Smallholders, Householders: Farm Families and the Ecology of Intensive, Sustainable Agriculture*. Stanford, CA: Stanford University Press.

———, R. R. Wilk, and E. Arnould. 1984. *Households: Comparative and Historical Studies of the Domestic Group*. Berkeley: University of California Press.

Nissman, D. B. 1987. *The Soviet Union and Iranian Azerbaijan: The Use of Nationalism for Political Penetration*. Boulder, CO: Westview Press.

North, D. C. 1991. Institutions. *Journal of Economic Perspectives* 5 (1): 97–112.

Nuijten, M., and G. Anders (eds.). 2007. *Corruption and the Secret of Law: A Legal Anthropological Perspective*. Aldershot, UK: Ashgate.

O'Ballance, E. 1997. *Wars in the Caucasus, 1990–1995*. London: Macmillan.

O'Brien, D. J. 2005. Marketization and Community in Post-Soviet Russian Villages. *Rural Sociology* 70 (2): 188–207.

Orlovsky, D. (ed.). 1995. *Beyond Soviet Studies*. Washington, DC: Woodrow Wilson Center Press.

Ortiz, S. 1967. The Structure of Decision-making among Indians of Colombia. In R. Firth (ed.), *Themes in Economic Anthropology*, pp. 191–228. London: Tavistock.

———. 2005. Decisions and Choices: The Rationality of Economic Actors. In J. G. Carrier (ed.), *A Handbook of Economic Anthropology*, pp. 59–77. Cheltenham, UK: Edward Elgar.

Orucov, X. H. 1990. *Muasir Azərbaycan Kəndinin Sosial-Mədəni İnkişafı Problemləri*. Bakı: Elm.

Orudzhev, G. 2003. Azerbaijan's National Minorities Today. *Central Asia and the Caucasus* 4 (22): 139–144.

Pardo, I. (ed.). 2004. *Between Morality and the Law: Corruption, Anthropology and Comparative Society*. Aldershot, UK: Ashgate.

Parkin, R. 1997. *Kinship: An Introduction to Basic Concepts*. Oxford: Blackwell.

——— (ed.). 2004. *Kinship and Family: An Anthropological Reader*. Oxford: Blackwell.

Pelkmans, M. 2006. *Defending the Border: Identity, Religion, and Modernity in the Republic of Georgia.* Ithaca, NY: Cornell University Press.

Perevedentsev, V. I. 1993. Population Migrations between the Republics in the USSR. In M. Buttino (ed.), *In a Collapsing Empire: Underdevelopment, Ethnic Conflicts and Nationalisms in the Soviet Union,* pp. 21–29. Milano: Feltrinelli.

Perrotta, L. 2002a. Coping with the Market in Rural Ukraine. In R. Mandel and C. Humphrey (eds.), *Markets and Moralities: Ethnographies of Post-socialism,* pp. 169–190. Oxford: Berg.

——. 2002b. Rural Identities in Transition: Partible Persons and Partial Peasants in Post-Soviet Russia. In P. Leonard and D. Kaneff (eds.), *Post-Socialist Peasant? Rural and Urban Constructions of Identity in Eastern Europe, East Asia and the Former Soviet Union,* pp. 117–135. New York: Palgrave.

Peters, P. 2006. Beyond Embeddedness: A Challenge Raised by a Comparison of the Struggles over Land in African and Post-socialist Countries. In F. von Benda-Beckmann, K. von Benda-Beckmann, and M. G. Wiber (eds.), *Changing Properties of Property,* pp. 84–105. Oxford: Berghahn.

Pfluger-Schindlbeck, I. 1989. *'Achte die Älteren, liebe die Jüngeren': Sozialisation türkisch-alevitischer Kinder im Heimatland und in der Migration.* Frankfurt: Athenäum.

——. 2005. *Verwandtschaft, Religion und Geschlecht in Aserbaidschan.* Wiesbaden: Reichert Verlag.

Pilkington, H. 1998. *Migration, Displacement, and Identity in Post-Soviet Russia.* London: Routledge.

Pine, F. 1993. 'The Cows and Pigs Are His, the Eggs Are Mine': Women's Domestic Economy and Entrepreneurial Activity in Rural Poland. In C. Hann (ed.), *Socialism: Ideals, Ideologies, and Local Practices,* pp. 227–242. London: Routledge.

——. 1999. Incorporation and Exclusion in Podhale. In S. Day, E. Papataxiarchis, and M. Stewart (eds.), *Lilies of the Field: Marginal People Who Live for the Moment,* pp. 45–60. Boulder, CO: Westview Press.

——. 2000. Kinship, Gender and Work in Socialist and Post-Socialist Rural Poland. In V. A. Goddard (ed.), *Gender, Agency and Change: Anthropological Perspectives,* pp. 86–101. London: Routledge.

——. 2002. Retreat to the Household? Gendered Domains in Postsocialist Poland. In C. M. Hann (ed.), *Postsocialism: Ideals, Ideologies and Practices in Eurasia,* pp. 95–113. London: Routledge.

Platz, S. 2000. The Shape of National Time: Daily Life, History, and Identity during Armenia's Transition to Independence, 1991–1994. In D. Berdahl, M. Bunzl, and M. Lampland (eds.), *Altering States: Ethnographies of Transition in Eastern Europe and the Former Soviet Union,* pp. 114–138. Ann Arbor: University of Michigan Press.

Pohl, J. O. 2007. A Caste of Helot Labourers: Special Settlers and the Cultivation of Cotton in Soviet Central Asia, 1944–1956. In D. Kandiyoti (ed.), *The Cotton Sector in Central Asia: Economic Policy and Development Challenges,* pp. 12–28. London: School of Oriental and African Studies, University of London.

Prodolliet, S. 1995. Subsistenzhandel und kleine Warenproduktion: Die fliegenden Händlerinnen von Muara Aman. In W. Marschall (ed.), *Menschen und Märkte: Wirtschaftliche Integration im Hochland Südsumatras,* pp. 177–208. Berlin: Reimer.

Quliyev, R. 2002. *Böyük Transformasiya: Azərbaycan Təşəbbüsləri.* Bakı: Nurlar Nəşriyyat.

———. 2004. *Postsosialist Iqtisadi Transformasiyası: Azərbaycandan Dəyərləndirmələr.* Bakı: Nurlar Nəşriyyat.

Quliyeva, N. M. Q. 1997. *Azərbaycanda Muasır Kənd Ailəsi və Ailə Məişəti.* Bakı: Elm.

Rəcəbli, X. n.d. *Şəmkir rayonu üzrə agrar strukturun və rəqabət qabiliyyətinin təhlili.* Unpublished report.

Ribot, J. C. 1998. Theorizing Access: Forest Profits along Senegal's Charcoal Commodity Chain. *Development and Change* 29: 307–341.

———, and N. L. Peluso. 2003. A Theory of Access. *Rural Sociology* 68 (2): 153–181.

Robotham, D. 2005. Political Economy. In J. G. Carrier (ed.), *A Handbook of Economic Anthropology,* pp. 41–58. Cheltenham, UK: Edward Elgar.

Rozelle, S., and J. F. M. Swinnen. 2004. Success and Failure of Reform: Insights from the Transition of Agriculture. *Journal of Economic Literature* 42: 404–456.

Sahlins, M. 1972. *Stone Age Economics.* London: Tavistock.

Savory, R. M. 1986. Kizilbash. In *The Encyclopedia of Islam, New Edition,* vol. 5, pp. 243–245. Leiden: Brill.

Schiffauer, W. 1987. *Die Bauern von Subay: Das Leben in einem türkischen Dorf.* Stuttgart: Klett-Cotta.

Schmidt, J. F. K., M. Guichard, P. Schuster, and F. Trillmich (eds.). 2007. *Freundschaft und Verwandtschaft: Zur Unterscheidung und Verflechtung zweier Beziehungssysteme.* Konstanz: UVK.

Schneider, D. M. 1980. *American Kinship: A Cultural Account.* Second edition. Chicago: University of Chicago Press.

Schroeder, G. E. 1996. Transcaucasia since Stalin: The Economic Dimension. In R. G. Suny (ed.), *Transcaucasia, Nationalism, and Social Change: Essays in the History of Armenia, Azerbaijan, and Georgia,* revised edition, pp. 461–479. Ann Arbor: University of Michigan Press.

Schulze, E. (ed.). 2001. *Alexander Wasiljewitsch Tschajanow: Die Tragödie eines großen Agrarökonomen.* Kiel: IAMO, Wissenschaftsverlag Vauk Kiel KG.

Schweitzer, P. P. (ed.). 2000. *Dividends of Kinship: Meanings and Uses of Social Relatedness.* London: Routledge.

Seabright, P. (ed.). 2000. *The Vanishing Rouble: Barter Networks and Non-monetary Transactions in Post-Soviet Societies.* Cambridge: Cambridge University Press.

Shaffer, B. 2002. *Borders and Brethren: Iran and the Challenge of Azerbaijani Identity.* Cambridge, MA: MIT Press.

Shahnazaryan, N. 2005. The Virtual Widows of Migrant Husbands in War-Torn Mountainous Karabagh. In H. Haukanes and F. Pine (eds.), *Generations, Kinship and Care: Gendered Provisions of Social Security in Central Eastern Europe,* pp. 231–266. Bergen: University of Bergen, Center for Women's and Gender Research.

Shami, S. 1994. Mobility, Modernity, and Misery: Population Displacement and Resettlement in the Middle East. In S. Shami (ed.), *Population Displacement and Resettlement: Development and Conflict in the Middle East,* pp. 1–10. New York: Center for Migration Studies.

Shanin, T. 1990. *Defining Peasants: Essays concerning Rural Societies, Expolary Economies, and Learning from Them in the Contemporary World.* Oxford: Blackwell.

Shnirelman, V. 2001. *The Value of the Past: Myths, Identity and Politics in Transcaucasia.* Osaka: National Museum of Ethnology.

Sidikov, B. 2007. Barth, 'Yeraz', and Post-Soviet Azerbaijan: Inventing a New Sub-Ethnic Identity. In T. Darieva and W. Kaschuba (eds.), *Representations on the Margins of Europe: Politics and Identities in the Baltic and South Caucasian States,* pp. 301–321. Frankfurt: Campus.

Sikor, T., Phang Ti, and Tuong Vi. 2005. The Dynamics of Commoditization in a Vietnamese Uplands Village, 1980–2000. *Journal of Agrarian Change* 5 (3): 405–428.

Smith, J., I. Wallerstein, and H.-D. Evers (eds.). 1984. *Households and the World Economy.* Beverly Hills, CA: Sage.

Spoor, M. (ed.). 2003. *Transition, Institutions, and the Rural Sector*. Lanham, MD: Lexington.

Stammler, F. 2005. *Reindeer Nomads Meet the Market: Culture, Property and Globalization at the 'End of the Land'*. Münster: LIT Verlag.

Stirling, P. 1965. *The Turkish Village*. London: Weidenfeld and Nicolson.

Strathern, M. 1988. *The Gender of the Gift: Problems with Women and Problems with Society in Melanesia*. Berkeley: University of California Press.

Suny, R. G. 1972. *The Baku Commune: Class and Nationality in the Russian Revolution*. Princeton, NJ: Princeton University Press.

——. 1993. *The Revenge of the Past: Nationalism, Revolution, and the Collapse of the Soviet Union*. Stanford, CA: Stanford University Press.

—— (ed.). 1996. *Transcaucasia, Nationalism and Social Change: Essays in the History of Armenia, Azerbaijan, and Georgia*. Revised edition. Ann Arbor: University of Michigan Press.

——. 1997. Living with the Other: Conflict and Cooperation among the Transcaucasian Peoples. *Caucasian Regional Studies* 2 (1): 1–7.

Swietochowski, T. 1993. Russia's Transcaucasian Policies and Azerbaijan: Ethnic Conflict and Regional Unity. In M. Buttino (ed.), *In a Collapsing Empire: Underdevelopment, Ethnic Conflicts and Nationalisms in the Soviet Union*, pp. 189–196. Milan: Fondazione Giangiacomo Feltrinelli.

——. 1994. The Problem of Nagorno-Karabagh: Geography versus Demography under Colonialism and in Decolonization. In H. Malik (ed.), *Central Asia: Its Strategic Importance and Future Prospects*, pp. 143–157. London: Macmillan.

——. 1995. *Russia and Azerbaijan: A Borderland in Transition*. New York: Columbia University Press.

——, and B. C. Collins. 1999. *Historical Dictionary of Azerbaijan*. Lanham, MD: Scarecrow Press.

Tadesse, W. G. 2005. Introduction. In T. Widlok and W. G. Tadesse (eds.), *Property and Equality: Encapsulation, Commercialization, Discrimination*, vol. 2, pp. 1–15. Oxford: Berghahn.

Tapdıqoğlu, N. 2005. *Şəmkir Rayonu və Onun Toponimiyası (qısa ensiklopedik dərgi)*. Bakı: Adiloğlu Nəşriyatı.

Tapper, N. 1981. Direct Exchange and Brideprice: Alternative Forms in a Complex Marriage System. *Man* 16 (3): 387–407.

Temel, T., W. Jansen, and F. Karimov. 2002. *The Agricultural Innovation System of Azerbaijan: An Assessment of Institutional Linkages*. ISNAR Country Report 64. The Hague.

Thompson, E. P. 1991. *Customs in Common.* New York: New Press.

Tomlinson, K. 2004. Meskhetian Turks: Displacement, Self-Perception, and the Future. *Bulletin: Anthropology, Minorities, Multiculturalism* 6: 11–38.

Torsello, D. 2003. *Trust, Property and Social Change in a Southern Slovakian Village.* Münster: LIT Verlag.

Trevisani, T. 2010. *Land and Power in Khorezm: Farmers, Communities and the State in Uzbekistan's Decollectivisation Process.* Berlin: LIT Verlag.

UNHCR Refugees Magazine. 1996. UNHCR Publication for CIS Conference (Displacement in the CIS): Conflicts in the Caucasus. Electronic document, www.unhcr.org/publ/PUBL/3b5580864.html.

Veliyev, I., and E. Asadov. 2003. Report on the Guiding Principles on Internal Displacement and the Law of the Republic of Azerbaijan. In R. Cohen, W. Kälin, and E. Mooney (eds.), *The Guiding Principles on Internal Displacement and the Law of the South Caucasus: Georgia, Armenia, Azerbaijan,* pp. 269–368. Studies in Transnational Legal Policy 34. Washington, DC: American Society of International Law.

Ventsel, A. 2005. *Reindeer, Rodina and Reciprocity: Kinship and Property Relations in a Siberian Village.* Münster: LIT.

Verdery, K. 1996. *What Was Socialism, and What Comes Next?* Princeton, NJ: Princeton University Press.

——. 2003. *The Vanishing Hectare: Property and Value in Post-socialist Transylvania.* Ithaca, NY: Cornell University Press.

Visser, O. 2006. Property, Labour Relations and Social Obligations in Russia's Privatized Farm Enterprises. In F. von Benda-Beckmann, K. von Benda-Beckmann, and M. G. Wiber (eds.), *Changing Properties of Property,* pp. 126–146. Oxford: Berghahn.

von Benda-Beckmann, F., and K. von Benda-Beckmann. 1999. A Functional Analysis of Property Rights, with Special Reference to Indonesia. In T. von Meijl and F. von Benda-Beckmann (eds.), *Property Rights and Economic Development: Land and Natural Resources in Southeast Asia and Oceania,* pp. 15–56. London: Kegan Paul.

——, and K. von Benda-Beckmann (eds.). 2006. *Dynamics of Plural Legal Orders. Journal of Legal Pluralism and Unofficial Law* 53–54 (special issue). Münster: LIT Verlag.

——, K. von Benda-Beckmann, and M. G. Wiber. 2006. The Properties of Property. In F. von Benda-Beckmann, K. von Benda-Beckmann, and M. G. Wiber (eds.), *Changing Properties of Property,* pp. 1–39. Oxford: Berghahn.

Wegren, S. K. (ed.). 1998. *Land Reform in the Former Soviet Union and Eastern Europe.* London: Routledge.

———. 2006. Review Article: Rural Responses to Reform in Post-Soviet Countries. *Journal of Peasant Studies* 33 (3): 526–544.

Weiner, A. 1992. *Inalienable Possessions: The Paradox of Keeping-While-Giving.* Berkeley: University of California Press.

Werner, C. A. 1998. Household Networks and the Security of Mutual Indebtedness in Rural Kazakhstan. *Central Asian Survey* 17 (4): 597-612.

———. 2002. Gifts, Bribes, and Development in Post-Soviet Kazakhstan. In J. H. Cohen and N. Dannhaeuser (eds.), *Economic Development: An Anthropological Approach,* pp. 183–208. Walnut Creek, CA: Altamira Press.

White, J. 1994. *Money Makes Us Relatives: Women's Labor in Urban Turkey.* Austin: University of Texas Press.

Wiesner, L. L. 1997. *Privatisation in Previously Centrally Planned Economies: The Case of Azerbaijan, 1991–1994.* Frankfurt: Peter Lang.

Wilk, R. R., and L. C. Cliggett. 2007. *Economies and Cultures: Foundation of Economic Anthropology.* Boulder, CO.: Westview Press.

Willerton, J. P. 1992. *Patronage and Politics in the USSR.* Cambridge: Cambridge University Press.

Wong, D. 1984. The Limits of Using the Household as a Unit of Analysis. In J. Smith et al. (eds.), *Households and the World-Economy,* pp. 56–63. Beverly Hills, CA: Sage.

Woodburn, J. 1998. Sharing Is Not a Form of Exchange: An Analysis of Property-Sharing in Immediate-Return Hunter-Gatherer Societies. In C. Hann (ed.), *Property Relations: Renewing the Anthropological Tradition,* pp. 48–63. Cambridge: Cambridge University Press.

Yalçın-Heckmann, L. 1991. *Tribe and Kinship among the Kurds.* Frankfurt: Peter Lang.

———. 2001. The Political Economy of an Azeri Wedding. *Working Paper* 28. Halle/Saale: Max Planck Institute for Social Anthropology.

———. 2005. Remembering the Dead and the Living of the Kolkhoz and Sovkhoz: The Past and Present of Gendered Rural Life in Azerbaijan. *Ab Imperio* 2: 425–440.

———, A. Behrends, and C. Leutloff-Grandits. 2003. Property Regimes in the Context of War and Displacement: Chad, Croatia and Azerbaijan in Comparison. *Working Paper* 62. Halle/Saale: Max Planck Institute for Social Anthropology.

———, and N. Shahnazaryan. 2005. Experiencing Displacement and Patriarchal Norms: Women in Postsocialist Armenia and Azerbaijan. Paper presented at the conference 'Displacement: Global Dynamics and Gendered Patterns', University of Bergen, 29 September–1 October.

Yunusov, A. 2000. *Meskhetian Turks: Twice Deported People.* Baku: Open Society Institute.

Yurkova, I. 2004. *Der Alltag der Transformation: Kleinunternehmerinnen in Usbekistan.* Bielefeld: Transcript.

Ziker, J. P. 1998. Kinship and Exchange among the Dolgan and Nganasan of Northern Siberia. In B. Isaac (ed.), *Research in Economic Anthropology,* vol. 19, pp. 191–238. Greenwich, CT: JAI Press.

Index